FROM ETERNITY TO ETERNITY

John Freeman

By the Same Author

THE DAWN OF WORLD REDEMPTION
A Survey of Historical Revelation in
the Old Testament

THE TRIUMPH OF THE CRUCIFIED
A Survey of Historical Revelation in
the New Testament

THE KING OF THE EARTH
The Nobility of Man according to
the Bible and Science

IN THE ARENA OF FAITH
A Call to a Consecrated Life

FROM ETERNITY TO ETERNITY

AN OUTLINE OF THE DIVINE PURPOSES

By

ERICH SAUER

Translated by
G. H. LANG

WM. B. EERDMANS PUBLISHING COMPANY
GRAND RAPIDS   MICHIGAN

First Published, 1954
Eighth printing, April 1978

ISBN 0-8028-1176-0

This Edition is published by arrangement with
The Paternoster Press, London, Eng.

PHOTOLITHOPRINTED BY EERDMANS PRINTING COMPANY
GRAND RAPIDS, MICHIGAN, UNITED STATES OF AMERICA

TABLE OF CONTENTS

PART III

THE COMING KINGDOM OF GOD: OBJECTIONS CONSIDERED

AUTHOR'S PREFACE TO THE
ENGLISH EDITION

THIS book appeared in Germany at the end of 1950. It consisted originally of Part I of this English edition. For the second German edition the book was considerably enlarged. The initial impulse to issue this book in English was a remark in the American magazine *United Evangelical Action*, Cincinnati, April, 1953,[1] which, while reviewing the Author's other two books, referred to this also.

These two books were *The Dawn of World Redemption* and *The Triumph of the Crucified*. They were issued in English in London (Autumn, 1951) and in Grand Rapids, Michigan, U.S.A. (Autumn, 1952), and found a kind welcome among serious students of Scripture. Twenty thousand copies of the two books were issued in the first twenty months.

The text and coloured Chart of the present book supply an outline of the basic train of thought of the other two books named. At the same time the train of ideas itself and the whole structure of this book is essentially new and different. It exhibits the unfolding of the history of salvation not in broad cross-sections of the development, showing the contemporary stages, persons, and events connected one with the other at any given time, but rather portrays them in the form of longitudinal sections, showing a number of distinct developments included in the whole course of history. These may be viewed as separate streams and single rivers flowing through the whole region, as, for example, the special history of the Divine methods of revelation in general, the history of the temples of God, the history of Israel, the history of the nations as to salvation, the history of the Messiah, the "days" of God, the various final judgments.

Thus in spite of the difference of Part I of the present book from the two books mentioned, it is nevertheless, like them, *historical* in character. To this are added two further Parts, the purpose of which is to establish by fundamental considerations the historical point of view set forth.

For this purpose Part II deals with the basic attitude to the question of the inspiration of the Bible as such, and thus to the foundation and justification of all study of Bible history in principle. For the whole study of the history of salvation stands or falls with the attitude taken to inspiration.

The official organ of the National Association of Evangelicals (N.A.E.).

Then Part III justifies the expectation of a visible kingdom of God (the Millennium). This is therefore more exegetical and eschatological. We deem it necessary to add this discussion because the entire nature and structure of our outlook upon the historical development of salvation depends in high degree upon the basic attitude taken to the Millennial kingdom. This applies as much to Old Testament prophecy as to the whole arrangement and texture of New Testament history, and in particular to the order and connexion of some chief and essential questions as to the original Christian hope.

Thus the three Parts of this book form a unity. Part I gives our actual *exposition,* Part II its basic *warrant,* and Part III the justification of the *character* and *structure* of our historical outlook.

This unites the present book with its two predecessors, so that they form together a *trilogy.* It uncovers the underlying pattern and roots of the two others, and endeavours to expand their message from new points of view and to support from the Scriptures the soundness of their basic position.

At the same time this book is so written that it is complete in itself, independently of the other two. It is not a supplement to them, but it includes in itself a complete, self-contained message for those readers who do not know the other books named.

I desire to express my heart-felt gratitude to the Translator, my esteemed friend Mr. G. H. Lang. I have read and carefully checked this English translation. It is accurate and excellent, reliable in all details.

I am very conscious of the difficulty of treating such a vast, all-embracing theme in so small a space. On this account only the chief points can be touched and these not even with approximate completeness. But if the Lord shall use this book to provoke to further meditation those who love His word, and to awaken and establish faith in Holy Scripture and in its personal and world-embracing message, the Author will rejoice and be well repaid. To proclaim His grace, to witness to His praise, to glorify Himself, this is the highest privilege and happiness of life.

ERICH SAUER

Bible School, Wiedenest,
  Rhineland, Germany.

INTRODUCTION

THE BIBLE—THE KEY TO WORLD AFFAIRS

THE Bible is the Book of the history of salvation. It is the most world-embracing of all books, the mightiest historical organism, *the* book of mankind. In the midst of the general history of mankind God begins a special historical revelation, in which He makes Himself present to the sinner as Redeemer and Lord. "The march of the gospel through the world is the proper theme of world history."

This His plan of salvation God carries out in ages and periods. What was eternally determined in Him *before* the ages will *in* the ages be carried through and perfected. Therefore Paul terms the plan of salvation the "purpose of the ages" (Eph. 3: 11), and praises God, the Lord Himself, as the "King of the ages" (I Tim. 1: 17).

Of this mighty unfolding Holy Scripture is God's testimony and record. Only he who reads it in this sense, and so allows it to work upon himself, does justice to its proper nature and chief meaning. But then there will rise before him a wonderful historical prospect. He will learn to regard the development of human history from the standpoint of eternity. He will perceive in history a uniform, universal plan, guided by God, which, in the course of millenniums, unfolds itself in living variety, regular order, and cosmic universality, moving surely to its goal. And the Bible, as the record of this totality, will become to him, not only the guide to personal salvation in Christ, but at the same time the universal call for salvation, the Book for all mankind, the key to world events.

DANGER OF AND WARRANT FOR CHARTS OF THE HISTORY OF SALVATION

The Chart here offered seeks to set forth this historical unity of the Bible. Its definite presupposition is faith in the Divine character and historical trustworthiness of the Holy Scriptures, including the literality of the ancient histories of the Bible, the genuineness of the prophecies of Daniel, and the reliability of the Old and New Testament prophecies of the End times. He who does not share this faith must reject in advance the study of the Bible history of salvation, and by consequence must refuse every attempt to set forth the periods of salvation diagrammatically. The Chart offered is not intended for such a one. But let this only be said, that Christ, the Son of God, Himself has confessed faith in the historicity of the first chapters of the Bible (Matt. 19: 8; 24: 37, 38), as well as in the book of Daniel (Matt. 26: 64: comp. Dan. 7: 13; Matt. 24: 15), and also in the expectations of the future of Old Testament prophecy (Acts. 1: 6, 7; Matt. 19: 28; 25: 31 ff.). Therefore they only can deny the historical unity of the Bible who do not acknowledge the absolute authority of the Lord Jesus.

But even one with a full faith in Holy Scripture may at first feel a certain reserve in relation to a pictorial setting forth of the historical Biblical revelation. It is not to be denied that every such drawing has in it the danger of rigidity and inflexibility, which can only be overcome if it be intentionally limited to the clearly perceptible, main, basic lines of the whole development of the history of salvation. But above all, how much seemingly learned but really confused and amateurish, not to say gnostic, trifling has often been connected with such drawings! How much over-refinement and artificial symbolic numbering, how many rigid schemes and often insipid drawings! How many times—especially in connexion with setting forth of the End-days —has prophecy been mistaken for mere prediction and has fallen—albeit unintentionally—under the ban of inquisitive striving to satisfy unwarranted curiosity!

Yet with all rejection of such extravagances one should endeavour to be just to the subject itself. If it is certainly true —and this is guaranteed absolutely to faith by the authority of our Lord and His apostles—that the Bible gives us reliable historical information as to the earliest times of the human race, and that its prophecies as to the general main divisions of the End-times are likewise reliable, why should it not be permissible, indeed useful, to set forth in one glance these historical periods of the past and the future, and to make their sequence easily perceptible to the eye through a diagram or a drawing? In the same way every dial of a clock is a diagram setting before the eye the sequence of sections of time. That these latter are so incomparably shorter does not invalidate this argument. For the question here is not the extension of the time but the principle adopted. Such a drawing or diagram makes it very much easier to perceive the simultaneousness or the sequence of certain historical events. In this sense it can be only useful to "read" such a chart of salvation as being like the dial of a prophetic world-clock.

Therefore it is rash and thoughtless to protest on principle against such charts, always supposing that these do really follow only general basic lines and also are set out in a dignified manner. To treat them all in advance ironically, as being "General Staff Ordnance maps" or "apocalyptic time-tables," is not only unjust but foolish.

Meaning, Purpose and Limitations of Prophetic Charts

Consciously restricted to what is clearly revealed in Scripture the Chart can make clear the historical unity of the Bible and the general, great periods of revelation.   At the same time, by means of the adjacent different coloured lines which run through it, it can show that certain persons, events, and developments were contemporary.   Finally, by following these single lines, it should show the chief stages in the individual progress of certain special developments in the course of their own history.   For example, the red line shows the history of Israel, the white the history of the idea of a temple, the golden the history of Christ, the green areas the history of the salvation of the nations, the black serpentine line certain developments in the history of demonism.

In this sense such a Chart of salvation can render a decided service to the believing Bible reader, and especially make it easier for the beginner and the young to gain comparatively quickly a certain historical survey of the development of Biblical revelation. As an object lesson it may thus offer help for both personal and united Bible study, for individual or common study in Bible weeks, Bible circles or other instruction for the young, as well perhaps for continuation classes for such as in any way work practically in the preaching of the Word in their churches or fellowships.   In occasional evangelistic or devotional sections, too, the text of the book makes it appeal also to the reader himself, summoning him either to lay hold of salvation or to give himself wholly to Christ.   While setting great value upon learning, it is ever the real and chief end of all true exposition of Scripture that, as Luther said, "God's word and the heart of man should become one thing."

The text that follows explains the Chart.   It therefore constantly refers to it.   At the end there is given special guidance as to how one should read the Chart.   But it would be good to consider this Appendix before beginning to study the book. The book is constructed on the supposition that the reading of the text will be accompanied by constant reference to the accompanying Chart, which we hope will render it materially easier to be understood and will quickly impart the desired general survey.

A detailed setting forth of the history of salvation is not in view in this book. For a closer study of the whole subject reference will be often made to the two larger books of the Author: *The Dawn of World Redemption* which goes through the Old Testament history of salvation, and *The Triumph of the Crucified* which surveys the New Testament history of salvation, but, in spite of numerous correspondencies and similarities in its contents, it is in its whole plan and structure otherwise laid out as the Table of Contents will at once show.

So now we send forth this simple work. Our prayer is that the Lord will use it to the awakening of true love to Holy Scripture, to advancement and ease in understanding it, to deepening of living insight into the historical unity of the Bible. May it be a contribution to growth in the perception of the ways of God in salvation, in their variety, unity, and consummating purpose: and above all may it serve the end that God's eternal counsel of love may be more clearly perceived and Scripturally testified, to the glory of the great God Himself, Who has made Himself known to us in Christ.

ERICH SAUER

Part I

GOD'S PLAN OF SALVATION IN CHRIST

CHAPTER I

HEAVEN AND EARTH IN GOD'S PLAN

The Eternal God

WHILE as yet no star traversed its course, no sun threw its flood of light and energy through space, no systems of stars and suns swept through infinity in mighty curves and uniform relations, there God was; He the eternal without beginning, He who is above the whole course of time, He who in harmony beyond explanation possesses unity and life, the Father, the Son, and the Holy Spirit, the basis of eternity, the Living One, the only God.[1]

Three divine Persons and yet one God; the Son one with the Father in essence yet voluntarily subordinate to Him (I Cor. 15: 28), the Cause of all causes, yet Himself uncaused—truly here are mysteries upon mysteries. Here the finite spirit stands always before the riddle of the infinite. To all eternity time-limited thought will never penetrate the sphere of the supra-mundane and supra-temporal, for like can be discerned only by like, and therefore God only by God.

I Co. 15:28

At no time to be explained, yet the divine mystery of the Trinity in Unity allows itself to be represented to the spiritual human eye by the mathematical figure of the triangle, and thus through that very region of human thought and perception with which more than with any other, it seems to be in contra-diction. The church fathers had already pointed this out early in the history of Christianity. For of all forms the triangle is the first. Neither the point as a mere object of thought, nor the line as mere extension, has shape. But the triangle, though containing three lines and three corners, is of all forms the first, or, so to speak, form "One," that has completeness and unity, thus uniting in itself harmoniously the numbers three and one and therefore it was early employed as a symbol of the God-head.[2] (See on the Chart, at the top of the whole circle, the

---

[1] Regarding the so-called "proofs" of God's existence see *The Dawn of World Redemption*, pp. 17, 18.

[2] *See over, page* 14.

faintly coloured "trinitarian" triangle as background to the A and O.)

The universal plan originated from God as Creator.   He is the Source of all that exists outside of Himself.   Everything arose through His will and lives by reason of His creative energies (Acts 17: 24, 28).

By consequence everything must belong to Him.   Because the universe is His work it is also His property.   Because each creature is His work it must be also His instrument.   All things must remain subject to Him and be always at His disposal.   Not only is everything *from* Him but at the same time *unto* Him (Rom. 11: 36; Col. 1: 16).

Thus the course of world affairs, in its ideal consummation, as the Bible pictures it, may be compared to a mighty moving circle which has its origin in God and in God its goal.   He is the Alpha and the Omega, the first and the last, the A and the O. (See the top of the circle in the Chart).

CHRIST SALVATION'S CENTRE

It is through the Son that God executes all His plans.   In the Divine Being the Son, precisely as Son, is the self-effulgence of the Godhead to Itself viewed inwardly and upward; and in an exactly similar way, from the moment that God completed the act of creating, the Son is the self-effulgence of the Godhead outwardly and downward (John 1: 3; Col. 1: 16; Heb. 1: 2).   He is the Mediator, the "Word" through which God speaks (John 1: 1–3, 14), the personal living Organ of manifestation concerning His nature and will.   Christ is the centre of the mighty moving circle

---

[2] Concerning the word "Trinity," both as to its content and as to the self-revelation of this mystery in the course of the history of salvation, see *Dawn of World Redemption,* pp. 18, 19.

The most detailed elaboration of the "trinitarian" triangle was that by Raymond Lull, the great and well-known missionary to Moslems (died as martyr, 1315).   It is a triangle with its centre of gravity and with lines which connect the corners of the three angles with this centre.   At the corners and the centre of gravity there are the words "Father, Son, Spirit, God," and on the sides and lines there are the small words "is" and "is not."

This is to indicate that the Father is not the Son; the Son is not the Holy Spirit; the Holy Spirit is not the Father.   But the Father is God, the Son is God, the Holy Spirit is God.

of the whole history of God's creation, the radiant central sun, the illuminating life-centre of all Divine revelation. (See the Chart, in the centre of the whole circle).

This was the purpose of God from eternity (Eph. 3: 11). Before the foundation of the world the Father had appointed the Son to be Mediator. It therefore followed that the creating of the world itself came to pass through the Son (Col. 1: 16; John 1: 1–3). The ages were called into existence in the Son (Heb. 1: 2); and because from eternity God foresaw the irruption of sin, before all time He appointed the Son to be Redeemer, to be the Lamb "foreknown before the foundation of the world" (I Pet. 1: 19, 20).

Therefore as the centre of salvation of the universe Christ must be viewed as connected with the cross from eternity. This central Sun of all Divine revelation and the cross belong eternally together. (See the cross in the centre of the Chart). Therefore also the later death of Christ on the cross, a self-offering to God, was "through the eternal Spirit" (Heb. 9: 14), a self-devotion in death, which the Son, although carrying it out in the midst of time, nevertheless offered to the Father as a supra-temporal act.

This Divine plan of redemption stretches from eternity to eternity. No God-given promise remains unfulfilled. In the events of the whole universe God displays Himself as the eternally Faithful, and Christ, as Himself God, revealing and revealed, is the living Guarantor of these eternal, Divine counsels of salvation.

Therefore the chief name of God in revelation is Jehovah. It comes in the Old Testament nearly 6,000 times, and, as derived from the Hebrew *hawa*, to be, to exist, it describes God as the Existing, Abiding, Eternal One, the One "Who is and always will be," or, as the exalted Lord Himself explains, the One "Who is and Who was and Who is to come" (Rev. 1: 4, 8; 4: 8)[3]

As symbol of this covenant faithfulness God has set the rainbow in the clouds (Gen. 9: 13–17). Every time we see the rainbow—this beautifully coloured bridge of light which unites heaven and earth—we ought to think of the trustworthiness and faithfulness of the gracious God, of the God who does not will the death of the sinner but even after the judgment lets His sun shine, who wishes to forgive him and to take him anew into His covenant. Therefore in Old Testament prophecy (Ezek. 1: 28), as well as in the picture-language of the *Revelation* (Rev. 4: 3), the rainbow appears not only as a half-circle in the natural firmament, but as a complete circle of light around the throne

---

[3] Concerning the names of God see *The Dawn of World Redemption*, pp. 187 ff.

of God, so as to signify that God is the perfect One, eternally
Faithful, the Rock of the revelation of salvation, the Reconciler
of heaven and earth, the God of the eternal covenant.

THE STARRY WORLD AS THE BACKGROUND OF THE HISTORY OF SALVATION

It is impossible for man to survey this whole universal plan
of God.   As finite and limited we cannot fully comprehend the
Infinite (Job. 38: 4–7; I Cor. 13: 9).   As fallen and sinful—and
because our very thinking lies within the circle of the curse upon
the Fall—we cannot press into the last and highest height of
that pure and holy super-world.   Therefore God, as the infinite
and eternally pure, is enthroned in unattainable height above all
His creatures (I Tim. 6: 15).

Therefore the Bible is free from all speculation.   In all its
utterances it everywhere concentrates on the message of redemption, even upon that which we men must know so as to attain to
eternal salvation.   Therefore its revelations are restricted on
the whole to God's government of earth and mankind in reference
to salvation.   Only so far as is occasionally necessary does it
give intimations concerning the cosmic, supra-earthly background
of this whole matter, and then only in mystery, without removing
the veil which still hides this supra-sensual world from our gaze.
"That which is secret belongs to the Lord" (Deut. 29: 29).

But we are at least permitted to perceive indubitably that God's
royal rule embraces the whole of His great creation, that cosmos
and supercosmos, visible and invisible, supra-earthly realities,
sun, moon, and planets (Isa. 30: 26; Luke. 23: 45), angels and
stars (Heb. 1: 14; Matt. 13: 39; etc.), cherubim and seraphim
(Rev. 4: 6–8; Isa. 6: 2, 3), partly as observers (I Cor. 4: 9; Eph. 3:
10), partly as servants of God (Acts. 12: 7; Heb. 2: 2; etc.), or in
some other relationship (e.g. Dan. 4: 13, 14, 23; I Pet. 1: 12),
stand in connexion with the history of the salvation of men as
it unfolds on earth.

Thus this, so to speak, circular movement from God to God,
which for earth and mankind has been given Divine revelation
in the Biblical history, unfolds itself at the same time against a
cosmic universal background.   The starry world of God en-
circles the events of earth.   The worlds of suns and stars, which
on a cloud-free night, out of a dark, blue-black firmament sparkle
upon man's earth, are in a certain sense cosmic world-frames,
observers and partakers of that which here below comes to pass
from God.

In ancient times these cosmic powers had been set forth under
the symbols of lion, ox, eagle, and man.   "Four are the highest

in creation: the lion among wild beasts, the ox among tame animals, the eagle among the birds, and man over all.   But God is the All-highest."   Thus ran an old, pre-Christian Jewish proverb.   Here the essentially leading kingdoms of created life, viewed in their chief members, are conceived as representatives and symbolic exhibitions of cosmic powers in general.   The ancient Babylonish astronomers have likewise applied these symbols to the stars, and in the four constellations of Man, Ox, Eagle, and Lion—distributed at the same time to the four quarters of the heaven—have seen the four chief representatives of the whole starry world and the Zodiac.

Ezekiel saw the four Living Beings as they bore, as it were, the throne-chariot of God (Ezek. 1: 5, 10, 15, 22–28); and John saw them as the representatives of the whole worshipping creation, surrounding in eternal praise the throne of the Most High (Rev. 4: 7–9; 5: 8–11).   In the highest view this whole symbol will declare that God is the Lord of the universe.   Everything should serve Him.   The whole realm of created things, in its members, heads, and representatives, should be subject to Him and should glorify Him, and in this sense the whole universe, as one entire kingdom of God, forms at the same time the cosmic background of God's saving acts on earth. (See the starry background on the Chart).

The Earth in the Universal Plan of God

The earth is the chief theatre of the revealed saving works of God.   Its history reaches back to a more remote period than the beginning of the human race.   There lies a veil of mystery over the details of the ancient time.   But the following can well be noted: The present condition of the world of nature on earth shows a fateful disharmony of splendour and terror, communion and confusion, life and death.   Gladness and misery stand in mighty conflict with each other, and permit us to perceive that behind this discord in nature lies discord in the kingdom of the spirit. But this cannot have first entered with the history of man; for the stratified rocks, showing the history of the earth, prove beyond doubt that death and destruction existed in unthinkable ages before the history of the human race begins.   The Bible itself allows us to see that before the fall of man there existed an adverse kingdom of evil, and in some way it was clearly interested in the earth and in man.   Therefore also the command given in Paradise itself that the man should not only cultivate the garden but "guard" it (Gen. 2: 15).   Therefore also, and very soon thereafter, the entrance of the Tempter (Gen. 3), who must have been the enemy of God before the temptation and fall of man.

B

When in the history of the universe this Power for the first time appeared in this attitude of hostility to God is wholly beyond explanation, as well as how he became so, seeing that originally, as a creation of God, he must have been otherwise. This original catastrophe must have entered like a fearful flash of lightning, tempestuous and destructive. (Compare the statement of Jesus in Luke 10: 18. See the flash of lightning on the Chart). But the manner and the time of the fall of Satan remains a secret. But it is obvious that it worked destructively upon that realm of creation which was subject to this Prince of God. In any case it is proved by the rocky strata of the earth that ancient destructions by death, wild beasts, and catastrophes, were connected with it. From this standpoint the prehistoric period of the development of the earth is divided into two chief and inconceivably long periods.

1. The original condition of the earth before sin broke in, and
2. The early further development of the earth to the entrance of man.

Closer investigation here is not the task of a history of salvation but of natural science.

How far at the time that sin entered the universe the work of creation had progressed in detail the Biblical account does not particularize at full length. We do not know whether that early creation had reached the stage of a completed development, either as "first earth," or "light earth," or "primeval creation." Therefore, since full information as to conditions on that prehistoric and pre-human earth is not available, we speak but quite generally upon that stage of earth's history.

Nevertheless, even this modest measure of knowledge opens to us mighty perspectives. Upon this earth God later set man. Therefore his appointed calling must be viewed in connexion with this ancient prior development. This earth he should subdue and thereby remain the servant of God (Gen. 1: 28). As "viceroy" of God he should extend authority. But this should have signified that in ever-increasing measure God's will should have been carried out on earth and the earth be more and more claimed for God. The extension of the rule of the earth by an earthly king who would remain subject to God would have been nothing less than the perfecting of the plans of God for the earthly creation and the triumph of His kingdom over the opposing kingdom of Satan.

This belongs to the higher call of man. This also explains the enmity of Satan against this new and special instrument of God. This explains also the mystery that there can be a new heaven and a new earth only by the perfecting of the plans of God for mankind, therefore only after the great white throne, after the conclusion of the history of redemption.

But on this account our tiny earth acquires significance for the whole universe. Upon this small planet will be fought the decisive battle between God and the Devil. Although a mere atom in comparison with the colossal stars of universal space, it is, though not as regards size and matter, but as regards the history of salvation, the centre of the universe. On *it* the Highest presents Himself in solemn covenants and Divine appearances; on *it* the Son of God became man; on *it* stood the cross of the Redeemer of the world; and on *it*—though indeed on the new earth, yet still on the earth—will be at last the throne of God and the Lamb (Rev. 21: 1, 2; 22: 3).

The whole course of revelation moves towards this goal. God does not abandon His plan for His creation, and even as in the beginning there was an earthly condition before sin broke in, so will there be finally a renewed and transfigured earthly creation, a perfected condition of the earth after sin has been overcome; and the last will surpass the first. The presence of God will be fully revealed. The heavenly Most Holy Place will be on the new earth, set forth in the *Revelation,* after the manner of the picture language of the Old Testament, as a vast *cube,* the expression of perfect harmony on all sides, and thus a symbolic shape representing absolute perfection.

The heavenly Jerusalem will descend to earth. The throne of God will be on the new earth. Thereby earth will become "heaven," for where the throne of God is there is heaven. Then, in this renewed, transfigured world, will God, "in the ages to come," show to His perfected saints the "unbounded riches of His grace in kindness towards us" (Eph. 2: 7). Out of His infinite inexhaustible fulness will He cause to stream forth one glory after another in an endless inconceivable sequence of God-filled ages.

Here also, as in the beginning, our gaze loses the detail in the whole ocean of the eternal. The circles of light of the ages fade into the radiant flood of the Divine. (Compare on the Chart the two areas of light on the two sides of the upper half of the whole circle with the gleaming but ever-receding light rings.)

Thus does faith view eternity. Looking back it sees the beginning in the eternal ages before time; looking forward it sees the perfecting in eternal ages. All comes forth from God; all returns again to God; He Himself is eternally inexplicable. He dwells in a light which no man can approach. Therefore to Him we consecrate our worship.

CHAPTER II

SEVEN CHIEF METHODS IN GOD'S REVELATION TO MANKIND

GREAT was the plan of God for man. As viceroy of God on earth, as the image of God, and His subject, he should have carried out the will of God. To reflect the image of God, by royal service to carry through God's creatorial plan for the earth, to glorify and worship God in His essential nature— this was his call and appointment in Paradise.

But then came sin and ruined all. The "tree of knowledge," through which man had to display his obedience to God, and should have won his victory over the Tempter, became the occasion of his overthrow (Gen. 3). From that time and by that catastrophe dark powers enter his history. It is as if from this happening at the tree of knowledge a black serpentine line takes its start, issuing in three chief directions (see Chart).

THREE DARK REGIONS OF THE DEMONIC

There is the dark line of *death*, in which ever after the course of man's history is embedded. For "the wages of sin is death" (Rom. 6: 23; Heb. 2: 14, 15).

There is the *demonizing of world history*, which, hissing like a serpent, to a shocking degree draws into its curse politics and religion, culture and civilization, invention and discovery, development and progress. Without belief in the existence of real demonic powers which somehow influence, inspire, and lead the actions of men, the history of the nations, on into our own time, is simply beyond explanation (see Dan. 10: 13, 20). Satan is the "god of this world" (II Cor. 4: 4; John 12: 31; 14: 30; 16: 11).

There are finally the spiritual powers of wickedness "*in the heavenly places*," who from this their station work out their activities on the earth (Eph. 6: 12), and against whom is our conflict; an organized kingdom of wickedness (Rev. 12: 7), with Satan at the head, the "prince of the power of the air" (Eph. 2: 2).

To conquer him, and to free the enslaved kingdom of the earth and men, is thenceforth the goal of the revealed history of salvation. Thereby must be shown to man the frightfulness of his fall, the insufficiency of his strength, and therewith the impossibility of all self-redemption. Only so can he be brought to see that God alone must be his Saviour, that everything must be given from above, that all must be of grace.

But for this it is necessary that ever fresh opportunities should be given to him to test from all sides his strength and so practically and irrefutably to perceive his own impotence. This is the meaning of the varied methods of God's revelation and the century-long development until the world-Redeemer came, indeed until is reached at last the final goal of the complete perfecting.

From this point of view the revealed periods of salvation divide plainly into three pairs.

Two Sections of Time in the Original Revelation

In the first pair God's revelation embraces the whole of mankind. It is the time of the original revelation. It lasts from the driving of Adam out of Paradise till the call of Abraham and divides into two chief sections.

At first God gave man liberty. In the time between the Fall and the Flood God spoke to fallen man principally through the conscience. An established, authorized control over the whole of human society, or its single groups, or a God-appointed moral and religious legal institution (as later through Moses) was not found at first. Man stood in the age of self-determination. But in spite of the believing testimony of individuals, such as Enoch (Jude 14; Gen. 5: 22; Heb. 11: 5, 6), viewed as a whole the end was licentiousness, self-will, brutality, a murderous spirit (see Lamech's Song of the Sword; Gen. 4: 19, 23, 24), and the conclusion therefore of this section of time was the Flood.

Now God changed His method, and gave to man the opportunity to test his strength by a principle at the opposite pole from self-determination, namely, that of human authority and control. Since Noah the individual was placed under the oversight and legal authority of the community: "Whoso sheds man's blood, by man's hand shall his blood be shed" (Gen. 9: 6). Thus the principle of authority was introduced. "All authority is from God" (Rom. 13: 1).

Here also man failed completely. He misused the principle of authority in the erection of world-kingdoms antagonistic to God. The earliest Babylonian kingdom—which by the erection of the Tower would show its own glory by independence of God (Gen. 10: 8–12; 11)—as well as Nimrod, are the beginning of a fateful world-development, which was retarded only by the confusing of the languages—a judicial act of God rendered necessary on account of His purpose to maintain the possibility of redeeming mankind. But mankind had in such wise failed that God no longer carried forward His revelation on this all-embracing scale but took a special way, in that He limited His revelation to a single man from whom there should come a people for God which as the "firstborn son" (Ex. 4: 22), was only appointed to be the beginning of an ever-increasing super-national family of sons of God (Isa. 19: 25; Mal. 1: 11; Mic. 4: 1-4).[1]

Two Sections of Time in the Preparation for Salvation

Thus there begins with Abraham the second pair of chief epochs in the history of redemption.   In especial manner it is the time of preparation for salvation leading directly to Christ. In harmony with the inner nature of redemption there must here be attained something twofold.   As a fact this came in the form of two new great sections of time, so that from the choice of Abraham the Old Testament preparation for salvation necessarily divides into two chief periods of revelation.

The sinner must be saved and be born again.   But this can be only by his conversion.   But conversion is a turning round, and this as such includes something twofold: a turning from the old and a turning to the new; a "No" to oneself and a "Yes" to God; therefore sorrow and renunciation as regards sin, and confidence in and devotion to the sinner's Saviour, or expressed Biblically, repentance and faith.

This is now in fact the real meaning of the two chief revelations given by God since His choice of Abraham.

Trust in God—this was the meaning and the dignity of the covenant-promise with Abraham (Gen. 15: 6); while the goal of the Mosaic law was the leading to repentance through the exposure of guilt and the working of the knowledge of sin.

Throughout centuries God spoke the word "Faith" into the history of salvation—this is the meaning of the covenant with

---

[1] This turning from the universalism of mankind as a whole to limiting the direct revelation to a special circle (Israel, church) is indicated on our Chart in that the main green area, which represents mankind in general, in the whole course from Abraham occupies only the half (the lower) space, while the upper half is shown by another (blue) colour as a separate special way of the Divine principles.

This twofold division in two-coloured sections ceases where the general course of the Chart reaches that section which represents the visible kingdom of God, that is, where, after the completion of the church, the special method of restricting the revelation ceases and merges into the restoration of the nations (Isa. 9: 23-25; Mic. 4: 1-3; Mal. 1: 11).   Consequently, this Millennial kingdom is then represented by an again undivided, single, continuous one-coloured (green), common area, with the gold-silver crown of the high priestly God-King of all mankind in the centre (Zech. 14: 9; 6: 11-13).

The parallel two-coloured sections indicate thus the special historical way of God with Israel and the church during the setting aside of the nations: the undivided, continuous, single-coloured section denotes the original and final universal revelation for the whole race.

Abraham. Through two thousand years it was an education in faith.

Throughout centuries God spoke the word "Repent" into the history of salvation—this is the meaning of the law of Moses. Through one thousand five hundred years it was an education in repentance.

"Repent" and "believe the gospel" said Christ, and thereby embraced both in a redeeming unity. This is the purport of the Old Testament as given in the New Testament.

But here again man failed. Instead of belief there came unbelief,[1] instead of confession of sin came Pharisaism, and when Christ appeared the people that had the revelation refused and rejected Him, the living Centre of salvation. "He came unto His own, and they that were His own received Him not" (John 1: 11).

Two Sections of time in the Accomplishment of Salvation

Therefore there came a new turn in the methods of Divine revelation. The third pair of the Divine dealings was introduced. At the same time they were the period of the fulfilment of salvation. First God builds His church; then He erects His kingdom. In the period of the gospel, witness is borne to the physically absent Christ; in the second (the Millennial kingdom, Rev. 20: 2–6) He reigns as visibly present. In the first all takes place through the Word and the Spirit, in the second through His direct kingly rule as well. The turning point is the *parousia* (arrival), the appearing of the Lord in glory (*epiphany*, II Thess. 2: 8), His unveiling and revelation in splendour (*apocalypsis*).

But what is the answer of man to these two methods of redemption in the New Testament time of fulfilment? Again complete failure! The period in which the Spirit of God glorifies the absent Christ ends with the turning away of cultured man to Antichristianism (II Thes. 2: 3–12; I John 2: 18; Rev. 13). The period in which Christ, after His return, will dispense to the world visible blessings through long centuries will end—after the release of the Devil for the testing of mankind—in the greatest revolt of all time, with a devilish inspiration never before known, an international rebellion against God led by Satan himself (Rev. 20: 7–10). The lost estate of man cannot reveal itself more catastrophically.

Nevertheless God goes victoriously on His way. Through world destruction, world judgment, world transfiguration will

[1]Comp. the ten times disobedient and murmuring Israel in the wilderness, at the end of the period of the basic, patriarchal promise to faith (Heb. 3: 17–19; 4: 6b .

the goal be reached: the eternal estate, the Day of God (II Pet. 3: 12, 13), the final perfecting (Rev. 20: 10–22; 5).

Thus the New Testament unfolding of salvation perfects itself by a mighty threefold ascent.   This embraces

the special activity of the *Spirit* of God during the absence of Christ, in the period of the church:

the visible kingly rule of the *Son* of God after His appearing in splendour to establish His kingdom in the period of the Millennium:

the eternal kingdom of God the *Father*, to whom the Son will at last give over all, "that God may be all in all" (I Cor. 15: 28).

Thus it will be clear that the New Testament unfolding of salvation bears a trinitarian stamp.   Out of the depths of the Divine Being the three Divine Essences come ever more clearly into view, and the ascending process in the revelation of redemption becomes at the same time an ascending self-revelation of the God of redemption.

But now the last—the kingdom of the Father—does not properly belong to the *unfolding* of salvation, but is its *goal* and is therefore not "history" but eternity.   On the other side, Paradise before the Fall—although, of course, not strictly *redemptive* history—is still *history* and must consequently be viewed together with the six historical periods of which the three above-named pairs of time-sections consist.   They all, together with the dispensation of Paradise, are *one* course of human history.   Therefore this whole course of development of salvation, as revealed in the Bible, stands before us as a series of *seven* great periods which proceed out of the pre-mundane eternity and merge into the post-mundane eternity.   These seven periods are:

1. The period of Paradise—
    from the creation of man to his fall.
2. The period of human self-determination—
    from the Fall to the Flood.
3. The period of human authority—
    from the Flood to the choice of Abraham by God.
4. The period of the (patriarchal) promise to faith—
    from Abraham to Moses.
5. The period of the Law—
    from Moses to Christ.
6. The period of grace (the church)—
    from the first coming of Christ to His return.
7. The period of the visible (Millennial) kingdom of God—
    from the appearing of the Lord in glory to the events of world perfecting, world destruction, world judgment, world transfiguration.

All that is beyond these seven periods of salvation is veiled to us. Out of the fulness of the Divine ages (Eph. 2: 7; Rev. 22: 5) the eternal God has revealed to us only this section.   With this we must be content.   But even this knowledge causes our hearts to worship.   Great is our God.   His ways are adorable.   Even this comparatively brief course of history between the eternities testifies how infinite is His fulness.

GRACE AS THE CHARACTER OF THE BIBLICAL WAY OF SALVATION AND ITS ONLY POSSIBILITY

At the same time it is grandly illustrated that salvation must be of grace.   In ever new forms it is shown that man can add nothing to his salvation.   By historical and experimental proof, that is at once continuous, powerful, universal, and embraces the millenniums, it has been set openly before the eyes of all the world that God is justified in the matter of redemption in having entirely excluded man's strength, and has made it to be wholly *His act* on the principle of a gift of grace (Rom. 3: 24–28).   In this way God stands before His whole creation, in heaven and earth, as justified in having appointed precisely this way of salvation (Rom. 3: 4).

His way of salvation in Christ now appears as not only the only way, but as also the only possible and necessary way, and the whole history and course of revelation becomes an irrefutable and obvious proof that there can be only *one* way which leads man to peace, that is, God's grace alone and the cross of Golgotha. "There is salvation in no other, also no other name under heaven given among men wherein we shall be saved" (Acts 4: 12). Hast thou laid hold of this Saviour as thy personal deliverer? Bethink thyself: there is no other way to God.   He only stands in salvation who has a living experience of Jesus Christ, and of Him as crucified and risen.   Jesus Himself says: "I am the way, the truth, and the life; no one comes to the Father but through me" (John 14: 6).   Therefore lay hold of Him, and with Him thou hast all salvation and happiness.

CHAPTER III

THE MYSTERY OF THE PEOPLE OF ISRAEL

ISRAEL is God's "chosen people" (I Chron. 16: 13; Exod. 19: 5). As a *red line* it extends its history from Abraham right through the ages. This line however is not always uniform, not direct and continuous, but repeatedly it subsides, indeed, in parts is broken and seems to disappear, but then again it emerges (see Chart). For Israel's affairs are more changeable than with any other people of the earth; now in the land, now out of it; sometimes in misery, sometimes in happiness, conditioned through sin and repentance, judgment and grace.

But in all this Israel has its duty and its God-given hope. At the appearing of Messiah it will recognize its sins and turn to God. Messiah will triumph and receive the *crown* (Zech. 6: 11–13. See Chart: the crown in the last green area in the central section of the drawing). The kingdom of God will be revealed and the whole of mankind be blessed. But all this will not be at all to the glorifying of any nation or creature but solely to the self-glorifying of the great Redeemer-God as the God of Jews and non-Jews. "Thus saith the Lord, not for your sake do I this, O house of Israel, but for the sake of My holy name" (Ezek. 36: 22, 32). "So that no flesh shall boast itself before God . . . but he who boasts let him boast in the Lord" (Jer. 9: 23, 24; I Cor. 1: 30, 31).

Not a single people was at God's disposal, so as to be able to make it His "chosen people," not a single community, nor even a single family. Hence the necessity of a completely new start and the call and choice of a single individual. Not immediately as a broad stripe, but rather as a *point* must this line begin (see Chart). But with this one man should commence a completely new historical leading, a separate stream in the midst of the whole ocean of the nations, which stream, with preliminary restriction of the revelation to the descendants of this one man, should lead direct to Christ, and by way of Christ and His cross to a world-embracing expansion of the redemption. Such is the meaning of the call of Abraham. And in this way would Abraham become the "father of all believers" (Rom. 4: 11).

MEANING AND TASK OF THE CALL OF ISRAEL

The meaning of Israel's call was threefold: moral education, historical revelation, missionary.

On the stage of world history by the example of Israel, there should be publicly shown to the nations what sin and grace, judgment and redemption are. In Israel's conduct and fate there should be given, in as it were a paradigm, an object lesson, not to be misunderstood or ignored, such as awakens the conscience and leads the sinner to the knowledge of himself, and then, through repentance and faith, to the knowledge of God.[1]

That the Divine revelation might descend to earth Israel should be the "People of the Ear," who heard God's word, the "receiving station" for the "waves" out of eternity. Theirs should be a calling which should find its final centre and crown in this, that at last not only God's word but God Himself should come, not only His prophets, but His Son (Heb. 1: 2). Thereby Israel becomes the place of arrival of the World-Redeemer, the bridgehead of His coming out of eternity, the home of the God-Anointed (Messiah), and through Him the birthplace of the Christian church. (John 4: 22; Eph. 2: 19, 20; Rom. 11: 17, 18; Gal. 3: 9, 14).

For the spread of salvation Israel should be God's witness and mouth, the channel of the revelation of salvation, the standard-bearer of the truth, God's herald among the nations. Herein lies its commission as prophet and missionary. The purport of its national history is associated with the universal: "in thee shall all the families of the earth be blessed" (Gen. 12: 3)[2].

ISRAEL'S FALL AND GOD'S WAYS OF JUDGMENT

Israel has never answered to its calling. Therefore its history becomes both crisis and judgment. Nevertheless God, for the sake of Abraham, His friend, holds fast to His goal (Rom. 11: 16, 24).

There were three principal periods of distress. Of these the first had the character of oppression only (Deut. 4: 20; Exod. 6: 6), but the two others that especially of judgment (II Kings 17: 7–23; Jer. 32: 31; Matt. 27: 25. "Exile" = banishment).

At the same time these principal periods of distress distribute themselves among the three chief branches of mankind since Noah, that is Ham, Shem, and Japheth. During these three periods the descendants of Abraham are out of their land, and the red line, speaking figuratively, sinks into the green area of the world of the nations.

In Egypt it was the Hamites (Gen. 10: 6), in western Asia, it was the Semitic Assyrians and Babylonians (Gen. 10: 22), and,

---

[1] Comp. *The Dawn of World Redemption*, p. 92, section "God's Wisdom," p. 151; Israel's course as an Object lesson.

[2] See *The Dawn of World Redemption*, p. 108ff "Israel's Call and Task."

since the destruction of the Jewish State by Rome, it is especially the Japhetic nations in general, in whose lands the descendants of Abraham have had to dwell and under whose authority they have again and again been given up to violence and oppression. The oppression in Egypt took place in the second millennium before Christ (between about 1700 to 1500 B.C.).

The captivity in Mesopotamia was in two stages: first, the ten-tribed kingdom, which had been separated from Judah after the death of Solomon (tenth century B.C.), was carried away by the Assyrians (destruction of Samaria 722 B.C.). From that time the ten tribes are missing and consequently have become the "lost" ten tribes. Then, a century-and-a-half later, came the judgment upon the southern kingdom. Nebuchadnezzar of Babylon destroyed Jerusalem and carried the population of the two-tribed kingdom to Babylonia (606, 597, 586 B.C.).

In a double sense the Babylonian captivity endured seventy years, politically and religiously.

Strictly the carrying away of the southern kingdom to Babylon took place in three stages. It commenced with the first invasion by Nebuchadnezzar in the year 606 B.C., and thus exactly seventy years before the later return of the remnant from Babylon (536). The result of this first expedition was the taking away of Jehoiakim and the leading nobles of Judaea (II Chron, 36: 5-7; Dan. 1: 1, 2). Then followed a second campaign of Nebuchadnezzar (597 B.C., II Kings 24: 8-17; II Chron. 36: 9-10). By the third invasion, that led finally to the destruction of the capital, the general body of the population was brought to Babylon (586 B.C., II Kings 25: 8-11). Thus although the whole captivity was not completed till 586 B.C. it had already begun in 606 B.C., and therefore it is entirely justified to reckon the Babylonian captivity from this first carrying away, so that from it till the return under Zerubbabel, by permission of the Persian king Cyrus (536), was exactly seventy years.

But also the destruction of the temple had lasted seventy years. Here naturally the year 586, in which the temple itself was destroyed, must reckon as the starting point. The close of the seventy years thereafter would then be the year 516, and this is the very year in which—after twenty years of interrupted building—the restored temple was consecrated and devoted to its true use. This was in the sixth year of Darius of Persia, whose reign began in 521 B.C.; thus it was 516 B.C.: comp. Ezra 6: 15. Darius reigned from 521 to 485 B.C.

In detail, to the three stages of the carrying away correspond three stages of the return.

First, there returned to Jerusalem, under Zerrubabel and

Joshua, a chief part of the captivity of the southern kingdom, so as to rebuild the temple according to a decree of Cyrus, the king of Persia (536 B.C.). Only a small number of the Ten-tribed kingdom returned with them; the chief portion of them remained behind and are missing until the present day. Only at the restoration of Israel, immediately before the arrival of Messiah's kingdom, will they emerge from among the nations (as, so to speak, the red band on the Chart reappearing from the green field of the nations). Then they will unite with the similarly new-appearing band of the Two-tribed kingdom (Ezek. 37: 15–22).

Seventy-eight years after the return under Zerubbabel, in the seventh year of the Persian king Artasasta (Artaxerxes I, 465–424), thus in 458 B.C., there returned under Ezra a certainly smaller group (Ezra. 7: 7), and soon thereafter, only thirteen years later, in the twentieth year of Artasasta (445), Nehemiah came to Jerusalem to build again the city and the wall. At the same time this was the commencement of the Seventy weeks of Daniel leading on to Messiah (Dan. 9: 25).[1]

Deeply affecting was the inward change experienced by the people during the captivity in Babylon. Until the exile Israel's chief sin had been idolatry (Exod. 32; Judg. 2: 17; 10: 6; I Kings 11: 5; II Kings 16: 3, 4); but now, largely under the powerful influence of Ezekiel, the "Moses of the Exile", the people were thoroughly healed of this sin. Since that time idolatry has never been a chief danger or cause of disaster. In Babylon Israel was healed of Babylon. Babylon itself, "the Mother of all harlotry and idolatry" (Rev. 17: 5), became the place of healing for the harlot people, and Israel returned to its homeland as a renewed people of God.

But then set in at once another false way. Life petrified. Dead formality gained the upper hand. Out of faith grew Orthodoxy, out of a striving after a holy walk with God came proud Pharisaism; and when Christ appeared, He, the crown and the star, the goal and the real meaning of its whole history, was rejected by the people and brought to the cross. In inconceivable blindness they themselves cried, "His blood come upon us and our children" (Matt. 27: 25).

God has taken them at their word. Judgment broke in. First, in A.D. 70, Titus destroyed the city and temple. Then sixty-five years later, after repeated outbursts of Jewish opposition, in the bloody insurrection of the false Messiah Bar Kochbar (Son of the stars, with appeal to Num. 24: 17), and after desperate conflict, the whole political structure was smashed to pieces and the

---

[1] This subject is treated more fully in *The Dawn o World Redemption,* p. 159f.

Jews were exiled from the land by the emperor Hadrian. By this, as our Chart symbolically represents, the red thread of the Two-tribed kingdom was snapped and sunk into the green area of the nations, as was formerly the red band of the Ten-tribed kingdom (722 B.C.). Since then Israel has been subject to dispersion and fearful sufferings and judgments (Deut. 28: 65, 67).[1]

ISRAEL'S HOPE AND READMISSION

But at the end of the time God will resume His dealings with Israel. Already tokens of this, flaming signs, are perceptible. The hand on God's world clock nears the midnight hour.

As regards Israel, up till now four chief events are especially prominent signs:

1791. Removal by the French National Assembly of all exceptional laws against Jews. Consequent swift development of Jewish influence in politics, press, and high finance.

1897. The founding of Zionism, and therewith systematic endeavours for the return to the land of their fathers.

1917. The Balfour Declaration. Palestine declared to be the national home of the Jewish people under British protection.

1948. Founding of the State of Israel.

These are all signs of the times. They retain their significance even should there be backward movements (see II Thess. 2: 7). (See the four dates on the Chart at the end of the green field of the nations, beneath the blue field of the seven golden Lampstands).

But this is to be marked with them all: the restoration of Israel does not become a reality simply by fulfilment of these signs of the times. For the kingdom of God in no wise comes through human progress. It is not the outcome of activities and developments on earth, but it is the gift of and comes by the powerful working of the Most High from heaven (Dan. 7: 13, 14).

Thus also with Israel. Its last development before the opening of the kingdom of Messiah will pass through catastrophes. God's judgment will be made manifest in the most terrific convulsions. The "great tribulation," the "time of Jacob's trouble," will burst in (Dan. 12: 1; Matt. 24: 21, 29; Rev. 7: 14; Jer. 30: 7).

But then Messiah will appear. The eyes of the remnant united in the land will be opened (Rev. 1: 7; Zech. 14: 4). They will turn to the Lord with repentance (Zech. 12: 10; Isa. 53: 3–6), and Israel, as well as the nations of the world, will be inwardly renewed (Isa. 11: 1–10; Zeph. 3: 9).

Christ will rule. Crowned with the double crown, of silver

---

[1] See *The Triumph of the Crucified*, p. 137, for a list of the greatest catastrophes and periods of distress in Israel's history since A.D. 70.

and gold,[1] (Zech. 6: 11–13), belonging to the royal priesthood of Melchizedek (Psa. 110: 4; Heb. 7), He will be the Divine King over Israel and the nations.

Conversion and reunion of Israel (Hos. 3: 5; Isa. 11: 9; Ezek. 37: 15–23), renewal of the nations (Zeph. 3: 9), peace among the peoples (Mic. 4: 3, 4), blessings upon nature (Isa. 11: 6–8; Hos. 2: 23, 24), heightened brightness of sun and moon (Isa. 30: 26)— these are some of the glories of that golden age.   But finally the visible kingdom of God on the old earth will, by mighty acts of God, be brought over into the eternal and perfect condition of the new earth, in the eternal kingdom and eternal glory of God the Father (I Cor. 15: 24–28).

Thus God reaches His goal.   In reference to Israel also His grace triumphs (Rom. 11: 26, 29).   In spite of all detail crises God's whole plan will be perfected.   The pilgrim goal of Abraham shines undimmed.   The saved descendants of the Patriarch—his bodily and spiritual seed through faith—share richly in the fulfilment of his longing.   For Abraham expected the "city which has foundations, whose Creator and Builder is God" (Heb. 11: 10), "Jerusalem above, of gold most precious built."   Truly, "The gifts of grace and the calling of God are not repented of" by Him.   "Oh the depth of the riches of the wisdom as well as the knowledge of God" (Rom. 11: 29, 33). To Him, the God of Abraham, Isaac, and Jacob (I Kings 18: 36, comp. 31), to Him, the God of the nations (Rom. 3: 29), "to Him, the King of the ages, the incorruptible, invisible, only God, be honour and glory from eternity to eternity.   Amen!" (I Tim. 1: 17).

---

[1] See the gold and silver crown on the Chart in the last green area of the middle section.   Gold, as it were the "red" metal, is the symbol of royalty (comp. red purple).   Silver, the "white" metal, is the symbol of priesthood.   In the Mosaic temple service it is plainly the colour of the priestly garments as referring to the holiness and purity, spirituality and light of the Divine and Eternal to which the priesthood stood in special relation.

CHAPTER IV

THE HISTORY OF THE TEMPLE OF GOD

THE central spring of Israel's calling was the temple service. According to the will of God Israel should have been a "royal priesthood" (Exod. 19: 6). Its God-given vocation was to effect just the very last and deepest experiences in the relation between God and man, even the restoration, cultivation, and perfecting of a holy, loving, and personal fellowship with the Lord.

THE POINT OF CONTACT OF ETERNITY AND TIME

But here opens the immense gulf between God and man. Not only that God is infinite and man the small and finite: not only that God is Creator and man His creature; but—God is the holy One and man, since Adam fell, is the sinner, God is the righteous One and man is laden with uncleanness and guilt.

And yet nothing but union with God can save the lost. For God is the fountain of life, and only fellowship with Him gives to the creature salvation and blessedness. But, on the other hand, for the sinner to encounter the holy and righteous God means for him the revelation of the righteousness that punishes. Thus precisely that which alone can help the sinner, even contact with God, must destroy him. Here lies the mighty tension which can only be relaxed if by some means this point of contact between eternity and time carries in itself at once the two elements—righteous judgment and salvation, that is, covering of guilt and foundation of a new life, forgiveness and sanctification.

THE MEANING OF THE MOST HOLY PLACE

Here now is revealed how, in simply magnificent manner, the symbolic meaning of the Old Testament temple service, and in general the whole Divine redemption, answers to the need of man.

This central point of union between eternity and time, between God and the sinful creature, is revealed symbolically in the central vessel of the Old Testament temple service, the ark of the covenant. Here in one vessel these two opposite aspects were harmoniously joined together. *Above* the ark there was the mercy seat (the *Kapporet*, the propitiatory cover) where the blood of the sacrifice was sprinkled once a year on the Day of Atonement for the forgiveness of sins, and *in* the ark were the tables of the Law which represented the demands and the kingship of Jehovah (Heb. 9: 4, 7).

By these two typical arrangements, *Kapporet* and *Thora* (law), the ark of the covenant included that necessary double-unity, a denying and an affirming, breaking down of the old life and introduction of a new, forgiveness and guidance, covering of sin and establishing God's rule in holiness (Exod. 25: 17–22). Indeed, this central foreshadowing of salvation could not more accurately correspond to the necessity for and the goal of redemption.

Here again is seen the clearness and logical consistency of the Divine revelation and how everything answers to its purpose.

Christ, then, has brought to completion this polar double-unity. His priestly offering brings the "putting away of sin" (Heb. 9: 26). His kingly office effects sanctifying and lordship. Thus both are fulfilled in One; the mercy seat and the tables of the Law: and also here, in the light of inward necessity and outward symbol, there is shown to us the demand for and the work of a world-Redeemer, who is Priest and King in one, who, as Zechariah says, is crowned with a crown of silver and gold (Zech. 6: 11, 12), who, as the New Testament declares, is the royal high priest after the order of Melchizedek (Heb. 7: 1–8:2).

Thus the Melchizedek priesthood of Christ—in its harmonious double-unity—is the fulfilment of *Kapporet* and *Thora*, the accomplishment and full exhibition of the most important type in the whole Old Testament temple service: the Ark of the Covenant in the Most Holy Place of Tabernacle and Temple.

Thus in the Most Holy Place contact between eternity and time is set forth in the most perfect symbol. Therefore it is at the same time, as also in its proportions (measurements), a symbol of perfection in general. This results from its being a cube, first in the Tabernacle, later in the Temple, and at last as a symbol of the heavenly Jerusalem (Exod. 26: 15–30; Ezek. 48: 16; Rev. 21: 16). For the cube is of equal size on every side, a harmonious whole, and therefore it expresses, so to say, "the ideal space"; as a space symbol it represents the idea of perfection.

THE BASIC IDEA OF THE TEMPLES OF GOD

On account of the invasion of sin it was not possible that the Divine perfection could reach its full manifestation from the beginning of history. Therefore it was necessary to represent the Old Testament Most Holy Place as hidden and veiled, as shut in by a curtain (Heb. 9: 3, 8), indeed as being mysteriously shrouded in darkness (Exod. 20: 21; I Kings 8: 12). And therefore it was also necessary to add to it graded anterooms and areas of less spiritual rank and importance, namely forecourt and holy place. Not till the perfection will God's plan and God's person

c

be brilliantly manifested. Not before then will the whole of God's people be *most* holy. Therefore only then will disappear both forecourt and holy place. Therefore also there will be no special temple area in the heavenly Jerusalem (Rev. 21: 22), for then the whole city will itself be the Most Holy Place, indeed a most holy place no more in the darkness of mystery but standing in the eternal brilliance of the complete Divine revelation (Rev. 21: 11).

Till then the three regularly graded temple areas correspond to the regions of the kingdom of God, as these, in their different positions in the history of revelation, are the theatre of Divine acts and the sphere of Divine powers and workings (Heb. 9: 23).

Seen thus the earth is the forecourt, where Golgotha was; heaven is the holy place; and the throne of God the Most Holy Place.

On earth God will work out two things: the justification and the sanctification of the redeemed. Therefore in the forecourt were two vessels: the altar of burnt offering and the laver of purification.

In heaven is the life and the light and the worship of the Eternal in the midst of heavenly spirits. Of these the shewbread (bread of life) testified, and the lampstand, as well as the altar of incense (see Psa. 141: 2; Rev. 8: 3) and the surrounding figures of the cherubim on ceiling and curtain (Exod. 26: 1).

But "above all heavens" is the throne of God Himself. There is the law that rules the universe, even as the tables of the law were in the Most Holy Place (I Kings 8: 9). There also is the grace which forgives the sins and turns the sovereign throne of God into a "throne of grace" (Exod. 25: 17; Heb. 4: 16; Rom. 3: 25); and above all there is light of the glory of God, which, like the Shekinah cloud, irradiates everything else (Exod. 40: 34, 35; I Tim. 6: 16).[1]

THE NECESSITY IN SALVATION OF THE SUBSTITUTIONARY SACRIFICE

The central act of the temple service is the offering. Only thereby becomes possible all this symbolic and saving activity. For if the point of contact of time and eternity, around which the whole temple service in general revolves, is to become an effectual centre of saving power, then must the work of grace which in it is perfected be at the same time justified in law. But this can only be if it is at once legal and effectual in dealing with sin, and therefore at the same time includes atonement.

[1] See *The Dawn of World Redemption*, p.137f. for further discussion of the "Tabernacle as a copy of the Universe," with special reference to Heb. 9: 12; 4: 14; 7: 26 with Lev. 16: 11–14.

[handwritten marginal note: Sin / Came in by man / I Separated God from man / II Brought death]

But sin in its nature is separation from God; and God is "the life"; therefore to be separated from God is to be separated from life, which is death: "death is the wages of sin" (Rom. 6: 23). But if an objective atonement is required it must correspond to the nature of sin, and thus likewise must consist in separation from the Creator and from life, and thus in death. Only through death can death be put to death (Heb. 2: 14; Eph. 2: 16): "without shedding of blood is no remission" (Heb. 9: 22).

The sacrifice of the Old Testament temple service refers to this central indispensable means of salvation. Systematically ordered by God it endured through the centuries, in hundreds of thousands of individual acts,[1] an always fresh and active educational institution pointing to the historical centre of salvation. Christ, as the "lamb of God," brought the true fulfilment (Heb. 9: 26). The devoting of Himself to God on Golgotha was the true offering, His cross the true altar, His blood the true redemption price, and thereby He Himself, in His person and work was at once the true temple, the true high priest, the true sacrifice.

WHITE, THE SYMBOLIC CHIEF COLOUR OF PRIESTHOOD

In the colour symbolism of the Old Testament service of God white is the chief and characteristic colour of priesthood. The garments of the priests were white, white were the working clothes of the Levites. White was also the chief colour of the high priestly clothing. For white is the colour of light and purity, the colour of feasting and joy, the symbolic colour of the world of blessed spirits, and the priesthood stood in special relation to that world beyond. It served the Lord of spirits, was to set forth and restore union with Him, should serve Him in holiness and purity, clearness and true light, and by its mediatorial service be a bridge leading to fellowship with Him and so to blessedness and joy. Therefore there could be nothing more suitable than that white should be prophetically the chief colour symbol of priestly service, and therefore on our Chart we have delineated the history of the temple of God by a white line.

THE CHIEF TEMPLES OF GOD (IN HISTORICAL SEQUENCE)

In the history of revelation there are to be recognized seven or eight consecutive forms of the temple idea.

1. *The Tabernacle.*

Erected by Moses about 1500 B.C. at the giving of the law at

---

[1] According to Num. 28 and 29 official annual offerings alone numbered 1,273, and thus were almost two millions from Moses to Christ, apart from the unnumbered millions of private offerings (Lev. 1: 3, 4, 5).

Sinai. This was the travelling tent of God in the wilderness, and was later, for several centuries, the central sanctuary of Israel during the interval between Joshua and Solomon, say from about 1500 to 1000 B.C. During the chief part of this period (till the time of Samuel) it was at Shiloh (I Sam. 1: 3, 9; Jer. 7: 12, 14).

2. The Temple of Solomon.

Built about 1000 B.C., incomparably grander than the Tabernacle, but following the same ground-plan (I Kings 6: 1). For centuries it was the centre of the worship of God, in spite of the concurrent apostate form of worship which began with Jeroboam in the Ten-tribed kingdom (I Kings 12: 25–33; John 4: 20). It was destroyed by Nebuchadnezzar of Babylon on his third expedition against Jerusalem (586 B.C.), and for seventy years the temple service in Israel entirely lapsed.

3. The Temple of Zerubbabel.

Only after the return from the captivity in Babylon under Zerubbabel and Joshua (536) could a beginning be made of a new temple, which nevertheless, after sundry further attempts, could not be carried forward for some time, so great were the difficulties that arose. Only after fifteen years, spurred on by the prophets Haggai and Zechariah (Ezra 5: 1), could the work of completing it be again undertaken. By five years' labour the building was completed in the second year of Darius of Persia (Hag. 1: 1). Thus it was exactly seventy years after the destruction by Nebuchadnezzar that in the sixth year of Darius this temple could be consecrated. Darius reigned from 521 to 485 B.C., so that this dedication was in the year 516 B.C. See Ezra 6: 15. It was a plain building (Ezra 3: 12), but it was signalized by special Divine promises (Hag 2: 7–9). Later, by forty-six years' labour, it was splendidly finished by Herod the king (John 2: 20).

But its real glory, by which it decidedly surpassed Solomon's temple, came to it in the fact that it was this very temple of Zerubbabel in which Jesus was a boy, and in which later, as Man and Prophet, he taught and fought (Luke 2: 41–50; John 2: 14–17). But still greater glory came in that it was this temple in which, in the death-hour on Golgotha, the curtain between the holy place and the Most Holy was rent, signifying that world-redemption was complete, that a fully valid sin offering had been set before God, and the direct way to God was thenceforth free (Matt. 27: 51; Heb. 9: 8, 9; 10: 19, 20). At the destruction of Jerusalem by the Roman Titus (in the same month, August, as before in the days of Nebuchednezzar) this temple also went up in flames. From that time Israel, who rejected the Messiah and invoked His blood upon themselves and their children (Matt. 27: 25), has been "without sacrifice, without altar, without ephod, without sanctuary" (Hos. 3: 4).

But God, whose plans of salvation can never be destroyed, even here holds steadily to His holy goal. Now also, in the midst of collapse and judgment, He did not abandon His principle, but rather brought it to a spiritual fulfilment, more wonderful, deep, and inward. He Himself called His church, and, by the indwelling of His Spirit, made it His temple.

The creative beginning of this new way was the Redeemer Himself. In Christ, the Son of God become man, "dwelled" the fulness of the Godhead "bodily" (Col. 1: 19; 2: 9). Thus has Christ, the centre of salvation, as the God-sent Immanuel, in His person and work brought to reality in perfect measure the truth expressed in the temple.

4. *The Temple of the Body of Jesus.*

If ever in the history of the universe eternity and time have harmoniously united it was in Jesus Christ who was God and was "manifest in the flesh" (I Tim. 3: 16). Therefore He was a moving "tent" of God and His body the true temple. So John described Him as "the Word became flesh and 'tented' among us" (John 1: 14, lit.). So characteristically He said of Himself: "Break down this 'temple' and in three days I will erect it again," This "He spake of the 'temple' of His body" (John 2: 19-22). He who was the Lord of the temple, and also in the Old Testament time its proper meaning and historical goal, in the fulness of time became Himself the full exhibition of the temple idea, simply and properly "the temple," in His person and His behaviour the ideal and perfect realization of union between heaven and earth.

The church is then the continuation of His life here on earth. "Christ in you the hope of glory" (Col. 1: 27). Therefore, through the indwelling of Christ through the Holy Spirit, is it also "temple of God."

5. *The Church, the Spiritual Temple*

In this realm of life the Lord unfolds this truth in three circles. Through His Spirit He dwells in the personality of the individual believer, whose body is now a "temple of the Holy Spirit" (I Cor. 6: 19). Through the Spirit He dwells in the local church of believers, which is thereby a place of His presence and "temple of God" (I Cor. 3: 16). And through the same Holy Spirit He dwells in the universal church, so that the whole body of Christ is "holy temple in the Lord," in which all individual members are built together to become "a dwelling of God in the Spirit" (Eph. 2: 21, 22; I Pet. 2: 4, 5).

Thus the church of the new covenant is God's temple in the present period of salvation.

The *foundation* is the Lord Himself. No one can lay another foundation than that which is laid (I Cor. 3: 11). The witness of the first generation has Him as its subject. Therefore what follows is built upon the foundation of the apostles and prophets (Eph. 2: 20).

The *stones* come from two quarries, and are Jews and Gentiles (Eph. 2: 11–22). They are joined together in one holy temple. They come as dead stones to the Living One, and are made to live by the Spirit of His life (I Pet. 2: 4, 5). Their faith *in* Christ is at the same time faith *on* Christ, a resting upon, a being built upon the Corner-Stone in Zion (Isa. 28: 16).

The *purpose* of this house is that it shall be a temple. It is a spiritual house, and the stones in the wall are at the same time priests at the altar (I Pet. 2: 5; Heb. 13: 10). Their life is a burnt offering (Rom. 12: 1), their service a drink offering (II Tim. 4: 6), their works a spiritual offering (I Pet. 2: 5), their worship a praise offering (Heb. 13: 15). They pray for others; they offer thanks for others (I Tim. 2: 1, 2), in their secret chamber they embrace the world. They are a blessing in their circle; they bring others into the presence of God, and so in each of them is fulfilled the promise, "I will bless thee and thou shalt be a blessing" (Gen. 12: 2).

In this indwelling of the Holy Spirit in the church lies its dignity and its responsibility. Through this great fact they become the dwelling-place of God in history, one point of contact between eternity and time, the anticipation of the great and true perfection, "Behold, the tabernacle of God is with men" (Rev. 21: 3).

But it appears that finally God will resume the history of the earthly visible temple.[1]

6. *The Temple of Ezekiel* (chs. 40 to 44)

At all events, in his prophecy of the Messianic salvation Ezekiel pictures a future sacrificial service with so many details[2] and such exact and particular statements and measurements[3] that

---

[1] If Rev. 11: 1, 2 should be taken literally then will Israel, returned to the land of its fathers, in the End-time and not yet converted, build again a temple in Jerusalem, in which case this will be a further temple to be named here. Including this building there will then be not seven but *eight* temples named in the histories of the Bible in which worship, whether true or false, will be offered to God.

[2] E.g. ch. 45. 23, 24; 46: 4–15.

[3] 40: 6–16; 41: 1–4; 43: 13–17.

THE HISTORY OF THE TEMPLE OF GOD

it seems scarcely possible to understand it all as simply symbolical and spiritual. The difficulty then is that, in spite of the instruction in *Hebrews* (10: 10, 14; 8: 13; 7: 18), there will then be a service of sacrifices *after* the completed work on Golgotha; and that this will include burnt offerings, meal offerings, thank offerings, and sin offerings,[1] a priesthood,[2] and a holding of special feasts (Passover, Tabernacles: Ezek. 45: 21; Zech. 14: 16). It is possible to resolve this difficulty by regarding these offerings as holding much the same status as Baptism and the Supper in this present time, that is, as tokens of remembrance, as representations of the now accomplished work of redemption. They will be symbolic pictures looking *backward*, just as the Old Testament offerings, done away by the Cross, looked *forward*, to a foreseen but then still future work of redemption, which at that time was not yet accomplished but which would be carried out in due time, even "when the fulness of time was come"[3] Gal. 4: 4).

But as last, as we shall now see, the accomplishment will come and with it the full exibition of the idea of a temple.

7. *The Heavenly Jerusalem as a Temple* (Most Holy).

In the picture language of the *Revelation* the eternal city of God is plainly pictured as the heavenly Most Holy Place. Therefore its form of a cube (Rev. 21: 16; comp. Ezek. 48: 16), because itself is the perfected temple of God. Therefore also there is no more an ark of covenant (Jer. 3: 16, 17), because the very throne of God is in the city (Rev. 22: 1, 3), and therefore the symbolical throne can disappear as having been fully realized. But whereas in the temple of the old earth the Most Holy Place was still shrouded in darkness (I Kings 8: 12; Exod. 20: 21; I Tim. 6: 16), as a token that God's revelation of Himself could not yet be completed, the heavenly Most Holy Place is brilliant with the radiance of the jasper-Shekinah (Rev. 21: 11; Isa. 4: 5; Exod. 40: 34–38). For perfection has been reached. God's name is on the foreheads of His redeemed, which means that each individual is not only priest but high priest (Rev. 22: 4; Exod. 28: 36; Zech. 14: 20, 21). His servants shall serve Him and see His face. God's self-revelation has come to full unfolding. Therefore all veiling disappears, and in place of the darkness of mystery there streams the light of the divine eternal sun.

[1] Ezek. 43: 18–27; 44: 11, 15, 27, 29; 45: 17; Zech. 14: 20, 21.

[2] Ezek. 40: 46; 43: 19; 44: 15.

[3] Concerning the lack in this temple of lamp, table of shewbread, curtain and especially the ark of the covenant (Jer. 3: 16, 17), and the typical significance of this fact, see *The Triumph of the Crucified*, p. 156.

CHAPTER V

THE TESTIMONY TO CHRIST OF THE OLD TESTAMENT

JESUS CHRIST is the innermost centre of the whole divine counsel of salvation. Everything which came to pass before Him took place with a view to His coming: everything in the history of the kingdom of God which is later than His coming is wrought in His name.

In the centre of His saving work stands the Cross. By the sacrifice of His life the Crucified paid the purchase price of redemption: "ye were bought with a price" (Cor. 6: 20).

THE SURPASSING GLORY OF THE NEW TESTAMENT PURCHASE PRICE

How greatly this purchase price surpasses all the world's standards and reckonings! "Ye know that ye were not redeemed with perishable silver or gold . . . but with the precious blood of Christ as of a guiltless and unspotted lamb . . . foreseen before the foundation of the world . . . raised by God from the dead, Who granted to Him glory" (I Pet. 1: 18–21).

Here Peter allows us to see five different facts:

1. All other payment is *temporal*, but the purchase of Golgotha is *eternal*. All money—silver and gold—had its beginning with the creation of the world; but we are purchased with the blood of a lamb "chosen *before* the foundation of the world."

2. All other payment is *earthly*, but the purchase price of Golgotha is *heavenly*. The metals, the common means of payment in general business life, come out of the earth, but Christ, the Son of the living God, came out of *heaven*. As He left heaven He said: "a body hast Thou prepared for Me . . . that I may do Thy will, O God". By this will we are now sanctified "through the offering of the body of Jesus Christ once for all" (Heb. 10: 5–10).

3. All other payment is *human*, but the purchase price of Golgotha is *divine*. In the mercantile life of the earth all values are settled by human agreement. Therefore there can be depreciation of the means of payment, inflation, change of values, indeed, departure from the gold standard, and it is *men* who determine the degree of these changes. But the purchase price

of Golgotha derives its glory, its value, from *God*. It is God Who has chosen and glorified this Lamb with whose precious blood we are purchased.

4. All other means of payment are *unclean* but the purchase price of Golgotha is *holy*. It is the blood "of a guiltless and unspotted lamb." To all earthly money there cleaves always some history of sin; if perhaps not in every case a sin of the present possessor, yet perhaps some sin of a former owner, or at least from the whole contact of the Mammon service of this world (Luke 16: 9). But Jesus is holy. He, the Holy One, gave His life for us, the unholy, and now we, purchased through His blood, are privileged to be transferred into the world of purity and holiness. And finally:

5. All other means of payment have an *end* but the purchase price of Golgotha is of *endless* efficacy. In the destruction of the world, in the burning of the elements, all silver and gold will be at last dissolved (II Pet. 3: 10). But Jesus in the glory, as the Lamb on the throne bearing the wound-marks of His love, will in all the endless ages be the central object of the praise and thanksgiving and worship of all the glorified (Rev. 5).

To lead to this centre of salvation was the task and meaning of the Old Testament. The Old Testament exists for the New Testament. Christ Himself is the goal and soul of the pre-Christian historical revelation. He is

the Goal of Old Testament history;

the meaning of the Old Testament worship of God;

the fulfilment of Old Testament Messianic prophecy;

already in Old Testament times the continually present and acting God in the whole Old Testament revelation.

CHRIST THE GOAL OF THE OLD TESTAMENT
HISTORICAL REVELATION

Especially since Abraham the pre-Christian revelation was planned to find its goal in Christ. "Abraham believed the Lord, and this He reckoned unto him to righteousness" (Gen. 15: 6). Abraham is the "father of all believers" (Rom. 4: 11, 12). Already, before circumcision, and so *before* any "religious work," he received the sentence of justification by the free grace of God (Rom. 4: 10-12). He reckoned that God is able to create life out of death (Rom. 4: 17-25; Gen. 22: 5; comp. Heb. 11: 8-19). He expected the coming "Seed" in Whom would be fulfilled all the promises given to him. He expected the city which has foundations, of which God is the Creator and Builder (Heb. 11: 10). Thus Abraham's faith was a faith on the free grace of salvation, on the resurrection power of God, on the coming Redeemer of the world, on the glorious goal of final perfection.

All this is fulfilled in Christ.   He procured the free salvation; He lives as the Risen One; He is the Saviour of the world; He guides His own to the heavenly city of God (Rev. 21: 14, 27). Thus Christ was the goal of Abraham's faith and of the promises given in God's covenant with him: "Abraham saw My day and was glad" (John 8: 56).

Four hundred years later God gave the Law.   Through Moses He revealed His holy will, and now what holiness is and what sin is was more clearly revealed than ever before.   "Through law comes knowledge of sin" (Rom. 3: 20; 7: 7).

Here, however, the reason for this exposing of man's failure was not so much that the sinner might be smitten and humbled, but rather that he might see his real state and come to repentance. Only so could his terrible need be taken at the root and by Christ, as the Substitute and Sin-bearer, be annulled and removed (Heb. 9: 26).   Thus the Law becomes our "tutor unto Christ" (Gal. 3: 24), and it becomes clear that even as Christ is the goal of the covenant with Abraham, so is He of the Mosiac covenant.

By reason of all this He is the goal of *both*, Abraham and Moses, and thus the uniting goal of the whole Old Testament history of revelation in its two-fold consummation and harmony.

Principally is Christ the meaning of the Temple.   In the Old Testament divine service a bridge was made by which the sinner, in spite of his helplessness and guilt, might pass into a measure of fellowship with God.   This was effected through the sacrifice, the central act in Tabernacle and Temple.

CHRIST THE MEANING OF THE OLD TESTAMENT DIVINE SERVICE

All the calling of the Old Testament priests, all holy anointings and official garments, all arrangements and appointments, all places and vessels, all acts in forecourt, holy place, and Most Holy Place, all festivals, sabbaths and sabbatical years, all served the one God-intended goal that God and man might "come together" (Exod. 25: 22), and man be received into the enjoyment of His covenant grace.

To effect this sin must be treated with full seriousness and justice.   But deed, however, can only be cancelled by deed, history only by history, actual sin only through actual atonement. This is the meaning of the Old Testament sacrifice of blood. In it are declared typically the basic truths of the sinfulness of man, the holiness of God, the substitution through holy atonement, the necessity of personal faith, the union of the sinner with the sacrifice (the sacrificial meal), and, on the ground of all this, the gift of the blessed assurance of the forgiveness of sins (Psa. 32: 1, 2).

But in this its most significant central act the Old Testament Divine service became a type of the Cross. For only as the "lamb" of God has Christ solved the question of sin, only as the Crucified is He the Bringer of salvation, only as the Substitute is He Immanuel, "God with us."

But because this saving act on Golgotha is so marvellously unique, so astonishing, so completely imcomprehensible, God, in the history of salvation, gave a preparatory school a thousand years long, a prophetic picture-book, a living exhibition, and the millions of sacrifices which in the forecourts of Tabernacle and Temple must lose their lives became a testimony repeated millions of times to the *one* sacrifice of the Son of God, Who through the offering of Himself once for all has made perfect for ever those who believe on Him and who through Him become sanctified (Heb. 10: 10, 14).

Without this application to Christ as their goal all the Old Testament temple sacrifices were unreal, indeed, horrible; but in Christ they acquire a redemptive significance reaching into eternity. Christ is the meaning of the Old Testament worship of God.

Thus all the institutions and arrangements of the Old Testament have their goal in a Person. The moral laws reveal the necessity of His redeeming work; the ordinances of Divine worship show its nature and manner. He *must* come, for otherwise everything falls under sentence of death; but when He comes it is as the "Lamb of God," for only so has His appearing redeeming significance.

Concerning this the Old Testament speaks not only of the necessity of faith, but quite as clearly it indicates the *expectation* of faith. He *will* come. This is the purport of that wonderful series of God-given oracles which we call the Messianic prophecies of Israel.

CHRIST THE FULFILMENT OF MESSIANIC PROPHECY

As a scarlet thread the announcement of the world's Redeemer runs throughout the pre-Christian revealed history. The circles become ever narrower, the specializing proceeds ever more distinctly. The Person of the Redeemer and His work, His deity and His humanity, His home town and time, His first and His second comings, His sufferings and the consequent glory, together with intimation of an interval and waiting time between His first and second appearings—this all is like a God-given beatifully coloured mosaic, or like concentric circles, or a pyramid ascending to its apex.

According to plan this rising to the summit moves forward in the course of the millenniums. There is first declared *what* must come to pass; then it is worked out ever more clearly *who* will complete it. Thus it passes from the general to the particular, from the matter to the Person, from office to the Bearer of the office, from expectation of Messiah (Anointed One, "Christ") to Jesus of Nazareth.

He comes out of mankind (Gen. 3: 15); from the race of Shem (Gen. 9: 26); out of Abraham's seed (Gen. 12: 1–3); out of the royal tribe of Judah (Gen. 49: 10); from the family of David (Isa. 11: 1; I Chron. 17: 11).

His home is in Bethlehem Ephrathah (Mic. 5: 2). He comes first in simplicity and lowliness, but then will be exalted to the throne of God, thenceforward waiting till all His enemies are set as a footstool for His feet (Psa. 110: 1).

Then He enters upon His royal rule. Israel is renewed (Ezek. 36: 25–27), the nations are blessed (Isa. 2: 1–5; 19: 24, 25), Nature rejoices (Isa. 55: 12, 13; Hos. 2: 21, 22), and finally there is a new heaven and a new earth (Isa. 65: 17; 66: 22).

THE SUFFERING SERVANT OF GOD IN ISAIAH 53

But as in the Temple worship, so here in Messianic prophecy, there stands as the centre of the whole the expectation of His work of atonement. Brightly there beams forth from Isaiah 53 (the most wonderful prophecy of the whole Old Testament) the picture of the Redeemer, the suffering Servant of God as the Lamb of God.

Here shine four chief truths, each of them expressed in three verses:

the fact of his suffering   —He *has* suffered: vv. 1–3;
the meaning of His sufferings—He has suffered as a *substitute*: vv. 4–6:
the manner of His sufferings —He has suffered *patiently*: vv. 7–9:
the victory of His sufferings —He has suffered for the *salvation of the world*. vv. 10–12.

This is the Christ of the Old Testament, the God-anointed Prophet, Priest, and King, consciously awaited by Israel, unconsciously longed for by the nations.

But in all this Christ is not only the Coming One but also, in that Old Testament time, is already the actually present One.

CHRIST IS IN PRE-CHRISTIAN TIMES THE PRESENT AND ACTING GOD

It was the Spirit of *Christ* Who was in the Old Testament prophets (I Pet. 1: 11).   It was *His* glory that Isaiah saw when he was honoured at his call to see the throne of Jehovah of hosts, the thrice holy One (John 12: 41; Isa. 6: 1–3).   *Christ* was the Rock which journeyed with Israel in the wilderness (I Cor. 10: 4). *He* was the Angel of Jehovah Who revealed Himself as early as the time of Abraham (Gen. 16: 7), the Angel of the Presence (Isa. 63: 9) the Angel of the Covenant (Mal. 3: 1), who already in the Old Testament came forth mysteriously, so that now He was addressed and worshipped as Jehovah, but now distinguished from Jehovah (Exod. 3: 2, with ver. 6: Gen. 22: 11 with 1; 16: 13 with 7; Judges. 6: 22 with 24).

It is in the New Testament that this mystery is first clearly opened.   It belongs to the mystery of the trinity yet unity of the Divine essence of the Father, the Son, and the Holy Spirit. The Messiah prophesied in the Old Testament is Jehovah-Jesus, the God *from* God yet *in* God, the eternal Son, the Word, Who in the beginning, Himself being without beginning, was with God and of like essence with Him (John 1: 1).

Therefore the Old Testament Word of God was a self-testimony of the coming Christ.   The Lord is not only the theme and goal but the Author and supporting Element of the whole Old Testament revelation.   The Old Testament entire is a "word of Christ."   Christ as God-Redeemer is both acting in the Old Covenant and expected under the Old Covenant.

LIVING SAVING FAITH AND JESUS CHRIST

Thus is He the object of all faith, under both the Old and New Testaments.   Attitude to Him determines all salvation for time and eternity.

In the New Testament the word "faith" is associated with the Person of Jesus Christ in a fourfold manner.

1.   We believe *on* Him, literally "*into*" Him (Gr. *eis*).   This means that He is the object of our faith, its living goal, its magnet. Faith is always in motion towards Him.   Although we have already come we are at the same time ever coming.[1]   In faith there is nothing static, but a dynamic.   Each grace is a living *movement* granted to us by God in Christ through the Holy Spirit.   Jesus Christ is the living magnetic centre who draws us into His fellowship by His word and His Spirit.

2.   We believe *in* Him (Col. 1: 4).   Here a different Greek

[1] Comp. I Pet. 2. 4: "to whom coming".

word is used which is employed to describe a determined place.[1] Christ is the sphere of our spiritual life. He surrounds us on all sides. We are *in* Him. A Christian is a man "*in* Christ." He experiences the blessed truth, "I in them and they in Me" (John 15: 1–7). He not only believes *on* Him and *into* Him: he practises his faith and the life of faith *in* Him. He lives and dwells in Him. Christ is our fortress of salvation, our castle, our dwelling-place, our element. What the water is for the life of the fish and the air is for man, that Christ is to our soul. He is in us and around us. He irradiates us as the sun. The sun is in heaven; yet on cloudless days we on earth are likewise "in" the sun, "in" the sunshine. Thus Christ Who dwells in heaven is at the same time here on earth flooding our being with light.

3. We believe *upon* Him. This also is a New Testament expression. "Believe upon the Lord Jesus, and thou shalt be saved, thou and thy house", so runs literally the well-known word of the apostle to the jailer at Philippi (Acts 16: 31). Under the influence of a psalm and a prophecy which speak of the Messianic "corner-stone" and "foundation" (Psa. 118: 22; Isa. 28: 16), Christ is described as the foundation of our life of faith "upon" (Gr. *epi*) Whom we believe (I Pet. 2: 6; Rom. 10: 11). "No other foundation can anyone lay apart from that which is laid, Jesus Christ" (I Cor. 3: 11). It is *upon* this eternal foundation that, in the power of the Spirit of God, we build the structure of faith. And finally:

4. We believe *Him*. Paul said, "I know *Him whom* I have believed" (II Tim. 1: 12). Here in the original language of the New Testament the word "faith" is joined to the dative case of the person trusted; "I know who He is to whom I have given my confidence" (placed my trust). Christ is not only the goal and the sphere, not only the supporting basis of our faith, but He is the *person* to whom our faith refers and in whom personally it centres.

He himself loves us. There is a secret but wonderfully strong bond that binds together Him and me, His great divine "I" and my small human "I". I am permitted to trust *Himself*. He stands before me as a *person*, and I stand before Him as a *person*. Jesus Himself is my happiness. He is my joy, my helper, my strength. *He* is my friend and counsellor. He knows all things most clearly, and He can do all things for the best.

I hearken to Him. I believe that He intends my good. I hold that His word and His plan is always wise. I do what He says. This means in truth that I believe—*Him*.

[1] In Col. 1. 4 the Greek word *en* is employed, not *eis*. *En* with the dative case does not, like *eis*, answer the question "whither?" but the question "where?"

This is the New Testament faith in Christ.   He was similarly the goal of the preceding Divine revelation of the old covenant. Thus in experience of Christ-Jehovah-Jesus there is revealed the oneness of both Testaments: the prophetic testimony to Christ of the Old Testament and the experience of Christ of the New Testament.

CHAPTER VI

THE NATIONS BEFORE GOD

GOD is the Lord of the world. As Creator and Ruler He is the God of the whole human race. In all times, including those since the call of Abraham and the introduction of His special ways with Israel and the church, He remained in personal relation to the whole human race and was the Decider of all national destiny and Lord of history.

Viewed from the standpoint of revealed history, there plainly run through the development of the whole human race certain quite determined chief periods, easy to distinguish. They are indicated on our Chart by the divisions of the green areas.

THE NATIONS IN THE ORIGINAL REVELATION
From the Creation of Man to the Call of Abraham

In this period the revelation of God was not restricted to a single people or to a single group of mankind otherwise associated (that is, spiritually, as the church), but was available for all simply as men. First in Paradise, then in the time of testing by human freedom, and afterward in the period of human authority, God's self-revelation was simply to all men universally.

After the Fall God at first gave to mankind the possibility of moral self-determination, without special Divine command or revelation of law, and without the setting up of human authority and control. Then, after the total moral failure of man in the Cainitic civilization and the judgment of the Flood thereby made necessary, He set man, by the appointment of authority, under corporate human order.

In Shem, Ham, and Japheth, the sons of Noah, there came, after the Flood, a new beginning (see Chart). Because Ham's descendants (on account of Ham's sin, Gen. 9: 21–25) were given over to an unblessed condition, and in Canaan, his youngest son, to even a curse (Gen. 9: 25), the blessing was concentrated upon the two other sons.

Japheth's blessing was of a more earthly kind: cultural and political expansion. "God give expansion to the Expander" (Japheth means "breadth," Gen. 9: 27).[1]

[1] As father of the Medes (*Madai,* Gen. 10: 2) and Greeks (Heb. *Jawan, Ionier*) Japheth is the ancester of the Teutonic race. For the Persians are a brother race to the Medes; the Romans are related to the Greeks. To the Persians belong the Indians (Aryas, Arians) and the Germans, to the Romans the French, Italians, Spanish, etc., and further, the Slavs and many others. Taken together they are all Teutons (Arians).

48

The blessing of Shem was principally connected with the history of salvation and led, through Abraham and David, to Christ. "Blessed be Jehovah the God of Shem" (Gen. 9: 26; 12: 1–3; Luke 3: 36; John 4: 22).

But in this section of history also man failed, as the tower of Babel made manifest (Gen. 11). Thus in both these early periods, that of Cain and the ancient civilization of Babylon, man showed himself incapable of agreeing to these two ruling principles of God. Freedom he abused to selfwill and licentiousness (see Lamech, Gen. 4: 19–24), and corporate authority to mighty political oppression and general vainglory (comp. Nimrod's world empire, Gen. 10: 8–12; also the tower of Babel, Gen. 11).

Therefore there became necessary a change in the methods of Divine revelation. In its madness, in collective strength and in vain self-glory, the human race had banded together to rob God of His glory (Babel, Gen. 11: 1–4); wherefore God destroyed this unity, set aside the whole race, and at the same time restricted the circle of light of His revelation to an individual and his bodily and spiritual descendants.

THE NATIONS DURING THE SETTING ASIDE

From the Call of Abraham to the Beginning of the Present Age of the Gospel

But God still remained the "God of the nations" (Rom. 3: 29). Not indeed in the sense of direct revelation and covenant, of Divine appointments and direct prophecies, of moral directions (laws) and theocratic civil constitutions,[1] but as Guide and Judge of their history (Prov. 14: 34). This He was through the influence of authorities (Prov. 8: 14–16), in both their political and military decisions,[2] through ordering of world conditions, determining of frontiers, overruling of historical events (Amos 9: 7), and through acting upon the spiritual and cultural life of the peoples, especially world outlook, morals and customs (Acts 17: 26). Even in his flight from God man could not escape from God. Even while set aside the peoples remained the object of God's activity and love.

With Nebuchadnezzar, the destruction of Jerusalem, and the end of the Jewish national life, there entered a further movement. After the nations, for nearly a millennium-and-a-half, had stood entirely in the background of Divine revelations, they now became again direct subjects of Divine prophecy. Hitherto indeed in the Divine messages to Israel (especially through Amos and

---

[1] Psa. 147: 19, 20; Rom. 1: 24, 26, 28; Isa. 45: 1–7.

[2] I Kings 11: 14–23; I Chron. 5: 26; Isa. 45:1–7.

D

Isaiah) there had often been remarks concerning the nations—in judgment and promise—but almost always Israel was the centre of gravity of even these prophecies. What God did with the nations He did principally "for the sake of Israel His servant" (Isa. 45: 1-7; esp. ver. 4). But now that Israel and Judah, through the destruction of Samaria by the Assyrians (722 B.C.) and of Jerusalem by the Babylonians (586), had lost their political individuality and were given into the hands of the nations, and thus "the times of the Gentiles" began (Luke 21: 24), it was but a natural consequence that now God gave also prophecies which dealt with the history of the nations not as in the background and mainly indirectly, but as in the foreground, as in themselves historical groups, as self-existing objects of the messages concerning them.

This came to pass in the dream-visions of Nebuchadnezzar and the prophecies of the world-empires by Daniel (Dan. 2: 4; 7: 8). Nebuchadnezzar, the heathen, saw the outward face of history as an imposing colossal image, in its unity, humanity, and magnificence (Dan. 2: 31-36), while Daniel, the prophet of God, perceived its inner essence, its wild-beast nature, disunity, and demonic nature (Dan. 7: 1-8).

Four world empires stand in the historical area of the prophecy.

The head of gold, the lion with eagle's wings (Dan. 2: 32, 38; 7: 4)—that is, the new Babylonian kingdom (612-538), especially under Nebuchadnezzar (605-562).

The silver breast (Dan. 2: 32), the bear, which lifted itself up on one side (Dan. 7: 5), the ram with the two unequal horns (Dan. 8: 3, 20)—that is the Medo-Persian empire, founded by Cyrus, destroyed by Alexander the Great (538-333), especially by his decisive victory in the battle of the Issus (333).

The copper belly and loins (Dan. 2: 32), the panther with the four wings and the four heads (Dan. 7: 6), the he-goat (Dan. 8: 5), with the one great horn (Alexander the Great)—that is, the Grecian-Macedonian empire, which, after Alexander's death (323), split into four chief states (*Diadochoi* = successors), which at last, especially in the second century before Christ, were conquered by the Romans.

Of special importance in the history of salvation and in prophecy were the two following kingdoms:

The kingdom of Egypt, the "king of the south" (Dan. 11: 5, 9, 11). In its territory was made between 250 and 120 B.C. the Greek translation of the Old Testament, which, on grounds not yet well known, is called the Septuagint (70, LXX), and which became later the world mission Bible of apostolic Christianity. And

The Syro-Babylonian kingdom, the "king of the north" (Dan. 11: 6, 7, 11). Here, in the second century before Christ, under Antiochus IV, Epiphanes (175–164), there came a fearful persecution of Jews who feared Jehovah, which brought the rising of the Maccabees in 168 B.C. The God-hating Antiochus was from that time a chief type in prophecy of the Antichrist of the End days, that is, the "little horn" of the third world-empire (Dan. 8: 9, 23), a type of the "little horn" of the fourth world-empire (Dan. 7: 8, 20, 24, 25).

There followed the fourth chief-world empire of the book of Daniel.

Its first stage was *the legs of brass and iron* (Dan. 2: 40), the terrible beast that crushed and devoured (Dan. 7: 7), the *Imperium Romanum* which included all civilized peoples of the then known world. Especially after the defeat of the Carthaginians at Zama (202 B.C.) the Romans in the course of the second century before Christ completed the subjection of most of the Mediterranean states. By 133 B.C. they were the lords of the world. Under their first sole ruler, Augustus (31 B.C.–A.D. 14), Christ was born. Under their second emperor, Tiberius (A.D. 14–37), the Lord appeared in public and completed His redeeming work (Luke 3: 1). Then the Romans became the instruments in the hand of God to complete the judgment on apostate Israel, who had rejected their Messiah (Matt. 27: 25). Titus, son and later successor of the emperor Vespasian, destroyed Jerusalem in the year 70. And again it was the Romans who, some decades later, after three years of fierce contest with the false Messiah Bar Kochbar,[1] in A.D. 135 destroyed the Jewish national life, and banished the Jews into complete dispersion, in which that people remain until the present time (comp. Deut. 28: 49ff.; Hos. 3: 4; Luke 21: 24).

Thus in the book of Daniel the parts of the monarchical image of Nebuchadnezzar correspond to the wild beasts of the vision of Daniel. We have indicated this agreement on our Chart, by each of the four beasts standing on a metal base, the kind of metal in each case corresponding to the four chief parts of the image, that is, the Babylonian lion stands on a pedestal of gold (as the golden head); the Medo-Persian bear is on a silver base (answering to the breasts and arms of silver); the Greek-Macedonian panther is on a copper pedestal (like the belly and loins of copper); and the fourth terrible beast is on a pedestal of iron (as the legs of brass and iron). Space forbade that in the Chart the image should be shown as standing.

[1] "Son of the stars," so named after Num. 24: 17.

The lowering of the position of the pedestals and their four beasts signifies that human development is no true upward and Godward movement, but on the contrary it is a downward way which, in spite of all progress in culture, moves terribly and ever increasingly away from God. This solemn truth was indicated in Nebuchadnezzar's image by the ever lessening value of the metals, gold, silver, copper, iron.

Thus in the meaning of prophecy the fourth kingdom lasts till the end of this age. In Nebuchadnezzar's colossus the iron reached to the feet (Dan. 2: 33). The setting up of the kingdom of the Son of man follows immediately upon the fourth Beast (Dan. 7: 7-14). Therefore on our Chart we have extended the line of the iron pedestal through the whole section of the present age.

It is a fact that, in spite of all detail changes, history has shown that the ideas of the fourth world empire have never died. Even after the collapse of the Western Empire (A.D. 475) and the Eastern Empire (1453), again and again it has displayed its vital energy, especially in the stability of the Roman Church, the continuance of the Roman (Latin) language in theology, law, medicine, science, military affairs, in the continuance and application of Roman jurisprudence, and indeed in quite distinct, clearly perceptible world developments, detail happenings, and singular political events. (See *The Triumph of the Crucified*, pp 132f.)

And during this period the gospel spreads through the world.

THE NATIONS UNDER THE CALL OF SALVATION

The Present Age of the Gospel until the Coming (parousia) *of Christ*

With the message of the Cross, of the full, only, present, and future salvation in Christ as our Representative and Surety, the messengers of Jesus go from land to land, and wherever men are found to open themselves to this message, and in repentance and faith accept Christ as their personal Saviour, they become partakers of His salvation and members of His church. The purpose of this proclamation is not the Christianizing of the masses, or of civilization, or the creating of "Christian" nations or groups of nations—this will come to pass only in the mission period of the coming visible kingdom of God (Isa. 2: 3, 4; 19: 21-25); but it is "to take out of them a people for His name" (Acts. 15: 14),[1] and is thus the creation of a new super-national people of God. In this people "there is neither Jew nor Greek, neither slave nor free . . . but all are one in Christ Jesus" (Gal. 3: 28; Col.

[1] See Titus. 2: 14; I Pet. 2: 9, 10.

3: 11). From this arises in place of the former *two* divisions of mankind known to historical revelation, a threefold division (I Cor. 10: 32), and to Israel and the nations is added the church as the "third race."

But what will mankind do at the end of this period of the gospel? After having heard for centuries the message of salvation in Christ they will decide finally for His foe, the Antichrist. There will be created a godless civilization, of the leading civilized peoples, united politically, centralized commercially, moulded alike in religious and world outlook. Only so is it practicable that at last "all," the small and the great, under threat of commercial boycott, will be forced to worship the Beast and thereby to deny the revealed faith of the Bible, so that at last "no one can buy or sell except those who have the mark of the Beast, the name of the Beast or the number of his name" (Rev. 13: 17, 18). Through this union of politics, business, and religion the Antichristian system will be a concentration of three lines of concentration, a monstrous spiritual revival of the tower of Babel. Our Chart expresses this in that the small green section which represents the Antichristian period contains a three-sided pyramid corresponding to and lying over against the ancient Babylonian tower. At the summit of this pyramid stands the mysterious number of the Beast, "666," which is not yet explainable beyond all doubt.

This will be the combination and final product of all God-estranged efforts of the world of nations severed from God, the sum of all world kingdoms of former times, of all the wild-beast kingdoms of Daniel's prophecies. Therefore the Antichristian Beast is represented as lion, bear, and panther at once, and the number of its horns (7) is the sum total of the horns of all four wild beasts of Daniel's vision (Dan. 7: 2-8). And finally, if the *Revelation* speaks of *two* Beasts (Rev. 13: 1-10 and 11-18), of which the first stands unmistakably in the foreground, while the second sees it to be his whole duty to secure all honour to the first Beast (Rev. 13: 12, 14, 16f), this is because the Antichristian world system will recognize two chief personalities who will unify the whole into one hellish organism embracing body and soul. These will be the political Leader and his religious-philosophical Minister of Propoganda. See on the Chart the two Beasts at the end of the iron line beneath the three-sided Babylonian pyramid.

But Christ will have the last word. Through the "outshining of His parousia" He will destroy the Foe (II Thess. 2: 8, 9; Isa. 11: 4) and will then set up His kingdom.

The Nations in the Visible Kingdom of God: The Millennium

As the God-King seen in visible glory will He then sit on His throne and judge all the nations of the earth. They will be gathered before Him and He will separate them as a shepherd divides the sheep from the goats (Matt. 25: 31, 32). As the place of this judgment of the nations the Scripture gives the valley of Jehoshaphat (Joel 3: 12). The point to be decided will be which of those who have escaped the late catastrophic judgments will find entrance to the visible kingdom of God, and, on the other hand, which, on account of his conduct, will be given up to the judgment of destruction (Matt. 25: 34, 46b).

Those who then are admitted to the kingdom of God will be covered with blessings. Then will the nations as nations be converted,[1] and for the first time in history there will be Christian nations and civilization in the meaning of Scripture (Isa. 19: 19, 23, 25). But to Christ, the God-King of mankind, crowned with the gold and silver crown of kingship and priesthood (Zech. 6: 11-13), will worship everywhere be offered (Mal. 1: 11).

The following will be everyday blessings enjoyed by all:
Renewal of the peoples (Zeph. 3: 9).
Peace among the nations (Mic. 4: 3, 4).
Blessing upon Nature (Isa. 11: 6-8; Hos. 2: 23, 24).
Social righteousness (Isa. 11: 3, 4).
Bodily health (Isa. 35: 5, 6).
Patriarchal age (Isa. 65: 20).
Fruitful daily labour (Isa. 65: 21-23).
Cessation of giant cities (Zech. 3: 10).

The Nations in the Final Rebellion

And yet! Here again, when the last and sharpest test comes, man proves himself a total failure. During this visible kingdom of God Satan has been bound in the Abyss (Rev. 20: 2, 3). See on the Chart the black serpent line below the green field area that represents human history. But finally he "must" be loosed, so that the results of this late period of salvation may be tested (Rev. 20: 8). And what happens? After enjoying for a thousand years the blessings of the visible rule of God man decides for—the Devil, and, under Gog and Magog, that is, still under Japhetic Indo-Teutonic leadership, marches in vast hosts to war against Jerusalem, the city of God (Rev. 20: 9; comp. Gen. 10: 2).

To this there can be but one answer from God: fire falls from heaven and consumes these God-hating men. The earth also,

Jer. 3: 17; Zech. 8: 20-22; Isa. 2: 3; 42: 4; Mic. 4: 2.

the theatre of this whole erring human development, is dissolved by fire, so that a new heaven and earth may arise (Rev. 20: 9–21; 1).

For man all this is extraordinarily humiliating. But it shows how God is justified that for the salvation of man He has from the beginning excluded all human strength and has appointed only *one* way of salvation: His grace alone and the Cross of Golgotha.

THE NATIONS ON THE NEW EARTH

On the new earth also there will be nations (Rev. 21: 24; 22: 2). The renewed mankind will still have organic structure. But then all will join in wonderful harmony. The heavenly city of God will be on the new earth (Rev. 21: 10). In it will be the throne of God and the Lamb (Rev. 22: 3), and on account of the King of glory, the centre and essence of all heavenly life, men will see in this city come down from heaven their capital and the centre of their worship. "The nations will walk in its light and the kings of the earth bring their glory into it" (Rev. 21: 24).

CHAPTER VII

THE HISTORY OF THE CHRIST

JESUS CHRIST is the redeeming Centre of the history of salvation. He was of old the creative basis of the Old Testament revelation, for His Spirit was in the prophets. He was in mysterious union with God His Father (Psa. 110: 1); He was the God of the history of Israel (John 12: 14; Isa. 61), the goal of the law (Rom. 10: 4; Gal. 3: 24; 19), as well as of all prophesying in the temple service (Col. 2: 17; Heb. 10: 1) and of all direct prophetic announcement (for example, of Messianic prophecy as in Isa. 53). As Lion of the tribe of Judah and Son of David (Rev. 5: 5; II Tim. 2: 8) He was the root and crown of the royal house of David (Rev. 22: 16; Matt. 1: 1-17), and therefore was basis, content, and meaning of all revelation even before He became man.

Then in the fulness of the time He Himself appeared (Gal. 4: 4). As the Star out of Jacob (Num. 24: 17) He arose in Bethlehem, as the "dayspring from on high" (Luke 1: 78), as the personal appearing of the goodness and love to man of God our Saviour (Titus. 3: 4). This is His first epiphany (appearing, II Tim. 1: 10), His coming for salvation, for the rescuing of the sinner, "to give His life a ransom for many" (Matt. 20: 28). As announced by John the Baptist He was the Lamb of God who carries and bears away the sin of the world (John 1: 29).

THE CROSS OF CHRIST THE CENTRE OF ALL TIMES

The Cross is therefore the central event of His work on earth. It is the central act of God in the whole history of the universe. It is the most marvellous revelation of the will of God to save, "so that each that believes in Him should not be lost but have eternal life" (John 3: 16). So though not in point of time yet in inner spiritual reality it is the central point of human history.

Jesus Nazarenus Rex Judaeorum (INRI), that is, Jesus of Nazareth, King of the Jews. This message, in Latin, Greek, and Hebrew, set above the cross by an unbelieving hand, stood therefore at the same time under the overruling of the world-governing Saviour-God. For in that this inscription in the three chief languages of civilization at that time—the languages of the State, of culture, of religion—was set over the cross, it did in fact, though not in human intention, express that Jesus of

Nazareth, of the people of Israel, stood in relation to all departments of human life, that His person and His work, outwardly and inwardly, is valid for all the world, that He, the despised, will yet wear the crown.

As matter of fact the outworkings of His saving work are marvellous. It is as if in the midst of the darkness of Golgotha the sun had shone out and illuminated with its brightness the whole past and the whole future. (Compare on the Chart the rays of light which stream out from the Cross on every side).

The effects of the original fall of Satan can be overcome only through the Cross. Therefore do the rays from Golgotha stretch back into those distant ages before man.

That on the threshold of the lost Paradise there was given to man the original gospel concerning the seed of the woman and the treader-down of Satan (Gen. 3: 15) can find historical out-working only in the saving work of the Crucified. Therefore the darkness of this word of promise receives its first clear light from Good Friday and Easter.

That God would not condemn but be gracious; that He would establish His covenant with men and have fellowship with them; all that He had testified in His covenant with Noah and had confirmed by the covenant-sign then appointed, the rainbow bridge of light which unites heaven and earth (Gen. 9: 12ff), all first became possible through the Cross. For only "through the blood of the eternal covenant" (Heb. 13: 20) was the wall of partition done away, the sin which separated God and man, for the removal of which through His sacrifice Christ appeared (Heb. 9: 26).

The promise given to Abraham of blessing for all peoples (Gen. 12: 3; Gal. 3: 13, 14), the justifying of Abraham through faith alone (Gen. 15: 6; Rom. 4: 9–13), the offering upon Moriah (Gen. 22), the faith of the patriarch for resurrection (Heb. 11: 19) —this all first receives full light from the saving work of the Crucified and Risen One (see Rom. 4: 23–25).

And finally, the whole Mosaic law, its moral demands, its appointments of Divine worship, its prophetic type and its an-nouncements of Messiah would, as regards at least their last and deepest meaning, remain for ever dark and incomprehensible if Christ had not come as the fulfilment of law and prophecy (Rom. 10: 4), and by one offering had illuminated, explained, and fulfilled all other offerings (Heb. 10: 14 and 9), and had thereby superseded the whole Mosaic law and temple service (Heb. 7: 18 and 12).

But the future also lies under the bright rays of the Sun of salvation risen after Golgotha.   For now there can be a church, a people for the personal possession of the Son of God, redeemed and purchased by His own blood.[1] Of this church the foundation, crown and star, strength, honour, and praise is the Cross alone (Gal. 6: 16; I Cor. 1: 18; 2: 2); that is, the Cross in connexion with the resurrection of the God-given Substitute and Surety, (I Cor. 15: 13–19), Who died for us and lives for us (Rom. 4: 25; 5: 10), Who on earth acquired for us salvation, and Who from heaven, through His Spirit and His royal high priesthood, bestows, maintains, and glorifies that salvation (Rom. 8: 34; Heb. 8: 1, 2; I John 2: 1).

Only thus can there be a visible kingdom of God; for only if sin be overcome can there be a renewed humanity truly serving God.

Certainly also for Christ personally the crown is attached to the Cross.   The same earth that was the scene of His humiliation must be the scene and witness of His exaltation and glory.   This simply belongs to the Divine justification of the Crucified before every creature.   Thus the appearing of Christ in glory is entirely a fruit of His appearing in humiliation and the Millennial kingdom stands out in the light of Cross and resurrection.

And at last the final goal will be reached, the eternal state, the transfigured universe.   And since all will be wrought through Christ, and through Him as the One who conquered sin by the Cross, then is it but a natural result that He as the Lamb will be the centre of worship for all eternity (Rev. 5: 6–9).   Therefore on the new earth the city of God that descends has the Lamb as its foundation (Rev. 21: 14, 27), the Lamb as its fountain of life (22: 1), the Lamb as its light (21: 23), the Lamb as its temple (21: 22), the Lamb as its object of blissful love (21: 9).   Therefore is He surrounded by the heavenly songs of praise as the Lamb upon the throne with the wound-marks of His love (Rev. 5: 6).   Therefore the seat of Divine authority in the glory is called "the throne of God and the Lamb" (Rev. 22: 1).

Thus the radiant sun of Cross and resurrection illuminates the whole history of the universe.   As regards the pre-Christian unfolding they break through as it were a generally gloomy and cloudy heaven, which only gradually and in parts clears; as regards the times after the completed work of redemption they shine through ever more clearly, overcoming all the clouds, the firmament becoming ever brighter, flooded with golden sunshine and brilliance.   (See on the Chart right and left the rays proceeding from the Cross over the background of heaven.)

---

[1] Acts. 20: 28; Titus. 2: 14; I Cor. 6: 20.

THE THREEFOLD OFFICE OF CHRIST

The historical unfolding of the redeeming work of Christ is amazing. It is inseparably united with the historical path taken by Christ personally after His incarnation, and which he still takes through time and eternity, through earth and heaven. Quite evidently this way, in its chief forward steps, corresponds to the three offices of the Redeemer, His offices of the Prophet, the Priest, and the King.

First, in the foreground stands the prophetic office (Deut. 18: 15–19). In life and teaching Christ proclaimed the will of God, and in the message of the kingdom of heaven showed Himself a "prophet mighty in word and deed" (Luke 24: 19).

Then this Prophet went to the Cross. He accepted the burden of the sins of the world (John 1: 29; I John 2: 2) and became at once the lamb for sacrifice and the priest (Heb. 9: 12, 14, 25). Thus there came this terrific hour on Golgotha in which Christ, the Holy One, at Passover in the year 30, on Nisan 15, (according to astronomical reckoning perhaps April 7th, 30), gave His life as propitiation for sinners. From the land of the living He descended to the black line of death (see the Chart), so as through death to bring to naught him that had the power of death, the devil (Heb. 2: 14).

But then God raised and exalted Him (Phil. 2: 9). He who was dead arose on the third day, ascended to heaven, and is now as King sitting at the right hand of God, whence He will come to complete His work (Heb. 2: 9; Rev. 3: 21). It is as if out of the black line of death there arises suddenly a golden line of glory, which soon after the event of the Cross mounts into the heavenly regions (Eph. 1: 20). There it remains, above all the course of the kingdom of God on earth, like a golden heavenly counterpart, until here below, in the field of world affairs, God's goal has been reached for this age of salvation, even the building of the church, the gathering of His redeemed, who here, in this interval and waiting time (Psa. 110: 1; Heb. 10: 13), as His witnesses, like seven golden lamps, shall glorify Him by raying forth brightly His message and His life (Rev. 2 and 3).

THE ROYAL HIGH PRIESTHOOD OF CHRIST

In this period, which is the economy of the gospel and of grace, Christ in heaven is at once priest and king. He intercedes on behalf of His own (Rom. 8: 34). He is their advocate with the Father (I John 2: 1): "We have such a high priest, Who sat down at the right hand of the Majesty in the heavens (Heb. 8: 1). He is priest for ever after the order of Melchizedek.[1] There by faith

[1] Heb. 7: 1–25; comp. Gen. 14: 22–24; Psa. 110: 4.

we see Jesus, who was humbled by becoming a little lower than the angels, precisely on account of His sufferings in death "crowned with glory and honour" (Heb. 2: 9).

CHRIST'S ARRIVAL (PAROUSIA) AND APPEARING (EPIPHANY)

In this the priesthood and kingship of the Highly Exalted One is perceptible only to faith. At present He is absent, invisible to the earthly eye. Therefore a day must come when this will undergo a change. Christ must return and set up His kingdom. He must come forth from His absence and make Himself to be present (arrival, *parousia*). He must take His people to Himself, conquer His foes, appear in splendour (*epiphany*), so unveiling Himself and becoming visible (Rev. 1: 7). He must make His people manifest before His judgment seat and make their life on earth to pass before His face in the light of heaven. He will decree crowns or loss (II Cor. 5: 10; I Cor. 3: 14, 15).

THE GLORIFIED CHRIST AND HIS GLORIFIED CHURCH

The golden line must at that time descend to the earth and the region of the air (I Thess. 4: 17), must unite with the ascending blue line of the perfected people of God, the seven lamps, and then must they both, the golden line of the glorified Christ and the blue line of the completed church, remain inseparable for all eternity (I Thess. 4: 17b). Therefore henceforth they experience all things in common. He who Himself came down first only to the region of the air, so as to come *for* His own, will then *with* His own Himself appear on earth (I Thess. 3: 13), so as then during the visible kingdom of God, united with them, to reign from heaven over the earth.

But finally this united gold and blue double line, above and beyond world rebellion (Gog and Magog), world destruction, and world transfiguration, will merge into eternity. On the new earth, and in the heavenly Jerusalem come down to earth, Christ will rule as Throne-Companion of the Father (Rev. 22: 1; I Cor. 15: 28). and His own will be with Him and share His. glory (John 17: 24; Rom. 8: 17). They will reign with Christ to all eternity (Rev. 22: 5; II Tim. 2: 12).

CHAPTER VIII

THE PRESENT COMPLETE SALVATION IN CHRIST

"THE voice of rejoicing and salvation is in the tents of the righteous" (Psa. 118: 15). Because Jesus has conquered, the fountain of life is open to us. Because He has overcome we also can live as overcomers. Because He has triumphed His triumph is our happy portion.

All His saving work is established in completeness and perfection.

THE MEDIATOR OF SALVATION

As the Christ, Jesus is the fulfilment of the Old Testament (Christ = Messiah = Anointed). As Bearer of the fulness of the Spirit of God (Acts 10: 38) He is the personal union of the three chief anointed offices of the old covenant. He is at once prophet, priest, and king. At the same time, His threefold work corresponds to all three powers of man's soul.

The corruption of man through sin was total. His understanding was darkened, his feelings became unhappy, his will evil.

Now as Prophet, Christ brings knowledge and releases man's understanding from the bonds of darkness.

As Priest, He presents the guilt offering, cancels both man's guilt and his consciousness of guilt, and brings his feelings to rejoice in the forgiveness of sins, and at the same time the blessedness of fellowship with God.

As King, He establishes His saving rule, governs the will of man by His own Divine holy will, and thus frees the will of man from the slavery of sin.

Thus His threefold office corresponds to the three powers of man's soul, and as before sin had conquered completely, so has Christ as Prophet, Priest, and King, now completely triumphed. No power of the soul is excepted. The whole man is drawn into the working of salvation. A full, free, total salvation is acquired.

THE GIFT OF SALVATION

On the ground of this all-sufficient work of salvation there can now be a life of richness and joy. The believer is brought out of the abyss of sin on to the high rock of salvation (Psa. 40: 2, 3). Out of hell's prison he is now set in heavenly places (Eph. 1: 3; 2: 6). He, the rebel, is pardoned by heaven's King and set among the nobles of the land (Psa. 16: 3). Indeed, he is made a member of the King's family (Rom. 8: 15), and shall at last reign

with Christ, the Son of God, in all the ages of eternity (Rev.
22: 5; I Cor. 6: 2, 3; Luke 12: 32).

What a salvation! Should it not incite our hearts to continual
exultation? Should we not in joyful thankfulness lay our lives
at His feet, devote ourselves wholly to Him, and freely and
willingly exert ourselves to be an ornament, a jewel, to the
message of the gospel, this most glorious proclamation to the
world (Titus 2: 10)?

Enriched in Christ, the practical realization of these riches is
now our duty. This is at once our task and privilege. The
redeemed must live as redeemed. Bearers of salvation must
walk as saved. They who possess heaven must be heavenly-
minded.

The Personal Experience of Salvation

But for an overcoming life certain definite spiritual pre-supposi-
tions are demanded. Only the Christian who responds to these
will rightly realize his full salvation and be preserved in holiness.
We mention certain of the most important basic conditions of
such an inward spiritual state.

1. *Faith on the finished work of Christ.* We must see once for
all how completely Christ has conquered. Not till then can we
experience a joyful life of victory. We do not need to torment
ourselves to effect our own salvation. We do not fight *for*
victory but *from* victory. The pre-requisite for victory already
exists. The Commander-in-chief has triumphed. Full salvation is now available in Him. "Jesus saves me now." In particular our eyes must be open to the high standing in grace which
we have received in Christ. We are "chosen, sanctified, be-
loved" (Col. 3: 12). We are a "temple of the Holy Spirit"
(Eph. 2: 21, 22; I Cor. 6: 19). We are sons of the Most High
(Gal. 4: 6, 7). Christ, the Firstborn, is not ashamed to call us
His brethren (Rom. 8: 29; Heb. 2: 11).

This knowledge of the high standing in grace does not make
us self-secure and self-contented, nor high-minded and satisfied,
but rather grateful of heart, and therefore devoted and dedicated
to God, always supposing that it is a truly spiritual knowledge
that is inwrought and interpenetrated by the Spirit.

But in whom this view of the freely granted fulness of grace is
lacking there will never be joy in his salvation. He toils in his
own strength, experiences defeat after defeat, perhaps at length
gives up the fight, and in practice sin carries off the victory.
Therefore is a Spirit-wrought view of full salvation in Christ a
pre-requisite for all true practical experiences of salvation.

2. *Full Surrender*. Faith is at the same time devotion. The original language of the New Testament has the same word for "faith" and "faithfulness" (Gr. *pistis*). Faith is not only assent to the doctrine, but at the same time practical consent by the life. As Luther said, faith is "life in God," or as Zwingli expressed it, "life in the Head." Faith is a dedication of one's self.

But here all depends upon the completeness of the dedication. Only entirely devoted Christians are entirely happy Christians. Someone has said that "a half-Christian is a complete absurdity." This is drastic but thoroughly justified.

Some Christians pray for devotion: "Lord, give me full devotion." But in this they overlook that their prayer is quite false. They ask that *God* will do something that He expects from *them*. Dedication is our responsibility. We have to say: "Lord, I devote myself to Thee," and actually to do it. Then will His victorious power stream into our life and the joy of full salvation will overflow in us.

3. *Attention to the Word of God*. Neglect of the Bible implies neglect of our own inner life. "Ignorance of Holy Scripture is ignorance of Christ" (Jerome). "As you deal with God's Word so God deals with you." God comes to us through the written Word. His Spirit accompanies His Word. The Catholic Bishop von Keppler has justly said: "The Holy Scripture is to us today the land that flows with milk and honey, and he who searches it as a spy can find there even today a fulness of new and surprising things." The Bible widens our vision. It shows us God's trustworthiness. It supplies holy objects for our thought and meditation. It sets before our striving noble objectives, and he who attends to the Word of God, and joyfully submits to it, will experience that

> "If a man hearkens God speaks;
> If a man obeys God acts."

4. *Faithfulness in little things*. "He who is faithful in that which is least, is faithful also in much" (Luke 16: 10). Only he who is watchful in the small everyday battle will grow strong and will steadily attain to a *life* of victory. Faithfulness means to be exact in little things, including when *no one sees it*. He who is ready to be faithful must be continually conscious of the presence of Christ. "Little is much if God is in it." Therefore in no wise despise the everyday life. In victory or defeat in the small everyday burdens and tests it will be decided how far experience of full salvation is a real practical possession.

5. *The life of prayer*. He who would have must take. But he who prays not receives nothing (Jas. 4: 2b, 3). Unfaithfulness in prayer means voluntary renunciation of victory. Only in the presence of God flow the living springs of salvation. Therefore wouldst thou be happy? Become a man of prayer. God only dispenses His gifts direct from His throne, He never dispatches gifts to a distance. Practical experience of salvation is known only in His presence.

6. *Courageous witness*. He who will be victorious must be a witness. "They overcame him [Satan] through the blood of the Lamb and through the word of their testimony" (Rev. 12: 11). He who confesses Christ becomes inwardly strong. In the storms the roots of the trees strike deeper. By bold confession the frontiers become clear. Discipleship and the world are made distinct from each other; in the follower of the Lord resoluteness and the consciousness of responsibility increase and the whole inner man becomes active and directed to Christ. Therefore courageous confession belongs to the practical presuppositions of experience of full salvation.

7. *Joyful counting upon the presence of Christ*. Practise the presence of Christ in thy life. Think of this: Where thou art, He also is. He sees every situation. He can help daily and hourly. He is Immanuel, "God with us." Grace has appeared: grace is therefore here (Titus 2: 11). What we need is to reckon practically upon the reality of the presence of the Holy Spirit here and now.

This was the special message which, some decades ago, a blessed revival movement called forth: "Jesus saves me now." It was the joyful message of the possibility of a victorious life, of sanctification through faith, of present and full salvation in Christ, which was set anew before the souls of the people of God in God-given authority. Full dedication to the Lord, freedom from not only the guilt but also the power of sin: what is this but rays of heavenly light able to illuminate the hearts of the redeemed and set us free from all feeble superficiality and daily experience of poverty or fruitless striving after holiness? Then is holiness no longer a wearisome effort in our own strength but a Divine working of the risen and glorified Christ. But for this one needs decided devotion, high aims, daily purifying, joyful energy, living freshness, and all this in Christ, the living and present One.

To the poets of the noblest treasures of song in the German language belongs the Lutheran Martin Rinkart, the "Ambrose of the Evangelical Church," writer of the hymn, "Now thank we all our God," which has been termed the German *Te Deum* (1586–1649).   This man of God, a Field Marshal in spiritual dress, had served his Lord and his church with heroic courage and great risk in the days of the pestilence and famine of the Thirty Years War.   He had a signet ring with the inscription "Musica."   He was a great friend of poetry and song and he gave this word a special meaning:

M.......V.......S.......I.......C.......A

MEIN   VERTRAUEN   STEHT   IN   CHRISTUS   ALLEIN
My   trust   stands   in   Christ   alone

And is not this in truth the experience of all holy men of God? Is it not so, that where trust on Christ is present there triumphant "musical" joy fills the soul? (Col. 3: 16; Eph. 5: 19).

But finally your present salvation in Christ will be glorified in possession of the future eternal salvation.   And as even now the soul of the redeemed has known only one basic melody, so will it then through all eternity ring out,

> "The Lord is my strength and my song
> And He is become my salvation"
> (Psa. 118. 14)

> "Nought have I to offer:
> Thou, O Lord, art all."

E

CHAPTER IX

THE CHURCH OF THE LIVING GOD

"IT is finished" (John 19: 30). This is the mightiest word that has ever been spoken on this earth. It was the most triumphant cry of victory in the hour of apparent catastrophic defeat. It is the creative spring of a God-given message which, world-redeeming and world renewing, goes forth to mankind.

With it there entered something quite new to the world outlook and religious thought of man. All merely human religious thought and work proceeds from the powers of man, from his spiritual, intentional, moral effort. In this, in spite of all differences in detail, lies the common factor in all heathen religions. But now all this is set aside. The starting point of all salvation lies entirely above, not at all below. Here it is God who effects all things. All human moral activity is faulty development. Salvation must be purely grant and gift, a revelation of the undeserved love of God, that is, it must be grace.

THE CHURCH AS A NEW CREATION OF GOD

The introduction of a heavenly new creation was a divine necessity. For through sin the old man is completely corrupted. Because man is not a stone but a spiritual organism, so soon as evil has forced itself into his life he works it out automatically into all parts of his being. Because of the organic character of the human personality, and by reason of the very height of his calling, at the entrance of sin there follows of itself so much the deeper a fall. Sin grips him radically, centrally, and totally; that is, as to root, centre, and circumference he is bound and lost, sold and enslaved.

Therefore he must be made a new creature. It cannot suffice that he makes only a complete change, turns himself around, and strives in practice after a new moral standard and direction in life. No, with the repentance and turning to God on man's side there must be united from God's side a creative act. The man who turns himself to God must, by the wonder of the new birth, be recreated in the essence of his personality. Not only his deeds and his life, no, he himself must become new (John 3: 7; II Cor. 5: 17). Thus out of the deep fall of the old man there arises the necessity of the new creating of a new man. The fleshly organism of the one lost must, by a Divine begetting, be replaced by the

66

spiritual organism of the one redeemed; and this new creation must be the dawn of a new world, according to its nature and being, the first step towards the final goal, a living prophet of the triumphant final promise, "Behold, I create a new heaven and a new earth." This is the church.

But this can only be effected by a work of God Himself, for when it comes to a creative act only the Creator personally can perform it. Neither angels nor archangels, neither cherubim nor seraphim, have creative power. As Creator and Imparter of life God the infinite is throned in solitary eminence above all His creatures, even the highest and most glorious in the heavenly world.

Therefore the church rests on a Divine ground. And therefore she *must* rest on it; and our faith is permitted to perceive that the sending of the Son, and undertaking of the work of redemption by a Person of the very Godhead, is not only a proof of the infinity of His love (John 3: 16; Rom. 5: 8), but is at the same time an outcome of an inner Divine necessity. Therefore Christ "must" suffer, on the third day rise from the dead, and enter into His glory (comp. Luke 24: 26, 46). But by this the church becomes forthwith the church of the *Son*. She lives by the work of the Son; the Son is her divine Head; and indeed, in the Son she is appointed to sonship (Eph. 1: 5; I Cor. 1: 9).

And now our eyes behold this mighty cosmic bow which the Son of God for our sakes trod as Redeemer. From the height of the throne of heaven to the depth of the earth and of death; out of the gloom of the dark night of the grave into the brilliant light above all the height of heaven (Phil. 2: 5–11; Eph. 4: 8–10; Heb 7: 26)—this is the path of the Redeemer for the sinner, the path of the Head for His members, of Christ for His church.

Therefore the church is the church of the Cross, the fruit of Golgotha. Christ died that "He might bring together in one the scattered children of God" (John 11: 52). Dying He became the Leader to life (Heb. 2: 10), in death the Conqueror of death (Heb. 2: 14), in the substitutionary sufferings under judgment the Cause of eternal heavenly salvation (Heb. 5: 9).

And because Christ, as the Risen One, has conquered the power of death therefore is His church a *living* church. She is an organism of risen ones, who have been made to live (Rom. 6: 5; Eph. 2: 5, 6), interpenetrated by His energies (Phil. 4: 13), pulsating with His life (Phil. 3: 10, 11), awaiting the revelation of the breaking forth of His full life: "When Christ, our life, shall be manifested, then will you also with Him become manifest in glory" (Col. 3: 4).

The Church as the Church of Christ, the "Body" of Christ

The men who believe in this belong to an entirely new world. Their life element is the Redeemer himself (Phil. 1: 21), their strength for victory is His grace (I Cor. 15: 10), their glory is His cross alone (Gal. 6: 14; I Cor. 2: 2). And because they are all organically joined to the same living Centre, Christ, therefore they form together a living unity, are one organism, suffused by the same spirit of Christ (I Cor 12: 13; II Cor. 3: 17). The church is "in Christ."

The New Testament sets this forth by the picture of the "body." This picture—used only by Paul—shows as no other the fulness of the New Testament riches of grace.

The church is "His" body (Eph. 1: 23). She is ruled by His will, for the head is the will of the body (Col 1: 18). In all her members she stands in direct relation to the Head (Col. 2: 19). From the Head she receives her strength. Out of the Head comes her growth (Eph. 4: 16). She is guarded by the Head; Christ, the Head, is the Saviour of the body (Eph. 5: 23). Indeed Paul, under the guidance of the Spirit of God, goes so far as to say that the church is "the fulness of Him who fills all things in all" (Eph. 1: 23). This means that, Christ, although not as a Divine person but as the "last Adam," would not be complete without His body. Without its fruit the corn of wheat would be "alone" (John 12: 24). A redeemer without redeemed were no redeemer. But now Christ has His church, now the Head has His members; therefore is the church as the body of Christ the "full complement of Him who brings to completion all things in all."

This is the church of Christ. With her there steps into history a completely new type of mankind (Eph. 2: 15), in which, as far as redemption is concerned, even now all former distinctions and standards (Gal. 3: 28; I Cor. 7: 19) have lost their validity: "there is no Greek and Jew, circumcision and uncircumcision, barbarian, Scythian, slave or free, but Christ is all things and in all" (Col. 3: 11). Already today the church is a piece of heaven on earth (Phil. 3: 20), a projection of the new creation amidst the old (II Cor. 5: 17), the sphere of God's life in history. She is the creaturely vessel of an eternal life born of God, a living prophetic setting forth of the great goal of redemption, "Behold, the tabernacle of God is with men" (Rev. 21: 3), "Christ in us the hope of glory" (Col. 1: 27).

THE CHURCH OF THE LIVING GOD

THE CHURCH AS THE CHURCH OF THE SPIRIT
The Twofold outpouring of the Holy Spirit in Jerusalem and Caesarea

From the historical revelation we see that in the development of salvation in Old Testament times there had been two groups of mankind; the one, inside the radiant circle of the Divine revelation in its direct preparation for redemption; the other group, since the call of Abraham and the setting aside of the nations, outside this sphere of light; even Israel and the nations, the "near" and the "far" (Eph. 2: 17). Therefore now the wonder of the new creating of the church, through the sending down of the Holy Spirit, must be effected as one *double* event, even by the outpouring of the Spirit not only on Israelites but also upon Gentiles. This is exactly what came to pass. In Jerusalem at Pentecost the descent of the Holy Spirit took place upon Jewish ground (Acts. 2): later, in Caesarea, in the house of the Roman Cornelius, the "like gift" was given on Gentile ground (Acts. 11: 17; 15: 8, 9; 10: 44–48). From then and onward all, whether by descent Jewish or Gentile, who have become partakers of the Holy Spirit are one spiritual organism in Christ (Eph. 3: 6; I Cor. 12: 13).

"MYSTERIES" OF REDEMPTION IN THE PRESENT CHURCH AGE

In the then following apostolic period three chief personalities, as the most notable standard bearers, have carried forward, among Israel and the nations, the truth of full salvation in Christ: Peter, Paul, and John. In this order they follow one another as the chief leaders of the apostolic time. First Peter begins in Jerusalem (esp. Acts 2–12); then follows Paul moving from Antioch out among the nations (esp. Acts. 13–28; I Tim. 27), and lastly John, especially in Ephesus and the churches of western Asia Minor (comp. Rev. 2: 3): Peter, the man of confidence and hope (I Pet.), Paul the herald of faith, John the apostle of love. So in this triple constellation of the most notable apostolic personalities there shines forth in historical unfolding the high moral trinity of all Christian holiness, "now abide faith, hope, love, these three."

To no prophet or saint of the old covenant was this wonderful spiritual organism fully made known by Divine prophecy (Eph. 3: 5; comp. Matt. 13: 17). That in the very time following the rejection of Messiah by unbelieving Israel God would carry out so magnificent, world-embracing and eternal a plan was a purpose which from before the ages He had hidden in Himself (Eph 3: 9), a mystery which had been kept in silence from the ages of time

(Rom. 16: 25). But now, in the New Testament time, there comes a revealing of the "mysteries of the kingdom of God" (Matt. 13: 11), an unfolding of Divine counsels formerly concealed. Now a whole fulness of mysteries is made known prophetically by His Spirit and is carried out historically through His working. The connexion of life and love between Christ and His own as His body (Eph. 5: 31), the inseparable oneness in the church between Israel and the believers from the Gentiles (Eph. 3: 1–6; 2: 11–22), the indwelling of Christ as the hope of glory (Col. 1: 27), the rapture, resurrection, and transfiguration in the perfection of a spiritual body (I Cor. 15: 51), the re-acceptance of Israel after the period of judicial hardening (Rom. 11: 25)—these all are mysteries of the Divine will[1] which He reveals and fulfils, and which He has entrusted to His own to be testified and administered (I Cor. 4: 1; Eph. 6: 19).

THE CHURCH AS A WITNESSING CHURCH

The Seven Golden Lampstands

With the message of full salvation the church has gone forth into the world. To witness for Christ is her high calling here on earth (Acts. 1: 8). Therefore her members are called "luminaries —heavenly lights" shining in the darkness of the world (Phil. 2: 15), a city on a hill that cannot be hid (Matt. 5: 14–16), and seven golden lampstands, with the glorified Christ in the midst, who is radiant as the sun, shining with eternal light (Rev. 1: 12, 14, 16; 2; 3). Therefore the church is commissioned to give a bright testimony. Christ and His Cross should be the theme of her life, and there must be practical carrying out of the truth, clear and perceptible to every man.

In word and work, in every deed,
May none see ought but Christ to read.

But thereby the church becomes also a prophet of Christ, as bearer of the life, a witness also of the life. She is proclaimer and interpreter of His life to the world. She is ambassador and confessor, messenger and mouth of God, and so, according to her entire inward nature, a church with a mission. Through the church shall be made known the manifold wisdom of God (Eph. 3: 10). Through His body the exalted Head extends His holy life here below. Thus is the church, as it were, through the Spirit the continuance on earth of the incarnation of Christ. She is not only in Christ, but Christ is also in her (Col. 1: 27). He acquires form in her, expresses in her His nature, and the Head reveals Himself through His members.

[1] Eph. 1: 9, 10; Col. 2: 2; 4: 3; Tim. 3: 9.

Why do we carry on missionary work?   Why must the church of Jesus Christ continually carry it on?   Why is she permitted to do it?

First, because Jesus Christ is the only Saviour of the world. "I am *the* way, *the* truth, and *the* life: no one comes to the Father but through Me" (John 14: 6).   Out of the solitariness and exclusiveness of the redemption in Christ arises its all-embracing application to the world and the unavoidable duty of the church to make known to the whole of mankind this one Saviour.

Second, because Christ has commanded it.   One has spoken rightly of a missionary "command."   The gospel is made known "according to the *commandment* of the eternal God" (Rom. 16: 26).

Third, because it follows out of the nature of the church as the "body" of Christ.   Just as our human physical body is the instrument by which our invisible, inner life, soul and spirit, reveals itself, so also is the church as the body of Christ, through the working of the Spirit the means and organ of the self-revelation of the indwelling Christ, and therefore the instrument for making known His life and saving truth.   "Ye shall be my witnesses" (Acts. 1: 8).

Fourth, because it is "gratitude for Golgotha."

The missionary duty which Christ has given to His own is world-embracing.   Four times in the great commission occurs the little word "all" (Matt. 28: 18–20).

"*All* authority is given unto Me."   This is the *foundation* of the work.   Without Christ, the Victor, the cause had long since been lost.   But His victory is our victory: His triumph leads to the triumph of His work.

"Teach *all* nations."   This is the *scope* of the work.   The gospel belongs to every man.   The church of the Lord is responsible to give its witness to the whole world.   We can form scarcely any idea of the greatness of the field.   There are living on earth about 2,300 millions of men.   If a modern express train at its average speed had to travel as many miles as there are men on earth—to each man a mile—then to arrive today at our town it must have started as early as the beginning of the first century before Christ (100 B.C.).   The inhabitants of Africa number more than the individual letters of 39 to 40 Bibles.   Thirty-nine large volumes!   And each individual letter representing a human soul, for whom Christ died!

"Teach them to observe *all* things that I have commanded you."   This is the *content* of our work.   We take to the whole world the whole Word of God, the whole Saviour, the whole salvation.

"And lo, I am with you *all* the days, even unto the end of the age." This is the *promise* of the work. The King not only sends forth but goes Himself with His soldiers. The Commander-in-Chief remains with His army, and His presence is their strength for victory.

But all this can be practical experience for the church only if she is a warrior church, if everything in her is marked by sanctification and testimony, action and growth, forward effort and movement, even by an experience of conscious responsibility, streamlined, God-wrought, filled and penetrated by the Spirit. What she *is* as to her standing, she must *become* in her walk. She is not an organization, only with "holy" institutions, but an organism of holy-acting persons. She is a society of active workers, serving and working, witnessing and bearing fruit. As redeemed she knows herself bound, in her freedom called to joyous service. She treasures the nobility of holy labour; she purposes to glorify Christ.

But in all this she walks contrary to the world. Therefore light is hated by the darkness, and the message of the church is despised and rejected. Indeed, at times it almost looks as if the saints will be overcome.

The Church as the Church of Hope

Therefore this tension must some day be released. Christ will come back and take His church to Himself. By exercise of divine power He will remove His people to His presence (I Thess. 4: 16, 17), and the Conqueror will unite to Himself His victorious warriors and heroes in eternal glory (John 12: 26; 14: 3). "Where I am there shall also My servant be. If any man serve Me him will the Father honour." The *ecclesia* is a church of hope. She is certain of her victory.

Christ triumphed on the cross. The goal of the church is her being glorified with Christ. She lives "from heaven, in heaven, and with a view to heaven. Her way is everlasting, her existence eternal." She is a waiting, expectant church, a church of first-born sons, whom the heavenly inheritance beckons. She is a victorious army of future conquerors.

Nevertheless all the redeemed will be made manifest before the judgment seat of Christ. Then each individual will receive according to what he had done in his life in the body (II Cor. 5: 10). Then will each one receive the rank in the glory which is his due (I Cor. 4: 5; II Tim. 4: 8).

From then on, from the time of its being rapt to heaven the church will be in inseparable union with Christ. It will appear with Him at the establishing of His kingdom (I Thess. 3: 13; Col. 3: 4). It will reign with Him in the period of the visible rule of God.   Indeed, it will be His "ruling aristocracy," His "administrative staff" in His kingdom in all the eternal ages. "Know ye not that the saints shall judge the world? . . .   Know ye not that we shall judge angels?" (I Cor. 6: 2, 3).   "Fear not, thou little flock; for it is your Father's good pleasure to give you the kingdom" (Luke 12: 32).

CHAPTER X

THE "DAYS" OF GOD

GOLGOTHA is the crisis of the ages, a world crisis, the dawn of an age in which a completely new world arises. From the victory of Christ on the Cross and His triumph in resurrection there begins a development which, advancing through millenniums, merges at last into the eternal world trans-figuration. All these ages are controlled by God as the supreme Lord of history and eternity and are therefore "hours" of God, "days" of God.

In essence the New Testament unfolding of salvation on into eternity appears as the course of three great days of God, the day of salvation (II Cor. 6: 2), the last day (John 6: 39, 40; etc.), and the day of eternity (II Pet. 3: 10; 12). But with this, in the Scripture certain sub-sections of the "last day" are also described by the term "day," so that the "last day" is presented as the combination and sum of several shorter days of God, as "day of Christ," "day of the Lord," "that day," "day of judgment." This free usage of the word "day" is a sign of the great range and freedom with which the prophets, when delivering their messages, under the guidance of the Holy Spirit, employed their terms.

The first of these three chief days is

THE DAY OF SALVATION (II Cor. 6: 2).

This is the age in which we at present live. Through the Word of God and the Spirit of God the message of redemption is offered to mankind, full salvation in the accomplished work of the Saviour, the undeserved gift of the free grace of God. Therefore the Lord says: "In an acceptable time have I heard thee, and in a day of salvation have I helped thee. Behold, now is the acceptable time; behold, now is the day of salvation" (II Cor. 6: 2). This "day" of grace will close when the full number from the nations is brought in and the church completed (Rom. 11: 25).

Looking backwards this New Testament time is the goal of the Old Testament preparatory development. All pre-Christian revelation was directed to the time of Christ. Therefore Christ is the final goal of the millenniums before the crisis of the ages. Therefore with His appearing the end age, that is, the goal age, had come—an organic united display of prophecy and fulfilment, of preparation and completion, which forthwith led early apostolic thought to describe the whole New Testament time of salvation from the first appearing of Christ as "End time," as the "last days." So Peter in his address on Pentecost ascribed the then events in Jerusalem to the "last days" (Acts. 2: 17). So John said in his epistle, "Little children, it is [the] last hour" (I John 2: 18). So Paul could say that upon us, the church of Christ, the "end points," the "goal points" of the pre-Messianic (pre-Christian) ages are come (I Cor. 10: 11). According to early Christian conviction the "End time" began with the incarnation of Christ (Heb. 1: 1, 2; I John 2: 18). His first appearing is the beginning of the End, and with His second appearing begins the end of the End. Thus in the sense of the New Testament the history of the End is not simply the history of the ultimate future, but the whole New Testament history of salvation is the history of the End as a progressive perfecting and arriving at the consummation. In Christ the beginning of the completion has appeared. Therefore ever since then everything is already the "End time" (*The Triumph of the Crucified*, pp. 102*ff*.).

But at length the close of this End time will come. This also will be completed in a mighty development embracing a lengthy period of centuries. This whole period from the close of the present age till the arrival of world perfecting the Holy Scripture calls a "day," that is "the last day."

THE LAST DAY

This expression is found in Scripture especially in the mouth of the Lord Jesus (John. 6: 39, 40, 44, 54; 12: 48), and also of one of His company (John 11: 24).

According to the words of the Lord there belongs to "the last day" the resurrection of those whom the Father drew to the Son and had given to Him, who, having believed, have eternal life (John 6: 44; 39, 40, 54). Also, according to the testimony of the Lord, the judgment of the lost belongs to the "last day" (John 12: 48). Now the *Revelation* of John explains that the "first" resurrection, in which only believers have part (Rev. 20: 5, 6), does not come together with the general resurrection; indeed, that the whole Millennium and the following "little time" (Gog and Magog) lie between: "And I saw thrones, and they sat upon them, and it was given to them to exercise judgment . . . and they lived and reigned with Christ a thousand years. The rest of the dead lived not till the thousand years were finished. This is the first resurrection. Blessed and holy is he who has part in the first resurrection" (Rev. 20: 4–6).

But if now, according to the words of the Lord Jesus, both

resurrections, the first and the general, belong to the "last day" it follows that this "day" is no single event but must be a long period which embraces first the introducing of the Millennial kingdom, then this itself, and finally the "little time" after the Millennium (Rev. 20: 3, 7), and the general judgment of the world before the great white throne.   Thus the "last day" is a day of God even as the present "day of salvation," which last has already included many centuries.   "With God a thousand years are as a day" (II Pet. 3: 8).

Now the members of the church belong to those whom the Father drew and gave to the Son, who stand in living organic fellowship with Him who for them died and rose again, who believe on Him and therefore possess eternal life.   And concerning these Christ says plainly that He will raise them "in the last day" (John 6: 39, 40, 44, 54).   Therefore the resurrection and rapture of the church must belong to the events of the "last day," with the contemporaneous manifestation before the judgment seat of Christ (II Cor. 5: 10).

The point of time of this manifestation of believers before the returning Lord Paul names the "day of Christ," "day of the Lord Jesus," "day of our Lord Jesus Christ," where, in all the six places in which he uses these expressions,[1] he speaks without exception of that which the final End time will bring judicially solely for believers of the New Testament church.[2]   Never in this connexion does he employ the term "day of the Lord."

The reason is as follows.   The term "day of the Lord" answers to the prophetic term "day of Jehovah."   Thus it is rooted in Old Testament prophecy, and from this, since the time of Joel (2: 1, 2; 3: 14), had a fixed and firmly impressed meaning. It denoted the time and manner of the coming of the kingdom of God and the kingdom itself.   But because, on account of the sins of Israel and of the nations, the visible kingdom of glory could only be introduced by severest catastrophies and displays of judgment, in Old Testament prophecy the term "day of Jehovah" (the Lord) signified the same as "the last tribulation," which breaks in as "great trouble" (Dan. 12: 1) for Israel ("time of Jacob's trouble," Jer. 30: 7) and for the nations.   In the New Testament, Christ in His discourse on Olivet (Matt. 24: 16, 21, 29), and the apostle John in the *Revelation* further spoke of this.   Occasionally Paul also wrote upon it (esp. II Thess. 1: 6–10; 2: 2–12).

But when at the end of his prophecy Joel cries: "Multitudes, multitudes in the valley of decision; for near is the *day of Jeho-*

---

[1] Phil. 2: 16; 1: 6, 10; I Cor. 1: 8; II Cor. 1: 14.

[2] II Cor. 5: 10; Rom. 14: 10; I Cor. 3: 13–15; 4: 2–5; etc.

vah . . .; sun and moon are darkened" (3: 14, 15); and when he then, in the same connexion, continues: "And it will come to pass *in that day* that the mountains shall drop with new wine . . . and all the brooks of Judah shall flow with water" (3: 18), then it is clear that he connects the term "day of the Lord" not with the gloomy time of judgment only, but also, and as concerns the length of the period, even chiefly with the glorious time of the visible kingdom of God. This is the reason why, in our Chart, we have not placed the expression "day of the Lord" simply in the section which represents the time of final (Antichristian) judgment, but have so set it that it reaches into the section of the Millennium.

In numerous places in the prophets the kingdom of glory is described simply with the expression "those days" (plural), because thereby this period is at once and in especial manner denoted as the desired goal to which all expectation is directed, and which is so much the object of all waiting and the chief theme of all prophecy that it simply did not need any closer description. There was only one series of blessed days which would bring true prosperity out of eternity into time, namely "those days" (Jer. 3: 16; Joel 3: 1; 2: 29; Zech. 8: 23).

The close, then, is the last judgment, the "day of judgment,"[1] in which all have to appear before God who did not have part in the rapture and the first resurrection. It is the ultimate event of the "last day," the final recompense of men and angels (Jude 6), the last settlement of accounts, at the great white throne.[2]

Thus is the final goal reached and eternity breaks in. In the Scripture this is described as

THE DAY OF ETERNITY (II Pet. 3: 18), THE DAY OF GOD (II Pet. 3: 12)

To introduce this the heaven must burst into flames and be dissolved, and the elements melt in fervent heat (II Pet. 3: 12). Then every sphere of sin is gone, and a new world stands forth in glory and holiness, with God Himself as its centre (Rev. 22: 3), so that "God may be all in all" (I Cor. 15: 28). And because this, God's day of perfection and completion, will never end, but will continue in all ages of the ages, the Holy Scripture names this "day of God" also "day of eternity."

This is the goal toward which we advance. Therefore it behoves us to press forward, to expect and to hasten the coming of the day of God, to "grow in the grace and knowledge of our Lord and Saviour Jesus Christ" (II Pet. 3: 18).

---

[1] Matt. 10: 15; 11: 22, 24; 12: 36.

[2] Rev. 20: 11-15; II Pet. 2: 9; 3: 7; Rom. 2: 5.

CHAPTER XI

THE JUDGMENT SEAT OF CHRIST AND THE GREAT WHITE THRONE

HOLY Scripture foretells two chief End judgments: the church being made manifest before the judgment seat of Christ and the general final judgment before the great white throne (II Cor. 5: 10; Rev. 20: 11-15).[1] These are far separated in point of time. Between them lies the Millennium (Rev. 20: 5).

DIVISIONS AND CLASSES IN THE RESURRECTION

The hitherto widely spread setting forth of the last day as one single event, with only one resurrection, simultaneous for righteous and unrighteous, and only one Divine judgment at the end of the world, does not correspond to New Testament prophecy. Much rather the Holy Scripture speaks of a resurrection *"From among* the dead" (Luke 20: 35), of a "first" resurrection (Rev. 20: 6), indeed, of a resurrection *"out* from among the dead" (Phil. 3: 11, lit.). It speaks of divisions and classes *within* the resurrection, and emphasizes that these are separated from one another by intervening periods. "As in Adam all die, so in Christ will they all be made to live. But *each* in his own class [the word also signifies military division]: the firstfruits Christ; *thereafter* those who belong to Christ, when He shall come: *thereafter* the end [that is, the end of the resurrection, namely of the rest of the dead]" (I Cor. 15: 22-24).

It is true that in the Old Testament both of these, the resurrection to "eternal life" and the resurrection to "eternal reproach and shame," are brought together in one picture (Dan. 12: 2, 13), and similarly in the prophecies of the Lord Jesus on earth (John 5: 28, 29; comp. Acts. 24: 15); but as prophetic revelation advanced (John 16: 12, 13) these appeared as *two* chief events and separated as to time: the resurrection of the righteous before the beginning of the kingdom of Messiah, and the general resurrection thereafter, at the end of the world. The key is Rev. 20: 5, 6: "These [the priests of God and of Christ] lived and reigned with Christ a thousand years. The rest of the dead lived not until the thousand years were finished. This is the *first* resurrection. Blessed and holy is he who has part in the *first* resurrection."

---

[1] Concerning the intervening judgment of the nations on earth at the beginning of the Millennial kingdom, see p. 54.

Connected with these stages of the resurrection there are two different chief final judgments.

THE JUDGMENT SEAT OF CHRIST

The first is the manifestation of believers before the judgment seat of Christ.[1] This takes place at the rapture of the church in the "day of Jesus Christ,[2] before the setting up of the visible kingdom of God. Here the walk of believers will be set in the light of the face of Christ, and each will receive according as he had acted when in the body, be it good or evil (II Cor. 5: 10). Loss or gain (I Cor. 3: 14, 15: Col. 3: 24), higher or lower position in heaven (Matt 5: 19), shame (I John 2: 28) or honour,[3] burning up or stability of one's life-work (I Cor. 3: 13–15)—upon all this decisions will be given at the judgment seat of Christ.

Let us take this seriously. It is indeed true that he who believes on the Son is free from final judgment (John 5: 24; Rom. 8: 1), for Christ, his Surety, has borne this judgment in his place (Isa. 53: 5, 126), and through faith he himself is become one with Him. But even so it is true, and of most momentous consequence, that the day in which believers will have to appear before the judgment seat of Christ "will be revealed in fire" (I Cor. 3: 13). Paul even speaks of the heart-stirring possibility that a believer, though saved personally, may suffer *such* damage to be compared to a man escaping out of a fire with his bare life (I Cor. 3: 15). Let us therefore live in practical faithfulness! That is the standard by which we shall be judged before the judgment seat of Christ (I Cor. 4: 2), and thus at last will be opened to us "richly" an entrance into the eternal kingdom of our Lord and Saviour Jesus Christ.

THE JUDGMENT BEFORE THE GREAT WHITE THRONE

The judgment before the great white throne is the proper general and final judgment. According to the testimony of the *Revelation* it comes at the end of the world after the Millennial kingdom and the following "little time" (Rev. 20: 11–15).[4] It follows directly after the extermination of the apostate race of the

---

[1] "We all"; (II Cor. 5: 10; Rom. 14: 10). In all, Scripture speaks in a threefold respect of the judgment of believers. "First of their judgment as sinners, second as children, third as servants. As sinners they were judged in the past on the cross. There in their Substitute their sentence was fully executed: the chastisement lay upon Him, that we might have peace. This is their blessed confession. As children they are judged in the present, when they are chastened by the Lord (I Cor. 11: 32). This is for their profit, so that they may attain sanctification (Heb. 12: 10). Lastly as servants, in the future, before the judgment seat of Christ."

[2] Phil. 2: 16; 1: 6, 10; Cor. 1: 8.

[3] "Crowns": II Tim. 4: 8; I Cor. 9: 25, 26; I Pet. 5: 3, 4.

[4] Comp. the connexion with ver. 1–14.

visible kingdom of Messiah (Gog and Magog), the general world destruction, and the final defeat of Satan (Rev. 20: 7–10). All have to appear before it who have not already appeared before the judgment seat of Christ, and thus mankind in general, including the nations of the Millennial kingdom. The result of the decision is inconceivably weighty. The Scripture says: "If anyone was not found written in the book of life he was cast into the lake of fire" (Rev. 20: 15).

Thus between these two judgments there lie many centuries. The one is at the beginning of the "last day,"[1] the other at its end. But for our gospel message and ministry both have significance also for all men living in the present age. With regard to these, that means:

Whoever has believed on Christ and has surrendered his life to Him as his Lord whom he serves, will have to appear before the judgment seat of Christ, and according to his faithfulness, he will have reward or loss. By Christ, the righteous judge, he will be set in that status in glory which is his allotted portion. As to his salvation there is nothing new to decide.[2]

But all others who may have heard, but not believed and obeyed the gospel, and consequently are not justified and sanctified (I Cor. 6: 11) on account of the work of the Redeemer, with all others of mankind of past and future, will be judged before the great white throne. How solemn if it shall then be shown that a man had heard the Gospel and had not believed, so that his name is not inscribed in the book of life! Therefore if thou hast not yet laid hold of salvation, make thy decision today! Bethink thyself that it concerns thy eternal destiny!   "Today, if ye should hear His voice, harden not your hearts" (Heb. 4: 7).

---

[1] Comp. ch. X: The "Days" of God.

[2] But certainly the perfected, both as assessors and under-judges, will take part in the final judgment. "Know ye not that the saints shall judge the world? Know ye not that we shall judge angels? (I Cor. 6: 2, 3).

CHAPTER XII

THE TRIUMPH OF THE KINGDOM OF GOD

"THIS is the victory that hath overcome the world even our faith" (I John 5: 4). The whole New Testament history of salvation is a mighty proof of the truth of this word. God's affairs do not move backward but forwards. The victory of living faith, in spite of various reverses in detail, yet viewed on the whole, strides irresistibly forward. This is proved unmistakably in every chief connexion and chief region of life of revealed history since Golgotha, in the Divine super-history as well as in the general history of man's redemption, in individual persons as in the final universal history.

THE DIVINE SUPER-HISTORICAL TRIUMPH
The Self-revelation of God as of the Holy Spirit, of the Son, of the Father

After completing the work of redemption Christ has gone to heaven. His witnesses carry the message of God's full salvation to mankind around. They are present in the world as visible representatives of their absent Lord (II Cor. 5: 20). But Christ himself is invisible.[1] In the present era of the kingdom of God everything that comes to pass is wrought by the Word of God and the Spirit of God. Therefore in a special sense it is the period of the saving activity of the *Holy Spirit*.

But herein lies a tension of extraordinary force. The puzzling "mystery" of the present age is that alongside of each other there is the publicity of the kingdom of Satan and the concealment of the kingdom of God, and this even today, in the period after Golgotha. Therefore God must introduce a day in which this contradiction shall be solved. This is the meaning of the return of Christ. Christ will become visible and establish His kingdom. Instead of His absence He will arrive and be present (*parousia*); instead of self-covering, self-uncovering; instead of concealment, revelation (*apocalypse* Col. 3: 4); instead of invisibility, brilliant outshining of His glory (*epiphany*). And then will set in a new period of salvation, the visible sovereignty of the *Son of God*.

But even this is not the final goal. The Scripture says that "He [Christ] must reign till He has put all His foes under His feet" (I Cor. 15: 25). Then He will pass the kingdom to God His Father, and the Son Himself will be subject to Him [the

[1] I Pet. 1: 8; Rom. 8: 24; II Cor. 5: 7.

Father] Who subjected all things to Him, that God may be all in all (I Cor. 15: 24, 28).   Then will have been reached the proper and actual end, the kingdom of *God the Father*.

Thus the New Testament history of salvation carries plainly a trinitarian imprint.   Out of the essence of the Divine Being the Divine Persons come forward ever more clearly, and since Golgotha the history of salvation becomes an ever ascending and advancing Self-revelation of the great God, the Holy Spirit, the Son, and the Father.   But thereby this super-historical line shows the invincibility of God's affairs and becomes to the whole earth and to all heaven a ringing testimony, that cannot but be heard, of the truth of the words, "Our faith is the victory that has overcome the world."

And the development of redemption on earth shows the same.

THE GENERAL HISTORICAL TRIUMPH
The Unfolding of the Counsel of God in Church, Nations and the Transfigured Universe

The goal of God in the present period is the creation of the New Testament church (*ecclesia*).   From all peoples men are called out to Christ through the gospel, and those who believe are united to Him and to one another as members.   Without doubt this is a mighty work.   When at last in the day of perfecting the church stands before Christ it will be thousands of thousands and ten thousands of ten thousands.   Yet compared with the millions and millions of men in general their number is but small.   It is the "little flock," as Jesus called them (Luke 12: 32).   Certainly this is no ground for doubt or despair; for truth remains truth quite independently of whether it is perceived and acknowledged by many or by few, and to precisely this "little flock" God has promised the kingdom (Luke 12: 32).

Nevertheless in this respect also God creates a broadening of the range of His salvation.   When Christ has appeared and established His kingdom on earth, the peoples as peoples will be placed under the blessing of His revelation, and Israel and the nations as a whole will be brought into the radiant light of the glorious kingdom.   Unmistakably this was the expectation of the Old Testament prophets.[1]

But finally the widening of the circumference of salvation proceeds to its world-embracing goal.   In the perfected state there will be a new heaven and a new earth (Rev. 21: 1), a transfigured universe, with the heavenly city of God, The New Jerusalem, on the new earth (Rev. 22: 3; 21: 10–27; 22: 1–5).   Thus also the developments within the creation prove that the

[1] Isa. 19: 23–25; Mic. 4: 3, 4; Zech. 14: 16; Mal. 1: 11.

business of the Lord is a triumphant victorious progress.   Not only the self-revelation of God, but also the history of the redemption of the creature, and thus both the super-historical and the historical, the eternal and the temporal—they all testify in common that the kingdom of God will triumph, that no power in heaven or on earth can annul God's counsel of salvation, that thus faith is the victory that overcomes the world.   " Jesus is Victor.'

But all this must have practical effects on our personal life.

THE VICTORY OF CHRIST IN THE JUSTIFYING AND SANCTIFYING OF THE INDIVIDUAL

As a matter of fact every time a soul of man submits to Christ and by faith embraces His completed salvation (Acts 26: 19), this is a victory of the exalted Christ through His Spirit (II Cor. 2: 14). And in the measure that the resurrection power of Christ, working livingly, effects practical sanctification (Phil. 3: 10), takes possession of the whole man for God, body, soul, and spirit (I Thess. 5: 23), and causes in his inner and outer life an actual experience of victory[1] this also is again a proof and result of this all-embracing truth, "Our faith is the victory that has overcome the world."

At last the final perfecting is reached.

THE UNIVERSAL TRIUMPH IN RESURRECTION AND WORLD TRANSFORMATION

The triumph of the kingdom of God will work out to a spiritual body.   Therefore the resurrection of the dead and the coming transfiguration of the body (I Cor. 15: 42–49).   Therefore also, after world destruction, the transforming of the universe (Rev. 22: 1) and the descent of the heavenly city of God (Rev. 21: 10). Only so will be perfected the victory of the affairs of the Lord: "when this corruptible shall have put on incorruption, and this mortal shall have put on immortality, then shall be brought to pass the word that is written, Death is swallowed up in victory. Death, where is thy sting?   Hades, where is thy victory? . . . But God be thanked Who has given us the victory through our Lord Jesus Christ" (I Cor. 15: 54–57).

Thus as an illuminated motto of the whole history of redemption from eternity to eternity, as a witness of Divine power, as a spur to a joyous confidence of faith, as an obligation to live a practical life of victory, as the expectation of a blessed perfecting, it stands forth that "our faith is the victory that has overcome the world."

[1] Rom. 8: 37; Rev. 2: 7, 11, 17.

CHAPTER XIII

SATAN, THE ADVERSARY OF GOD

SATAN also has his history. It is the clear, well recognizable teaching of Scripture that Satan is no mere abstract idea, but is a concrete, personal, transcendental Reality, gifted with the highest intelligence, fallen indeed, but none the less an exceedingly powerful spirit being.[1] To destroy his work, and to win back the fallen creation to God, and in God and for God to transfigure it, was the chief end of the redeeming work of Christ (I John 3: 8).

According to revealed history we can discern six consecutive chief stages in the history of salvation and the development of the demonic. These differ in length.

LUCIFER IN THE HIGHEST HEAVENLY WORLD

Although Holy Scripture indicates but little of the transcendental background of universal affairs, and speaks only with the greatest reserve of the origin and permission of evil, it is evident that Satan, now the great Adversary of God, cannot always from of old have been in this condition. For if God is the Creator of the whole universe (Col. 1: 16) then must the existence of Satan be traced back to Him. But then it is clear that because the holy God cannot allow anything sinful and imperfect to proceed direct from His creator hand, this creature cannot have been from the beginning evil, but must originally have been spotless and pure. Therefore only later, at a point of time beyond our perception and in a manner wholly inexplicable by us, must Satan have conceived the first evil thought and have fallen away from God.

Certain hints of Scripture allow the supposition that pride was the essence of this first demonic sin (comp. I Tim. 3: 6; Ezek. 28: 14-17). For originally Satan was a Lightbearer (Lat. *Lucifer*) of the Divine glory. Indeed it appears that to him, as a special angelic prince, a large part of the universe had been entrusted to rule (Luke 4: 6). In this original state of light this angel prince of God was in the highest heavenly realm.

SATAN IN THE LOWER HEAVENLY PLACES

Then came this ancient event which lies at the root of all the misery in the universe. Lucifer fell away from God and since

[1] Matt. 4: 1-10; Luke 10: 18; Rom. 16: 20; Rev. 12: 7; etc.

84

then stands as Prince of an organized kingdom of darkness opposed to God and His kingdom of light. He had become an Enemy and Adversary.[1] With this moral fall was connected his being cast out from the highest heavenly regions. "I saw Satan fall as lightning from heaven," declared Christ (Luke 10: 18). Satan's realm was involved in his fall. He himself remained in the lower regions of heaven (Eph. 6: 12), the "prince of the authority of the air" (Eph. 2: 2). Yet the history of Job (Job 1: 6; 2: 1), the prophecy of Zechariah (3: 1), and the *Revelation* (12: 10), show that on appointed occasions he has access to the throne in heaven. In the lower heavenly places (Eph. 6: 12) he will remain until the time of the End, when Michael the archangel will cast him down to the earth with his angels (Rev. 12: 7-13). See on the Chart the great flash of lightning representing the ancient fall of Satan and the flaming Divine judgment connected with it, and also the black serpent-line.

In this whole immeasurable period there may be perceived three chief sub-sections.

(*a*) Satan as the adversary of God in the period of the pre-Adamic earth, that is, from his fall to the creation of man. In this period Satan was the lord of the ruined creation.

(*b*) Satan as the Adversary of God in the pre-Christian human ages. In this period after his victory over man (Gen. 3) Satan is the unconquered lord of the human race he had conquered. This is from the fall of man to the death of Christ.

(*c*) Satan as the Adversary of God in the period of the Christian church. This endures from the victory of Christ on the Cross till Satan shall be cast down to earth by Michael (Rev. 12: 7-13). In this period he is conquered by the Cross in principle,[2] but, outside of the church (Col. 1: 13) he is still ruling on earth:[3]

Thus with the fall of man there enters human history likewise a black serpent line. Thenceforth it issues in three directions:

in the underworld—for it creates the death line; the wages which sin pays is death.

in the human world—for there it effects the demonizing of national and cultural history (Dan. 10: 13, 20); and

in the upper world of spirits—there Satan thenceforth, and also in reference to the development of man, is the "prince of the power of the air" (Eph. 2: 2).

[1] The Hebrew word Satan means Enemy, Adversary; quite in general, I Kings 11: 14, 23, 25; in a court of law, Ps. 109: 6: in Num. 22:22 even of the angel of the Lord. The word Devil comes from the Greek *dia-ballo* to throw across, to censure with words, with the adverse purpose to prove one guilty, either by lying (II Macc. 4: 1) or by speaking the truth (Dan. 3: 8; Luke 16: 1; comp. Rev. 12: 10).

[2] John 12: 31; 16: 11; Col. 2: 15; Heb. 2: 14.

[3] I John 5: 19; II Cor. 4: 4; Acts. 26: 18; Eph. 2: 2.

But at length there entered this mighty event: Satan was in principle conquered at the Cross. The Prince of the world was judged (John 12: 31; 16: 11), the strong one was conquered by the Stronger (Matt. 12: 29), the head of the serpent was trodden underfoot (Gen. 3: 15). And with the Prince of Darkness his realm also was conquered. Through the Cross He whose heel had been bruised (Gen. 3: 15) threw off from Himself the principalities and powers, robbed them of their armour, set them in the pillory, and openly triumphed over them (Col. 2: 15). From then there goes on a progressive deliverance of mankind from the power of demons. For every time that a man by faith claims his title in the saving work of the Crucified, his personality, which is a part of Satan's realm, is wrested from the Evil one; the Prince of this world is cast out (John 12: 31), a portion of his kingdom is freed from demonic control, and the saved man is translated out of the authority of darkness into the kingdom of the Son of God (Col. 1: 13; Acts 26: 18). Thus Satan is the great loser.

It is true that he continues to be a Prince, if fallen and darkened (Jude 9); it is true that still he seeks by power and deceit to delude man (II Cor. 4: 4), to rule and destroy him (Eph. 2: 2); it is true that still he also attempts to burden and accuse even the redeemed and saved.[1] Nevertheless it stands fast that Christ is the Victor and His own will share His victory.

SATAN ON EARTH

All things ascend to climax. Therefore the antagonisms will not gradually be smoothed out but will get sharper. Therefore the end of nominal Christianity is not a gradual Christianizing of civilization but Antichristendom. Therefore the final development will be the deciding battle between God and the Devil. Therefore will Satan, in spite of all his rage, be then the suppressed. There arose "a war in the heaven," and Michael and his angels cast the dragon and his angels down to the earth (Rev. 12: 7–9). This will mean indeed that Satan now in quite special degree will rage on the earth, so as to demonize unbelieving men, and will incite an antichristian international system to a devilishly inspired rule and power (Rev. 13: 4). But this bluster and rage are but the convulsive spasms of a wild revolutionary given over to defeat and fetters (Rev. 12: 12).

At length the final blow falls. Christ appears, and with Him the hosts of heaven (Rev. 19: 11–16), and though Satan and the rebellious antichristian nations will be allowed to have the last word but one in the history of man, yet Christ will now have

[1] Rev. 12: 10; Zech. 3: 1f.; Job 1: 6; 2: 1.

the very last word: "And the Beast and the false Prophet were seized . . . and cast alive into the lake of fire, which burns with brimstone" (Rev. 19: 20); and as regards Satan himself John the prophet says; "I saw an angel come down from heaven who had the key of the abyss, and a great chain in his hand; and he seized the dragon, the old serpent, who is the Devil and Satan, and he bound him a thousand years, and cast him into the abyss and locked and sealed it over him" (Rev. 20: 1–3).

Satan in the Abyss during the Millennium

Satan remains in this imprisonment during the Millennial kingdom. Now mankind can again breathe freely, for the power of the Devil to tempt is eliminated (Rev. 20: 3). The black serpent line on the Chart which, since the time when Michael cast Satan from the lower heaven to the earth, turned sharp downward and for a time (Rev. 12–19) wound around upon the earth, now is forced to the underworld, *beneath* the history of the Millennium, and coils and twists itself there during the whole period of the thousand years (Rev. 20: 3, 7). But it can have no influence upon the events taking place on earth. This means for mankind an extraordinarily great relief and easement in submitting to God. On the other side it means a heightening of responsibility if man nevertheless sins. From this arises the liability to sharper judgment in the Millennial kingdom.[1]

Satan Again on Earth: Gog and Magog

But at last this brilliant period of the visible kingdom of God must be tested by the results. Even the peoples of the Millennium shall have the possiblity of a free decision. No one shall be compelled to serve God in eternity. Therefore after the thousand years Satan *must* be set free, if only for a short time (Rev. 20: 3b, 7).

The effect is shocking. Men reject the gracious God Who, during a thousand years in which peace ruled, had showered upon them an inconceivable fulness of blessings, and choose His deadly Enemy, the Devil. Therefore world judgment and world destruction is the only answer the holy God can now give (Rev. 20: 7–15).

Satan in the Lake of Fire

But the Devil who seduced mankind will be cast into the lake of fire and brimstone, where also the Beast and the false Prophet are (Rev. 20: 10). And at the last judgment before the great

[1] Ps. 2: 8, 9; Rev. 2: 26, 27; Isa. 11: 4; Zech. 13: 3; 14: 17, 19; Mic. 5: 7, 8.

white throne all will follow them whose names are not found written in the book of life (Rev. 20: 15).

Holy Scripture knows nothing of an escape from the lake of fire and a final salvation of those condemned in the last judgment. Therefore in our Chart the lake of fire stands alone and is not merged into the universal circle of the history of salvation moving from God to God. The Bible shows no connecting line from the lake of fire back to God. This is intensely serious. It behoves us to remain bound by the Divine Word. How affecting is all this! How fearful are the powers that stand behind all the sin and misery of fallen mankind. But how powerful and just is God! He conquers the foe, makes manifest His own victorious power, and to those who take their stand on His side He gives eternal life.

Therefore the solemn question: On whose side standest thou? On the side of God or His adversary? Here there is no neutrality. Either Christ is thy bliss or Satan thy fate! On thy personal attitude depends thine eternal destiny. Therefore choose Christ, the life, that thou mayest live!

CHAPTER XIV

GOD'S UNIVERSAL PLAN OF THE KINGDOM AND THE CHURCH

THE ROYAL SOVEREIGNTY (KINGDOM) OF GOD IS THE CHIEF CONTENT OF THE WHOLE BIBLICAL HISTORICAL REVELATION

ALL these mighty developments in the realm of the Divine, human, and Satanic belong to the history of the kingdom of God. The "Kingdom" is the real basic theme of the Bible. It is the surrounding historical frame in which the whole course of revelation is being consummated. All ages and periods of the Divinely revealed ways; all groups and persons addressed, whether Israel, the nations, or the church; all temples, sanctuaries, and redeeming acts; all heavenly and demonic activities, whether in the foreground or background, stand in some way, either positively or negatively, in connexion with the history of the kingdom of God. The kingdom itself is the royal saving work of God to the carrying through of His counsels in creation and redemption.

Therefore the most correct and inclusive translation of the Greek word *basileia*, used for "kingdom," is rather kingly *rule* than kingly *realm*.[1] It signifies far more than merely the *sphere* of a king's rule, king's territory, province, district, state, or area.[2] It is nothing static, but a dynamic; no mere motionless circle but rather to be compared to a line; no mere enclosed section of time, but a continuous acting and becoming. It is the kingship of the Most High working salvation, that is, quite generally, it is the royal authority of the Saviour God, His government as a living and powerful Divine action, revealing itself in ever new forms of self-manifestation, in the course of many dispensations and periods.[3]

[1] In this connexion the Greek word *basileia* has a double meaning in Holy Scripture. It signifies:
  (a) the territory of a king: e.g. Matt. 4: 8, therefore the plural "kingdoms of the world"; 12: 25; Mark 6: 23.
  (b) "empire, kingdom, kingship," in the sense of existence, state, dignity, ruling activity of a king, thus kingly government, kingly authority; e.g. Rev. 17: 18.

[2] The bare translation "state" does not sufficiently express the *kingly* significance of the word. The Greek *basileia* is connected with *basileus* a *king*. Therefore the verb *basileuein* means not only *rule* but rule as a *king*, e.g. by Paul in Rom. 5: 21.

[3] Concerning the different consecutive forms in which the kingdom has appeared see *The Triumph of the Crucified*, p. 23f., including the footnote; also Ch. XI.

89

It is the kingly rule of God as, coming down from heaven, it will be set up on the old earth by way of redemption, and in perfected form will be continued on the new earth for ever.

But then "kingdom of God" is more than "Millennial kingdom" (see *The Triumph of the Crucified*, p. 27). Already in the Old Testament God's rule was termed "kingdom of God," even the kingdom which must be taken away from its then possessors, the Jews, because of their unbelief (Matt. 21: 43). Also the present age of the church is termed "kingdom of God," hidden indeed in a mystery (Matt. 13: 11), but nevertheless full of power and activity.[1] And the eternal state, the final perfecting, is "kingdom of God" in the fullest sense of the term, even the heavenly kingdom, unto which the apostle expected to be preserved (II Tim. 4: 18).

And because all this comes from heaven, carries heaven in itself, and has in God, as the King of heaven, its creative base and its dominating summit, therefore is this kingship of God at the same time the kingship of the heavens. For where God is there is heaven, and where He reigns He brings heaven in His person.[2] Therefore the message of His kingly rule is at the same time the "gospel [good news] of the kingdom," that is, the joyful message, which saves and blesses, that God is King.

That the expression "the gospel of the kingdom," in this special sense, is not used by Paul, bears nothing against the above explanation. Apart from the term "passover" in I Cor. 5: 7, Paul nowhere uses the term "Lamb of God," but no one will infer from this that for him the message concerning the Lamb does not dispensationally apply to this age of the church. In matters of expression each of the inspired writers has his own personal, God-wrought characteristics, peculiar to each, but all having in common that they set forth the same New Testament truth of salvation.

For us who live in the present age of the church, and who as believers on Christ belong to the New Testament church, it is of great importance, at the close of our explanations as to the

---

[1] Rom. 14: 17; Col. 1: 13; 4: 11; Acts. 20: 25, 28, 31.

[2] For more detailed treatment of the relation between the expressions "kingdom of heaven" and "kingdom of God," both by the rabbis and the Lord Jesus, see *Triumph of the Crucified*, pp. 22ff.

The expression "kingdom of heaven" is used by Matthew only, and by him 32 times. He used it in numerous places where Mark and Luke, on the same occasions and in the same statements by the Lord, employ the term "kingdom of God"; for example:

> Matt. 4: 17—Mark 1: 15.
> Matt. 5: 3—Luke 6: 20.
> Matt. 11: 11—Luke 7: 28.
> Matt. 13: 11—Luke 8: 10.
> Matt. 19: 14—Luke 18: 16.

Divine plan of redemption, to enquire *in what attitude the New Testament church stands to this kingdom.*

In view of the fact that this kingdom is such a tremendous reality which in the course of the Millenniums reveals itself in ever new forms, this question can only be answered by further asking: In what relation does the church of the New Testament stand to these single manifold revealed forms of the kingdom in the various dispensations of past, present, and future? Here in fact the Holy Scripture gives an unusually full answer.

The Relation of the New Testament Church to the Old Testament Rule of God (Theocracy)

This is threefold:

(*a*) internally: the relation of substance and shadow (Col. 2: 17; Heb. 10: 1):

(*b*) externally: the relation of universality to national limitation. The gospel is the breaking through the national bounds of the Mosaic law by the promise to Abraham of blessing for all nations (Gen. 12: 1–3).

(*c*) historically: the relation of goal and preparation. Upon the church have come the "ends" [appointed goals] of the [pre-Christian] ages" (I Cor. 10: 11).

The Relation of the New Testament Church to the Present Kingdom

This also is manifold. We think now of the present form in which the kingly rule of God appears in its full spiritual sense as the kingdom in mystery, that is, of the sovereign rule of God in the period between the first and second comings of the Lord. In this sense we say:

All members of the body belong to the kingdom and all true citizens of the kingdom belong to the church. Dead professors belong only to the sphere of influence of the kingdom (Matt. 7: 21–23; 13: 41; 22: 11–14). as do all effects of Christianity in morals, art, culture, laws, and world-history; but to the real kingdom itself belong only those who have been born anew (John 3: 3, 5). In the present age these form the church. Therefore in the various periods of history the respective generations of the church, living at any time on earth, represent at the same time the *citizens* of the kingdom (Eph. 2: 19; Phil. 3: 20; Col. 1: 13).

Further; the church is the fruit of the kingdom, in that she is the eternal outcome of the activity of the present kingly rule of

God in Christ through His Word and His Holy Spirit. For by the preaching of the "word of the kingdom" as the joyful message of the redeeming sovereignty of the Saviour God, and by its being believed, there arises the church (Acts 20: 25; 28: 31). According to Paul the preaching of the gospel is a *command* to repent.[1] and conversion is an act of obedience and submission (Acts 26: 19). Thus conversion is both the acknowledgment of the kingly rule of God, and at the same time—in its inseparable connexion with the new birth—the entrance into the membership of the church; and so, with the establishing of God's kingly rule in a human heart the building up of the church is effected. Therefore the church is the fruit of the kingdom.

The church perfected is, then, the total of all who in all times and places have accepted Christ as their LORD (I Cor. 12: 3), and who thereupon have been translated out of the authority of darkness into the kingdom (*basileia*) of the Son of God's love (Col. 1: 13). This means that the New Testament church in its entirety is the full number of all citizens of the kingdom in the present age, the sum of all generations of believers under the present form in which the kingdom of God appears.

As regards the spiritual life, the relation of the church to the present rule of God is that of a living *organism* for the Spirit. The church is present where Christ is acknowledged as Lord by redeemed men. Thus the kingly rule of God is its spiritual essence. The church is the organism in which the kingly rule of God through His Holy Spirit is recognized in principle and realized in practice (I Cor. 12: 3). Therefore Paul compares the *ecclesia* to a political state (Phil. 3: 20). The redeemed are a "people" (Acts 15: 14), fellow "citizens" with the saints (Eph. 2: 19), a "kingly" priesthood (I Pet. 2: 9), and Paul, the especial apostolic standard-bearer of the truth of the church (Eph. 3: 1–10), describes his fellow-workers in the church as being at the same time his fellow-workers unto the "kingdom of God" (Col. 4: 11). And finally

In the present age the members of the church are the *ambassadors* of the kingdom. We are ambassadors for Christ (II Cor. 5: 20). The church has to represent its heavenly government in this world as in a foreign land, that is, God, its Lord, and Christ in whose kingdom she is (Col. 1: 13). This is their life-work on earth.

Thus the relationship of the New Testament church to the present form of the kingly rule of God has chiefly a fourfold aspect:

As to their persons they are citizens of the kingdom:

[1] Acts. 17: 30; Rom. 16: 26; I Cor. 7: 19; Gal. 6: 2; Rom. 5: 21.

as to their existence they are the fruit of the message of the kingdom:

as to their nature they are the organism of the kingdom:

as to their task they are the ambassadors of the kingdom.

Thus behind the whole history of the church stands the authority of the kingdom. Furnished with this royal and full authority of the King of all kings (Matt. 28: 18–20) she can proclaim the royal and saving command of God (Acts 17: 30; Rom. 16: 26; I Cor. 9: 16) and can do so in the triumphant certainty that the Lord of all Lords is with us. Our kingdom cannot be shaken (Heb. 12: 28). The Coming One will come and will not delay (Heb. 10: 37), and at last we shall "see the King in His beauty" (Isa. 33: 17).

THE RELATION OF THE NEW TESTAMENT CHURCH TO THE ETERNAL KINGDOM

The kingdom of God in its form as the kingdom of glory will be the sphere of the *active rule* of the church: "Know ye not that the saints shall judge the world" (I Cor. 6: 2, 3): "Fear thou not, thou little flock, it is your Father's good pleasure to give you the kingdom" (Luke 12: 32). The church is thus the ruling aristocracy, the official administrative staff, of the coming kingdom of God.

The kingdom of God as the future kingdom of glory is the *inheritance* of the church. The sanctified in Christ will *inherit* the kingdom (I Cor. 6: 10; Gal. 5: 21; Eph. 5: 5). They will enter into it (Acts 14: 22). It is the goal of their pilgrimage. They are called unto this kingdom.[1] (I Thess. 2: 12). It is their reward. They will be "counted worthy" of the kingdom for the sake of which they suffered in the present time. (II Thess. 1: 5).

Thus as regards the future the church will be "in" the kingdom. She is one circle in a greater circle, but among the separate circles which make up the whole circle she is of all the highest.

Thus the church stands in a living relation to all forms of the kingdom. The kingdom of power shall become the kingdom of glory: between lies the kingdom of grace, whose essential content is the redemption. But the church is at the centre of the whole. All revelations of the kingdom are joined to her essence and existence. The whole course of time is bound up with this people of eternity. But above all, the King Himself is her own:

---

[1] "Called" in the sense that peers are summoned by the sovereign to attend at the House of Lords. [Trans.]

for Christ her Head, is at the same time given to her as Head over the universe (Eph. 1: 22).

Therefore it becomes us to walk worthily of this high calling (Eph. 4: 1). We have, with Paul, to proclaim the kingly authority of God (Acts 20: 25; 28: 31). It becomes us to be witnesses and evangelists so as to win souls for Christ, that obedience of faith may be found among all nations (Rom. 1: 5, 15, 18; 16: 26).

Thus our message of the gospel is at the same time a proclamation of the Kingdom (Acts 20: 25). We proclaim both the present and the future kingdom.[1] In this sense gospel workers of the church are "fellow-workers unto the kingdom" (Col. 4: 11).

THE KINGDOM MESSAGE OF THE CHURCH

As regards the *moral conduct* of men we proclaim the kingdom as a *totalitarian claim of God.* To preach the gospel means to proclaim as a herald, with Spirit-filled authority, God's announcement of remission of sins.[2] Behind the saving command stands the royal authority of the supreme Lord of the universe. God offers to man His gift of salvation, and at the same time commands him to accept it (Acts 26: 19; 17: 30). And has He been able to show to a man His grace, then from that time this grace will rule him royally (Rom. 5: 21, lit.; I Cor. 7: 19). His whole being and existence, in all its connexions, spheres of life, and circles of activity will thenceforth come under the sole and total rule of his kingly Lord.

In view of man's *poverty* we proclaim the kingdom as the *gift* of God. The Scripture teaches that not on earth but in heaven will the future kingdom be handed to Christ (Dan. 7: 13, 14; Luke 19: 12). Its course is not from below to above, but from above to below. It is not a payment for human merit, but a free gift of the grace of God. It comes not from progress but through collapse, not from moral activity but by Divine renewal. Not Christianizing the world until civilization has been Christianized, but increasing enmity of the world until Christianity is expelled by civilization— this is the course foretold by prophecy (II Thess. 2: 3–12; Rev. 13). Thus completely does man himself display his utter incapacity to enter into God's royal thoughts concerning salvation and His kingdom. Not by reconciliation, but by increasing conflict, not by alliance between God and the vainglory of man, but by the smashing of the God-estranged kingdom

---

[1] Rom. 14: 17; I Cor. 4: 20; Col. 1: 13; I Cor. 6: 9, 10; I Thess. 2: 12; II Thess. 1: 5; Acts 14: 22.

[2] "Proclaim": Gr. *kērussein*, from *kēryx*, a herald. I Tim. 2: 7.

of the world by the kingdom of God (Dan. 2: 34, 44, 45)—thus will arrive the completion of the present age.

This truth has also a high apologetic value.   Far from being a reason against the message of the Bible, this very increase of the general unbelief becomes an unwilling proof of the accuracy of Biblical prophecy.   But finally, after the judgments of the End time, the kingdom of God will be to men His—*gift*.

In the light of the utter *weakness* of men we proclaim the kingdom as the *power* of God.   Only the kingdom of the Divine King, when He appears, will be in a position to solve the political and social problems of mankind.   Christ alone will be the Arbiter who will bring peace to the nations (Isa. 2: 2–4).   He will be the first to pronounce true justice for the poor and the widow, and introduce a just distribution of property (Isa. 11: 3–5).   He first will overcome evil in man and give to the peoples pure lips (Zeph. 3: 9).   Thus will He introduce a true human fellowship, and by the power of God His kingdom will be one of peace, righteousness, holiness, and love.

As regards the *longing* of men we proclaim the future kingdom as God's *goal for mankind*.   The kingly rule of the Eternal alone can bring the fulfilment of all man's ideals.   Then first will arrive the realization of a true, noble humanity.   Therefore in Holy Scripture the promised kingdom is described as the "kingdom of the Son of man," that is, as the kingdom that shall no more have as its motto and escutcheon the wild beast but the countenance of man.   It will be the kingdom of the God-King who will then free mankind from its sub-human, wild beast character, and for the first time set on the throne of international history true humanity in the meaning of the Creator, even the image of God (Gen. 1: 26, 27).[1]

In the light of the *enmity* of man we proclaim the kingdom as the *victory* of God.   The stone which shattered the colossus of Nebuchadnezzar went on to fill the whole earth (Dan. 2: 35, 44; Rev. 11: 15; 19: 11–21).   Therefore it becomes the believer to have a confident spirit, an assurance of victory, and courage.   Therefore away with all fear of ruin and all little faith!   Away with all fear of man and all cowardice in witnessing!   The gospel is no hole-and-corner affair!   Eternal victory belongs to the affairs of the King!

Finally: In view of all human *greatness* we proclaim the kingdom as the *glory of God*.   Therefore we praise Jesus Christ, declare His excellencies (I Pet. 2: 9), show the greatness of His royal

---

[1] See in Dan. 7 the symbols of the world empires, lion, bear, panther, and terrible beast, and then (v. 13) the appearing of the kingdom of God in the form of a Son of man.   Upon the title "Son of man" see *The Triumph of the Crucified*, pp. 21f.

power and the majesty and exaltation of His person.   He Himself is the content of our message: "we preach not ourselves but Jesus Christ, and Him as Lord" (II Cor. 4: 5).

"Now to Him [the Father] the blessed and only Potentate, the King of kings and Lord of lords, who only hath immortality, dwelling in light unapproachable, whom no man hath seen nor is able to see, to Him be honour and power eternal.   Amen." (I Tim. 6: 15, 16.)

PART II

THE BIBLE AS THE RECORD OF GOD'S DEALINGS WITH MAN

CHAPTER XV

THE LIVING AND THE WRITTEN WORD

GOD—THE LORD OF HISTORY

THE nations are like the roaring sea, like breaking billows in raging tumult (comp. Isa. 17: 12, 13). Nations and civilizations come and go. Kingdoms and cultures are built up and destroyed. Philosophies are highly praised as rock-like truths and—are swept away. And streams of blood flow in the age-long war of men and ideas.

But God, the Lord of all, is enthroned above it all. "The Lord is King. He hath clothed Himself with majesty . . . Thy throne stands fast from the beginning. Floods lift up, O Lord, floods lift up their roaring . . . but mightier than the thunder of mighty waters, mightier than the breaking billows of the sea, is the Lord in the height!" (Psa. 93: 1–4).

From this His unassailable throne on high the Eternal surveys the whole historical development. As above time He sees through and through all time. As the creator of the course of history and the governor of heaven and earth He controls the universal process. Therefore as the Lord of history He, and He alone can explain history.

This He does by His revelation in word and history. In spite of all self-veiling, in the course of the development, He testifies of Himself through the mouth of His prophets, through His rule in judgment and in grace in the life of individuals and of peoples, through combining events according to the law of sowing and reaping.

The Bible is the record of this. Therefore the Bible is "the Book of mankind," the key to world events. All understanding of the whole of human affairs depends upon attitude to it.

God has wonderfully ordered this His Book. "Holy men spake from God being moved by the Holy Spirit" (II Pet. 1, 21). "All Scripture is God-given" (II Tim. 3: 16). "The words of the Lord are pure words, as silver fired in a furnace . . . purified

G

seven times" (Psa. 12: 6). "Sanctify them in the truth; Thy word is truth" (John 17: 17).

"Word of God" and "Book of God"

As regards range of meaning "Word of God" and "Book of God" are not precisely the same. The former expression extends beyond the latter. At the same time it encloses it in itself.

We have to speak of the "Word of God" in a threefold sense.

1. Christ is the *personal* word, the living Divine *Logos*. From eternity *before* all creation, without beginning He is the "Word" *in* God and *with* God, in His nature and essence equal to God, even Himself "God." Then, by and *since* the creation of the world He is the "word" which God speaks, the Revealer of the thoughts and acts of God, and as such the mediator of world creation and world preservation, of world redemption and world consummation.

2. Of Him testifies the *proclaimed* "word," the word of God as a general message, as the all-inclusive contents of Biblical truth, simply as a proclamation, as the sum and total of all that which God says. In this sense all proclaiming of the testimony of Jesus by word of mouth should be, not man's word, but "God's word" (I Thess. 2: 13), both testimony in the gospel and ministry in the word in the church (I Pet. 4: 11). This is the meaning of *all* places in the New Testament in which the term "word of God" is used. In no place in Holy Scripture does the expression "word of God" attach itself to its written permanent form, to the "Book of God," because at that time the canon of the New Testament was not yet formed.[1]

3. Of this proclaimed word, under the leading and in the name of the personal Word, and through the inspiration of the Holy Spirit, has the *written* word, the *Book* of God, come into being. But although, as to the range of its meaning, this encloses a narrower circle, since the cessation of direct prophetic, apostolic revelation, it has just on this account unique significance of the highest conceivable order. Thenceforward all proclamation of God's word by the mouth is simply a drawing from, an explaining and applying of, the written Word of God, and the written Word is rule and standard (formative and corrective) for all right proclaiming of God's word by the mouth. Therefore the original written Biblical Word has full validity, is God-given, and of absolute, inescapable authority.

[1] Comp. I Thess. 2: 13; Heb. 4: 12; Acts 4: 31; I Pet. 1: 23; 4: 11; etc. Rev. 22: 18 applies in direct manner to the book of the *Revelation* of John himself, and is no utterance concerning the whole canon of the Old and New Testaments.

Seven chief grounds constrain us to this attitude of faith. From limits of space we can mention here only the most basic. Details would extend beyond the scope of our work. Not scientific establishment of details or defence of faith, but simple personal testimony to faith is our object.

CHAPTER XVI

THE INSPIRATION OF THE BIBLE
NECESSARY BECAUSE OF THE FALL OF MAN

*W*E *believe that full inspiration is necessary because of the absolute insufficiency of man.*

For how otherwise shall we be in a position to attain a God-given outlook? Were the Bible a mixture of truth and error we should have ourselves to attempt to decide what in it is to be acknowledged as from God and what in it must be refused as an admixture of human error. If man has no plain standard given to him by God Himself how shall his spirit decide what is Divine and what human? How shall our spirit be emboldened to analyse God's book, or indeed to dissect it—mostly on purely subjective impressions or feelings, or on the basis of insufficient historical knowledge—and thereupon to sit in judgment and decide which statement of the Bible deserves to be believed and which not? We, the fallen! We, who not only morally, but in spirit and capacity for understanding have thrust ourselves through sin into darkness and mist! "Darkened in their thinking, aliens from the life of God in consequence of the ignorance which dwells in them" (Eph. 4: 18). "A natural man receives not what comes from the Spirit of God; he is not in a position to understand it" (I Cor. 2: 14). Who then will draw the dividing line? Who will recognize the frontier? Not even the moral judgment of so sanctified and chosen an instrument (Acts 9: 15) as was Paul offers to the inward man an absolute guarantee to perceive beyond doubt all the will and judgment of God. The apostle himself testifies: "I know nothing against myself, yet am I not hereby justified" (I Cor. 4: 4). So far is the human judgment removed from being a "voice of God"; so difficult is it to effect a clearing and enlightenment of man's spiritual understanding.

It is a necessary result from such a condition that all Divine matters must be made known to man by revelation from above; so that there must be given to him from heaven an objective basis of knowledge.

Here lies the decisive starting point for the doctrine of Biblical inspiration. That which fallen man thinks about God is untrustworthy and mostly erroneous; it is "religion." What he needs to perceive is what the Most High thinks about him, and what He testifies concerning Himself and His way of salvation.

This objective basic reality is not, as to its essential nature, a book but a Person. It is the crucified and risen Christ, exalted to the right hand of God, with Whom the Holy Spirit unites us organically. Christ is the living "Truth," the personal "Light," the Fountain of all knowledge; and, at the same time, as the Giver of light, He is also the Saviour Who delivers us from darkness and makes us children of light.

The first generation bore witness to Him. There was testimony to the sacred history of Jesus by those who had seen and heard (Luke 1: 2; II Pet. 1: 16; I John 1: 1-3); there were Spirit-given revelations in the gatherings of the first Christians (Acts 11: 27, 28; I Cor. 11: 23; Eph. 3: 5); there were exact historical accounts of the events by believing men who had been present or had drawn their knowledge from original sources. Through all this the first generation, who, as regards the sacred Book had at first only the Old Testament but not yet the New Testament in its present complete form, possessed nevertheless a clear acquaintance with the objective foundation of salvation and spiritual knowledge.

But with the departure of the first generation this direct message and witness more and more receded. Therefore, as the perpetuation of this apostolic testimony, the substance of this objective foundation of wholly reliable historical and doctrinal knowledge must be preserved to future generations. Only so could these be protected from gradually increasing darkness and be preserved clear, fresh, and healthy in knowledge, faith, and life.

Therefore God added the New Testament to the Old Testament already existing, and this was done in the apostolic period itself. Thenceforth this complete Holy Scripture is the fully reliable, prophetic, apostolic message given to us from above concerning the effectual salvation of God in Christ Jesus.

Thus the Bible is the book of the Truth, testifying of life and imparting life, given by the Holy Spirit and accompanied by the Holy Spirit. Without it the church of God would be given up to hopeless wandering and ignorance. Instead of light and faith there would come religious twilight, in place of sobriety, fanaticism, instead of clarity, a misty obscurity, and more and more would God's word be exchanged for the subconscious voice, the so-called "inner light," and in the course of centuries the objective testimony of God would evaporate into a general subjectivism.

But no: exactly as we need *grace* because of our moral incapacity, so do we need *inspiration* because of our intellectual and spiritual incapacity, *i.e.* we need an absolutely reliable record of God's revelation, a fully inspired Bible; and this especially since the cessation of the direct prophetic, apostolic Divine testimony. Against this fact not even the most zealous agitation against the Bible as being a "paper Pope" can help. All contention against such an absolute objective element in the revelation rests upon a lack of self-knowledge. It is an instance of self-confidence and self-deification, though no doubt unconscious and unintentional.

Without belief in a full inspiration we open wide the door to arbitrary subjectivism. Rationalism mounts the throne, and finally our imperfect human understanding, darkened through the Fall, stands as judge over God's Book and God's Word. This be far from us! The accused sinner in the dock can never have the capacity or right to take the place of the Judge on the bench and to decide what God may or may not have said. This applies to the whole organism of the Divine revelation, and to the Bible as its record, down to its smallest particular.

First, and above all, this applies to the doctrine of the Scripture. But as the revelation is at the same time history the doctrinal and historical elements simply cannot be separated. Much doctrine of Scripture depends directly on the question whether the connected Biblical report is historically accurate; for example, whether Jesus did or did not make this or that statement and did or did not teach this or that doctrine. With uncertainty as to such historical accounts there would be joined uncertainty as to certain doctrines. No doubt the Bible is not a textbook of history just as it is not of science; but because of the inseparable connexion of doctrine and history it must be strongly emphasized that its historical information is reliable. The natural history references of the Bible must be regarded in the same way, for in the giving of the law to Israel the seven-day-week is referred back to the six days and the sabbath at creation, and also certain miracles, in Old and New Testament history, such as the standing still of the sun in the days of Joshua, set forth clearly a connexion between Nature and history.

> If Thy Word no more is valid
> Where shall then my faith repose?
> Not a thousand worlds I covet,
> But to do Thy Word I choose. (Zinzendorf).

CHAPTER XVII

INSPIRATION—LOGICAL IN VIEW OF THE USE OF HUMAN WORDS

*W*E believe in full inspiration because of the inner connexion of thought and word.

For the unmistakable expressing of thought there is necessary a careful choice of corresponding words. In human speech words are indeed first of all mere symbols and signs for conceptions or thoughts; for the thinking of man does not arise from words, but from indistinct notions, sensations, and conceptions. But this does not contradict the fact that everything spiritual, if it is to attain to *clear* unfolding of a real thought or "idea," reveals itself in *words*. A thought only becomes properly a conscious thought if out of the subconscious realm of sensation and the indeterminate impression of will and feeling a word is born. As only through the birth the germ of life becomes a man or a beast, so only through the word does the spiritual possibility or the spiritual sensation become a clear spiritual actuality. The word may be regarded as the body of the thought, giving the spirit "visibility" and form. Therefore if the word is blurred the thought is blurred and all becomes foggy and indistinct. The saying "spirit without word" is therefore a "word without spirit," that is, a spirit-less (meaningless) word.

In reference to the inspiration of the Bible the foregoing means that if the thoughts are inspired then must the words also be so. Without inspiration of its words the thoughts of the Bible would be without distinct form. A certain change (variation) of the words always includes a more or less definite change of the thoughts. Now it is exactly the delicacies and shades and stresses which quite often constitute the special beauties of the words of the Bible. Luther justly said that "Christ did not say of His thoughts but of His words that they are spirit and life" (John 6: 63), and J. A. Bengel declares that "All the words which they should speak and write were prescribed exactly to the prophets . . . with the ideas God at the same time gave them the words." The Prince of preachers, Spurgeon, said: "We contend for every word of the Bible and believe in the verbal, literal inspiration of Holy Scripture. Indeed, we believe there can be no other kind of inspiration. If the words are taken from us, the exact meaning is of itself lost." As Monod said: "The Bible is heaven in words."

The fact that the writers of the New Testament when quoting the Old Testament do not always repeat verbally the Hebrew text[1] is not at all to be regarded as inexactness or as a refutation of the inspired character of Holy Scripture. For the proper and uniform Author of the whole Bible is the Holy Spirit. Now an author has the right to repeat his own statements in freer form, without being compelled to retain their exact wording. Moreover he has the right to make a statement which may follow closely the contents of a former statement but which, to suit some new situation, contains variations. Now when quoting the Old Testament Christ and the Holy Spirit were taking words out of His own Book (I Pet. 1: 11; II Pet. 1: 21; Heb. 3: 7).

Even in the region of human art true inspiration (using the word in the wider sense) creates for itself a corresponding form of expression which extends to the details. Handel, the great contemporary of J. S. Bach, whom the British people so honoured as to bury him in Great Britain's most renowned resting place, Westminster Abbey, and who composed his greatest work, the oratorio *The Messiah*, in the incredibly short time of twenty-four days, has in like manner applied to this his work the word of the apostle Paul, "Whether I was in the body or out of the body I know not: God knows" (II Cor. 12: 2). And Joseph Haydn, the great composer of "*The Creation*," testified: "If I think on God and His grace in Christ my heart is so full of joy that the *notes* dance and spring from the pen."

God's acts and self-revelations do not float as bodiless ideas above all earthly happenings but are woven deep and directly into concrete history. Therefore spirit and word are not simply *near* to one another but are united organically and *in* one another.

Let us not be mistaken. We do not speak of a stiff, mechanical, dictated inspiration of the word. This would be completely unworthy of a Divine revelation. A mechanical inspiration (automatic dictation) is found in occultism, spiritism, and therefore demonism, where the evil inspiring spirit works by setting aside (substitution) and excluding the human individuality. Divine revelation, however, has nothing to do with such suppression of the human personality. It will not sanction the annulling of the God-given laws of human consciousness, nor transforming the man into an automaton; it causes rather the intensifying and heightening than the excluding of the human faculties. "Light cannot produce darkness, but rather acuter sight." The Divine revelation desires fellowship between the human spirit and the Divine Spirit. It seeks the sanctifying and transfiguring of the

[1] For example, Heb. 10: 5 "body" with Psa. 40: 6 "ears"; also Acts 15: 16 with Amos 9: 11, 12; or Heb. 13: 5 with Deut. 31: 6.

personality and setting it to serve. It desires not passive "mediums" but active *men* of God, not dead tools but living, sanctified co-workers with God, not slaves but friends (John 15: 15).

Therefore its inspiration is not mechanical but organic, not magical but divinely natural, not lifeless dictation but a living word wrought by the Spirit.   Only so can God's word be man's word and man's word God's word.   Only so can God's word meet us as man's word, that is, in the garment of human languages, Hebrew, Aramaic, Greek.   In a completely mysterious, inexplicable manner, in which it corresponds in general to the mystery of the Divine-human element in the whole kingdom of God, there are found in Holy Scripture the distinctions between the writers as to character, disposition, literary style, spiritual labour, with also the differences of their contemporary culture, surroundings and personal life history, but all this overruled and thereby thoroughly guarded by the inspiring Spirit of God.[1]

One need only compare the powerful style of an Amos or Isaiah with the mournful tones of the melancholy Jeremiah. How very different are the thought-structure and literary style of Paul from those of John.   At the commencement of his Gospel Luke tells quite plainly as to his own intellectual work in compiling his account of the gospel.

As to the surrounding civilizations, the Old Testament, especially in its arrangements of temple service and Divine worship, is full of references and parallels to the religious and cultural conditions of the ancient East; while the New Testament, viewed culturally and historically, is a thoroughly Hellenistic book, with hundreds of parallels and references to the mode of thought of the Greek-Roman world of the Mediterranean area. Paul especially, the evangelist to the great cities, has a pronounced Hellenistic picture-language from city life.   Observe his numerous pictures and references from the Greek-Roman life, military, sport, amphitheatre, and law court.

Also the personal life history of the writer is reflected; for example, in the picture-language of the countryside of the shepherd Amos (7: 14; 2: 13; 3: 4–6), in the prophetic utterances as to nations by the Minister of State, Daniel, in the portraying of the future priestly temple service by the priest Ezekiel (Ezek. 1: 3 with chs. 40–48), in the summons to the building of the Temple, also through a priest (Zechariah).

Quite unmistakably there is thus a human factor in the Bible.

[1] Concerning this interweaving of the eternal and temporal, and the uniform Divine-human character of the inspiration of the Bible, see *The Dawn of World Redemption*, pp. 144ff.

But it must be clear to faith that this human factor does not consist in a measure of failure in the original text, that is, that the sacred text is a mixture of errors from personal, contemporary, historical, or scientific sources, but it (the human factor) arises from this interweaving of the Divine and human in the history.

That the sacred writers as individuals were not on this account themselves free from mistakes is evident. As children of their time they shared with their contemporaries in numerous, especially scientific, errors. The Holy Scripture never attributes to them personally an absolute moral perfectness (see Peter in Gal. 2: 11ff.), or freedom from mistakes in natural knowledge. But when it is a matter of the special, strictly "official" service of the inspiration of the written Bible, then faith must postulate that here there is freedom from error in the original text. The decisive point is that the personal errors of the human instrument of inspiration did not obtrude into the sacred text itself.

It has been rightly pointed out that Scripture itself uses popular expressions in regard to astronomic, geologic, and other scientific matters, even as do most of our modern scholars in everyday intercourse. And it must be expressly said that the inspiration of the Spirit preserved the Biblical writers from declaring as true anything, historical or scientific, that in fact is false. "Moses was instructed in all the wisdom of the Egyptians. What preserved him so that when writing the Pentateuch he did not accept the ancient Egyptian chronology, which later Manetho laid down definitely in his writings, and which began 30,000 years before Christ? What influenced Daniel, who was skilled in Chaldean science, to shut his ears to the monstrous Chaldean fables as to the creation of the world? Paul was acquainted with the best science of his time. Why do we find nothing in his speeches or letters similar to Augustine's scornful rejection of the teaching that there are Antipodes or to the opinion of Ambrose, that the sun draws water up to itself that it may thereby cool and refresh itself from its extraordinary heat?"

It is indeed the mystery of the inspiration of the Bible that it allowed its human instruments to be thoroughly active, yet nevertheless watched over and guarded each thought and each word so that the result is an absolutely trustworthy Divine Word free from error and fully interpenetrated by the Spirit. "God," said Dr. Saphir, "without whom no sparrow falls from the roof, and whose wisdom is declared by the smallest of His works, was surely able to watch over the utterance of Scripture; and microscopically to search into the wonder of His word is less the sign of a small mind than much rather of a thoughtful spirit."

In all this we must distinguish clearly between revelation,

illumination, and inspiration.   Revelation is the uncovering of Divine mysteries, to the understanding of which illumination leads.   The sacred writers did not need that to be "revealed" which they had experienced with eyes and ears or which they could get to know by inquiry (Luke 1: 1-3).   In such case the Spirit of God used their knowledge and purified it from all error.

Biblical inspiration then is that further activity of the Holy Spirit through which He mysteriously filled the active human spirit of the Biblical writers and guided and overruled them, so that there arose an infallible Spirit-wrought writing, a sacred record, a Book of God, with which the Spirit of God evermore organically unites Himself.

Of course, clearly all these remarks attach to the *original* texts of the Bible.   The number of variant readings in later text transmission is not small.   Yet no one need be alarmed.

Dr. B. Kennicott in his edition of the Hebrew Bible (*Vetus Testamentum Hebraicum*, published at Oxford) deals with consonantal variants in more than six hundred manuscripts.   These have, according to Dr. R. D. Wilson, about 284 *millions* of letters. Among these letters there are about 900,000 variants, 750,000 of which are the quite trivial variation of "w" and "y".   So there is, as Dr. Wilson remarks, only *one* variant for 316 letters and, apart from the insignificant "w" a·.d "y" variations, even only one variant for no less than 1,580 letters (comp. Professor I. K. Skilton, *The Infallible Word*.   Philadelphia-London 1946, pp. 139, 140).

In particular, the accuracy of the Jewish Massoretes (copyists, from Heb. *massora*=transmission) proves that the sacred book of the Jews is the most carefully transmitted book of all antiquity. For preserving the correct consonantal text each copyist had to accept, among other, the following rules: He counted exactly how often one and the same word occurs in the whole Old Testament or in parts thereof.   He made notes of how similarly sounding sentences differed from one another.   He counted how often one and the same word comes at the beginning, middle, and end of a verse.   It was ascertained which was the middle letter of the Torah (the law); indeed, at the end of the Old Testament it was shown how many times each letter came in the whole book.

The high quality of the traditional (Massoretic) text has been newly established by comparison with the manuscript of Isaiah found in 1947 in a cave near the Dead Sea.   This comes from the second or first century B.C., and so is about a thousand years older than the most ancient of the previously known manuscripts of the Old Testament.   These last come from 900 to 1000 years after Christ.

Comparison has indeed shown that the number of variations is certainly not small. But many of them are only different orthography or older forms of the endings of the same Hebrew words. But above all this, exact comparison has demonstrated yet again the eminently reliable work which the Massoretes and their predecessors of the early centuries after Christ put into their copying of the sacred text. From them we derive the Hebrew text which is the basis of our present editions of the Old Testament.

As regards the New Testament, according to Professor Skilton, the 200,000 variants in words distribute themselves among more than 4,000 manuscripts of earlier and later date, a part only fragmentary or very small, a part larger or almost complete. But a single complete or nearly complete New Testament manuscript contains almost 150,000 words. This shows that the percentage of the variants in their relationship to the whole text must certainly not be over-emphasized.

Dr. F. J. A. Hort was one of the most distinguished investigators of Biblical manuscripts. He was joint-Editor with Bishop B. F. Westcott of the very best edition of the Greek text of the New Testament. According to them "the proportion of words virtually accepted on all hands as raised above doubt is no less than seven eighths of the whole. The remaining eighth, therefore, formed in great part by changes of order or other comparative trivialities, constitutes the whole area of criticism."

Speaking of this small part—this remaining eighth—Dr. Warfield, another authority on New Testament textual investigation, states that 95% of all variations in the New Testament text "have so little support that their adoption or rejection would cause no appreciable difference in the sense of the passages where they occur." Indeed, with absolute certainty it can be affirmed that not a single complete sentence of the original text has disappeared from the manuscripts. For our faith all these thousand readings have not the slightest significance. Dr. Hort and Dr. Westcott in their epoch-making Introduction to their standard work, *The New Testament in the Original Greek* even declare: "What can in any sense be called substantial variation is but a small fraction of the whole residuary variation, and can hardly form more than *a thousandth part* of the entire text."[1]

So also states Sir Frederic G. Kenyon, a front-rank authority in the English-speaking world in the field of New Testament textual criticism: "The authenticity and the general integrity of the books of the New Testament may be regarded as finally established. . . . The Christian can take the whole Bible in

[1] *The New Testament in the Original Greek*, 1882. Appendix Introduction, p. 2.

his hand and say without fear or hesitation that he holds in it the true Word of God, handed down without essential loss from generation to generation throughout the centuries."[1]

Nevertheless it is true that God has suffered the introduction of certain faults in the copying of the sacred text. The history of the formation of the texts of the Old and New Testaments shows this beyond contradiction. We need only refer to the critical apparatus of the Nestlé Greek Testament, as well as to the corresponding references in all scientific commentaries and editions of the original Greek text.

A widespread objection against belief in full inspiration is drawn from this. It is said that the whole question of full inspiration is in consequence shown in advance to be more or less fruitless, more historical and theoretical than in any sense practical, more a question of the past than the present. The original texts of the Bible are in any case no more available. Also, that no one whose judgment is to be taken at all seriously will assert that the translation he uses, however careful and distinguished it may be, or in whatever language, is in all details without mistakes, absolutely perfect and unexceptionally clear. Indeed, that this last cannot be said without limitation of even the very best of our existing ancient texts of the Hebrew and Greek Bible. Only evident ignorance of the actual facts of textual history could assert otherwise. In view of all this, so it is asked, does it not follow that there is *no real difference* whether one does now believe in a full inspiration of the original texts or not, it only being pre-supposed that we do in general acknowledge Holy Scripture to be fundamentally God's Word, even if, under the circumstances, it were linked from the beginning with certain human imperfections? It is a clear fact that no one today has the actual original text.

Our answer runs:

We do not at all underestimate the weight of this objection. A mathematical refutation is not possible, nor at all necessary. Even as in our relation to the "living Word," Christ, so here in our relation to the written Word, the Bible, we find ourselves entirely on the ground of personal faith. At the same time faith sets against this objection quite definite and clear postulates. We point the reader to the seven chief arguments of our discussion

---

[1] F. G. Kenyon, *The Bible and Archæology*, 1940, p. 228. F. F. Bruce (University of Sheffield), one of the most widely read men of our generation in the field of Biblical history, archaeology and literature, says: "There is no greater authority in the field of New Testament textual criticism than Sir Frederic Kenyon." The testimony of such a scholar and specialist as Kenyon is therefore in our connexion all the more worthy of consideration.—F. G. Kenyon, *Our Bible and the Ancient Manuscripts*. London 1939, p. 23. F. F. Bruce, M.A., *The Books and the Parchments*. London 1950, p. 180.

concerning the inspired character of the Bible as the God-given record of the history of salvation.[1]

Nevertheless we must assert with emphasis: *There is a vast difference between the two attitudes!*

It is something distinctly different whether one declares:

(*a*) that in creating the Holy Scriptures God gave a record of salvation originally free from mistakes and fully inspired, which now, in connexion with Christ the living Word, and with the continual operation of the Holy Spirit, is the rock foundation for our life of faith, and to which we, through most careful searching as to the text, through scientific and spiritual translating and exposition, bound under the authority of Christ, shall strive to approach as nearly as possible: or

(*b*) that God never has given such a *fully* inspired Divine Book, and that therefore even the most scientific inquiry as to the text, and the very best conceivable Spirit-filled translating and expounding, can never penetrate to such a final, completely binding, fundamental Divine record, simply because such a book of God, as a rock foundation, never in *this* form has existed.

This difference is consequently of the highest significance, and precisely in reference to our present attitude to the Bible.   Therefore, and for this very reason, he who believes in the full inspiration, of the original documents will doubly endorse scientific labour on the history of the text and its investigation.   Indeed, the more we reject unbelieving criticism as to the *contents* of the Bible the more we endorse critical inquiry as to its *text*.   Precisely because of such a believing attitude we wish to know with the *utmost possible exactness* what God originally said in His perfect written Word.

And in general, there is further difference whether one, in digging a foundation comes at last to a solid, unbroken, vast stretch of rock or only to a subsoil which, indeed, in a high measure is firm but yet in certain places is mixed with sand.   Moreover, under given circumstances, to one who doubts full inspiration, each according to his subjective attitude—one more, the other less—even such longer or shorter passages of Scripture may appear as not completely binding, though textual criticism has proved them to be undoubtedly genuine.

To the question why God permitted the original manuscripts of the sacred writers to be lost we reply, *first:* Were they still in existence they would by some be doubtless honoured as relics, and would have indeed been almost worshipped, as the Israelites did with the serpent of brass, which in a similar way had been originally connected with a wondrous work of God (Num. 21: 8;

[1] pp. 100 to 136.   The seven are placed together in the Table of Contents.

II Kings. 18: 4). And *secondly:* In any case doubt would never have been silenced as to whether these in fact were or were not the original manuscripts. So certainty would never have been reached by the presence of those original writings. They could rather have been a danger of religious confusion than a reliable help. Thus there lies Divine wisdom in the absence of the original manuscripts.[1]

[1] Moreover, what if a holder of one or other of those manuscripts had cunningly falsified them and so had been able to claim Scriptural authority for deadly error? [Trans.]

CHAPTER XVIII

INSPIRATION IN ANALOGY WITH GOD'S REVELATION IN NATURE

*W*E *believe in a full inspiration as worthy of God in view of the fact that in the Creation, which is the Divine revelation in Nature, the minutest objects are ordered with the greatest care and exactness.*

From its greatest representatives in the starry world down to the minutest creatures and plants, indeed to the molecules, atoms, and electrons of which it is composed, Nature is built up with inconceivable exactness according to most refined and powerful laws. Therefore we ask, shall the Most High, seeing that He has so wonderfully ordered in the lower form of His self-revelation, that is, in Nature, have employed less care in the infinitely higher and nobler revelation, that is, His testimony in the written Word?

Every butterfly wing, with its hundred thousand pellicles; the eye of every fly, with its six to seven thousand lenses; every spider thread, with its three hundred single threads, is a witness to this exactness. And the 306 armour plates of a beetle, the 8,000 pairs (!) of muscles of a silkworm, the 700 strokes per second of the wings of a gnat, the sperms of the 300,000 species of mushroom which are so minute that one of each sort would not even fill one thimble—are they not all a direct, irrefutable proof that not only is it not unworthy of God, the Greatest of all, to control the tiniest of all things, but that, on the contrary, it most fully and in the highest degree displays His greatness? Or we may think of the marvellous structure of the bee; 31,000 sensitive hairs are on the feelers of the drone, 5,000 facets (lenses) are set together on each eye of the bee, all exactly hexagonal. The 440 strokes of the wing per second enable it to attain a speed of forty miles per hour, almost the average speed of a fast train. And finally what shall we say of the Infusoria, some of which are so small that of one variety in Bohemia not less than 225 million armour plates are found in one single cubic centimetre? to say nothing of the marvellous power of that ten thousandth gramme of animated matter which we call the brain of the ant, or of the wholly inconceivable atomic planetary systems which are the basis of matter, or of the other millions upon millions of wonders of the tiny world of the most minute things. And lastly, seeing that, as the Lord said, the very hairs of our heads are all numbered (Matt 10:

30), will God be less concerned as to the details of His Word by which He wishes to guide millions of human beings with un-ending existence to salvation, blessedness and glory in all the ages of eternity?

CHAPTER XIX

INSPIRATION DEMONSTRATED BY THE HARMONY OF THE WHOLE SCRIPTURE

*W*E *believe in full inspiration because of the harmony of all the single parts of the whole Biblical testimony.*

God's book is written in three distinct languages, Hebrew, Aramaic, Greek. The New Testament was written by nine different writers, the Old Testament by at least thirty. They differed in culture, class, age, and profession, being prophets, kings, officials, ministers, shepherds, a tax gatherer, priests, fishermen, theologians, judges. Their books differed in places and lands of origin—in Babylon and Ephesus; in the bustle of the seaport of double-harboured heathen Corinth (epistle to the Romans), as well as in the peaceful starry night under the open heaven in the Holy Land (Psa. 8); in Rome, the centre of the world-empire, as well as in Jerusalem, the centre of God's chosen people; in the wild, cleft, jagged mountains of the deserts where David found refuge, as well as in the nobly decorated cities of Greece where Paul preached; in the fruitless, arid deserts of Sinai, as well as in the land which flowed with milk and honey. And finally, though a millennium and a half passed from Moses to John, the seer of Patmos, in the course of which God permitted the perfecting of this noblest of all books, and though all these manifold circumstances pressed closely one upon another, there is nevertheless a harmony which, even under the most critical dissecting knife of unbelief, knows how to assert itself again and again.

Against this reference is made to the many supposed "contradictions" in the Bible, especially in the Gospel narratives, as for example, in the miracles of the Lord and the accounts of the resurrection. But how often, and in the most surprising manner, it has been found that, by more exact knowledge of the period, or of the individual surroundings, or of the idiomatic expressions of the historians, such "contradictions" without any ingenious forcing dissolve into harmony. Therefore faith, by a variety of proofs, has a thoroughly tested and certain ground for joyful confidence that, even in those matters in which we have not yet perhaps the full explanation, it nevertheless already exists: either somewhere else another already has it, or sooner or later either we ourselves will find it or perhaps another will do so. In either case we shall all see it clearly in the perfect day.

Quite often we shall be surprised how extremely simple the explanation was, only *we* had not seen it sooner for lack of clear knowledge of certain local, linguistic, or historical details. Therefore faith is sure of this, that the Bible, which has so often been justified in spite of its critics, will in like manner be found correct in all those questions which today we cannot answer. For the believer the thousandfold past victories of the Bible are justification and pledge of his confident expectation that yet further victories will follow in the present and the future. Such an expectation, based upon innumerable experiences, is certainly not unjustified, "unscientific," or out of date.

Let us suppose that in the course of long years there arrived at a certain place parcels of marble of very different and often most irregular shapes. Also that these came from three different continents and from more than forty different sculptors, who for the more part had never seen one another nor exchanged letters. But at last it became possible to construct of these strange shapeless pieces a single, magnificent, beautiful statue, in which the various pieces so exactly fitted together that not the smallest gap was to be found. Would this not be an irrefutable proof that these single pieces in their several forms, corners, angles, and shapes, had been made from one common plan and been determined by one common intelligent designer? No one would doubt this. Now in a spiritual manner this is precisely the case with the Bible.

Or would it be possible to cure today a sick person by means of a medical book that had been compiled from forty different doctors who had lived in the times of the ancient East and of classical antiquity; being men of Asia Minor, North Africa, and Greece; professional doctors and laymen, scholars and artisans; to which book had been contributed receipts which had been applied during the course of fifteen hundreds of years, say from the middle of the second millennium B.C. to the close of the first century A.D.? We think not. But the Bible is actually the medicine for all the world, the medicine for our souls. Millions upon millions in all times and lands have experienced its healing power; and although its earliest parts are already more than 3,300 years old, yet is their healing power as strong today and their healing word as effective and life-giving as if the whole book had been written just now.

The whole Holy Scripture carries one doctrine and shows one way of salvation for our inner life. Though the revealed ways of God in different periods have been very manifold, yet there is but one life-principle that permeates the whole, and this oneness found in all these many varieties and different forms proves that there is a consistent, underlying Divine pattern and plan.

CHAPTER XX

INSPIRATION TESTIFIED BY THE UNIFORM STRUCTURE OF THE HISTORY OF SALVATION

*W*E *believe in an organic, self-unfolding, full inspiration because of the historical unity of the revelation testified by the Bible.*

This is the most wonderful thing about the Bible: in spite of its most astonishing variety it is a united organism, a harmonious system, full of life and animated by *one* spirit.

Because the revelation of God is a connected historical progress, its record must also be a connected, historical, systematic whole, a well-ordered prophetic and historical system. Therefore as in the development of salvation itself so also in His Book, God sets forth the truth of redemption not in abstract, intellectual, philosophical form but in concrete, comprehensible, living and natural instruction and in graded, progressive, historical unfoldings. It is therefore but just that men in the Evangelical Church, such as Bengel, Oetinger, Beck, and Blumhardt, and before them, as their common root, the Dutch expositor John Cocceius of Leyden, have conceived of Holy Scripture as a skilfully constructed building, the ground plan of which was prepared in advance, and of the whole of which Christ is the end, a system with measure and proportion, in which each separate part is organically incorporated as a member of the whole. All is radiant with the wisest order without any confusion. The harmony of every part constitutes the transparency and clearness of the whole.

Therefore all the books set forth one truth and one doctrine, on which account they mutually expound one another, and Scripture explains itself by Scripture. The subject of the kingdom of God, and its planned dispensations, is the leading melody of this whole Divine symphony. "But we have to bow down, observant and attentive, to comprehend the given harmony," and in the measure that this comes to pass in humility, faith, and obedience, the Divine glory of the Bible will ever anew rise before us, and from point to point, from detail to detail, will be livingly established, and the historical unity and the greatness of Holy Scripture, reaching even to the smallest matters, will ever afresh prove its character as inspired.

In addition to many details, smaller and greater, in the agreement of prophecy and fulfilment, this is seen especially in the general inner formation and consistent structure of the whole as revealed in the sequence of periods and economies with their respective goals.

Indeed, could the preparation for salvation in the Old Testament be more clearly formed to move to a consummation that it was?

First, in the ancient Bible history, as the historical foundation of the whole course, there are two chief periods of revelation which, in the form of a polarity, are harmoniously opposed and joined to each other.

After the exclusion from Paradise, during the course of many centuries, there was in force the principle of *self-determination* without any revelation of Divine law and without God-ordained human authority (from Adam to Noah).

Then, when this principle had shown men's failure, there was introduced its harmonious opposite, the principle of *control by authority* ("Whoso sheds man's blood by man shall his blood be shed." Gen. 9: 6), and then followed the development of human history with human authority and the building up of Kingdoms and States (see Racial Table, Nimrod, Gen. 10).

Then, as this also was falsely perverted by man (Babel), came God's change from the universalism of the original revelation to the particularism (separate part) of the revelation limited to Abraham and later to Israel. But the goal, the blessing of all peoples, and therefore the yet certain attaining of the glorious end of universalism, remained unshaken (Gen. 12: 3; Gal. 3: 8). Is not this, at the very beginning of history, a most consistent, systematic, inwardly connected, educational working clearly directed to a goal?

And what harmony and consistency in the additional further guiding of the preparation for salvation from Abraham to Christ! Just here there is seen an absolutely clear, indeed, completely unsurpassable directing of history to the Redeemer and His work as its goal!

There are again two chief periods, two chief covenants (Abraham and Moses) in harmonious contrast, comprising

first, an education of *faith* lasting through two thousand years (the covenant with Abraham);

and then, as supplementary, through a millennium-and-a-half, an education in *repentance* (by awakening of consciousness of sin through the Mosaic law).

Could there be a more suitable preparation for the New Testament unfolding of salvation? Was not this the great object, that the sinner should be saved? And this could not be effected save on condition of his turning to Christ as his personal Saviour, that is, on condition of his conversion.

And is not conversion simply the sum of turning from and turning to, of "No" to self and "Yes" to the Lord, that is, of repentance and faith?

And now we see in the Old Testament revelation just these two periods with these two chief goals, faith and repentance. Therefore is not conversion, as the unity of these two, quite evidently the educative centre and goal of the entire Old Testament preparatory revelation?

Can there be a more transparent historical system in the world than this, in which we see just two such outstanding time-sections (Abraham and Moses) which contain, as their respective educational goals, just these two central requirements (faith and repentance) which are indispensable in man's *subjective* attitude to God if he is to obtain God's free salvation?

And is not the whole Old Testament, just precisely in these same two objectives, likewise directed with wonderful system to the *objective* work of the Redeemer Himself?

As the main feature in God's covenant with Abraham (seen especially in the birth and the offering up of Isaac) there is faith in the *life*-giving grace of God and His *resurrection* power. In the law of Moses, there is the *death* sentence of God upon the sinner as the deepest and gloomiest result of God's judgment.

Thus the latter quite clearly points to Golgotha and the former to the resurrection of Christ. Thus are they both (Abraham and Moses), in their contrary unity, visibly and perceptibly directed to the two chief sides of the saving work of the Redeemer, and it becomes manifest that the whole Old Testament is directed not only to the subjective end of the conversion of the sinner (repentance and faith), but also to the objective end of the redemptive work of the sinner's Saviour (death and resurrection), and thus to the central human *experience* of salvation as well as to the central God-wrought *event* of salvation.

One must verily be blind not to see in all this a perfect Divine plan, established in advance, with a definite foreseen goal, clearly seen and consistent.

And how organically and inwardly connected is also the structure of the New Testament unfolding of Salvation!

First, in the testimony of the Word and the Spirit, there stands in the centre the *absent* Christ, who has gone to heaven, during the period between His first and His second appearings. Then after the *parousia* (arrival, return, presence) there reigns as revealed in glory, the *present* Christ. Thus first covering, then uncovering; first concealment, then revelation; first, misunderstanding, then acknowledgment; first humiliation, then exaltation; first the crown of thorn, then the royal crown of triumph. And with regard to the human side, first salvation known by faith, then salvation seen by all.

Furthermore, regarding the expansion of the circles of light within the areas and spheres of the creation, we see clearly three stages: first the gathering of the church, then the blessing of the nations, and lastly a new heaven and a new earth, the transfigured universe. So also here there is clearly perceptible a harmoniously graded, progressive, magnificent plan.

But above all this, surpassing indeed everything in the highest and most impressive degree, the progressiveness and consistency of the Divine plan shows itself in the gradual unfolding of the personal self-revelation of the Redeemer-God Himself.

First in the present period of the church, the special activity of the *Spirit* of God: then in the visible kingdom of God in the End-time, the period preceding the consummation, the kingly rule of the *Son* of God: finally, in the eternal state, the kingdom of glory of God the *Father* (I Cor. 15: 28).

This means that the whole New Testament revelation is a threefold, rhythmical, progressive self-revelation of the eternal God as the Holy Spirit, the Son, the Father, and it becomes evident that the whole historical course of redemption since Christ, salvation's centre, bears a trinitarian stamp; so that in this universal course of history there is not only deliverance and salvation but above all the God of deliverance and salvation Himself shines forth ever more brightly and radiantly.

There can be no plan of history more logical, clear, purposive, harmonious, magnificent! But exactly this clarity of purpose and unity of the whole makes this history of salvation a universal, historical self-evidence of its Divine character. And because the Bible is the record of this historical revelation, this harmony of the whole proves also at the same time its proper inner historical God-ordered unity and thus the Divine inspiration of the Holy Scriptures (for further treatment see Part I, chs. II and XII).

It is such an attitude of faith in the Scriptures that alone makes possible the study of the Biblical history of salvation. But whoever, through unbelief or half-belief, takes up a lame attitude to the Scriptures, and especially to the first chapters of the Bible, the prophecies of Daniel, the saving significance of the Cross, the bodily resurrection of Christ and His personal return, to him the beginning, middle, and end of the Divine plan of redemption will be unintelligible, and the marvellous Divine temple of the history of salvation will remain to him a closed building.

In an especial manner early history and final history belong together. He who denies the one will usually doubt the other. Thus Paul Althaus (Prof. of Theology in Erlangen) declares:

"The history of salvation does not begin with an original historical Paradise and therefore does not close with a final historical kingdom of God on earth. The Paradise on this earth and the Millennial kingdom belong together. Theologically they stand and fall with one another." Here is seen that accepting or rejecting the history of salvation is directly connected with the personal attitude to the inspiration of the Bible, either positively or negatively.

One has called belief in a full, organic, historically unfolding inspiration a "levelling fundamentalism." It has been said that "in a false understanding of the doctrine of inspiration every word is put on one level without taking in account that the time is fulfilled, that Christ has come . . . that only from this one middle point of the line, even from the history of God's revelation in Christ, must past and future be viewed and estimated." But nothing can be more erroneous than this verdict. It is precisely belief in full inspiration which, with Christ and His apostles, acknowledges indeed all the fundamentals of revelation, that knows at the same time, with the Lord Himself, how to distinguish between "great" and "small" commandments of God (Matt. 22: 38; 5: 19), between God-inspired statements concerning things necessary to salvation[1] and God-inspired arrangements of historical information of lesser significance.[2]

Further: it is precisely belief in full inspiration, historical and developing, that distinguishes between dispensations and periods of salvation, between preparation and fulfilment, between Old Testament dawn and New Testament noontide. This is, indeed, just the contrary to "levelling"! Much rather it is here plainly testified, that on the basis of Biblical revelation there is progress from lower to higher, from twilight to clear day, a manifold articulation, a chain of periods richly coloured, an ever upward ascent. Just this *non*-levelling of Scripture statements and periods is the precise presupposition for all study of redemptive history in which faith in full inspiration has always perceived the goal and crown of its spiritual and intellectual efforts in searching into Divine truth.

And without any compromise we add: Even these words of God which rank lower as revelation are of full value, and allowing for all differences and non-levelling, we have no right to overlook them or to esteem them lightly. God's word always remains God's word, whether it speaks as to things necessary

---

[1] Such as the incarnation of the Redeemer, His substitutionary work, bodily resurrection, the demand for repentence and faith, and the reception of the Spirit.

[2] Such as Christ's statement regarding the tithing of mint, dill, and cummin (Matt. 23: 23), or Paul's word as to his cloak with Carpus (II Tim. 4: 13) or his dietetic advice to Timothy (I Tim. 5: 23).

to salvation or of things external, of things eternal or temporal, or whether it be instruction by the Lord on a higher or lower plane of revelation. Here man has no right to make a difference, perhaps in the sense that he believes and follows one as important and rejects the other as wrong or superfluous. If anywhere there applies here the principle that Christ Himself declares, that one should do this and not neglect the other (Matt. 23: 23).

Moreover what appears to one unessential may have essential significance for another. Concerning Paul's word as to his books and parchments (II Tim. 4: 13), there is an interesting incident that shows the value of every word of Scripture. One asked J. N. Darby what loss there would be if that remark had not been preserved. He replied that he at least would have been the loser, because in his ascetic days as a clergyman he had thought to get rid of his library, but it was the care of Paul for his books that had restrained him. When the vast benefit to the church at large that resulted later from Darby's use of his extensive and valuable library is considered, there is a remarkable example of the value of each word of God's book.

In an organism the less important members are penetrated by the same life. Now the Bible is a spiritual organism permeated with the life of God. A heathen Chinaman asked a missionary for a Gospel. The latter had at hand only a Gospel by Matthew. He regretted this: he would rather have given him the Gospel by John. For Matthew begins with its long genealogical table, which is so extended but contains, as it seems, so little that is interesting. Might not the reader after a few lines lose pleasure in the book and cease to read?—But what happened? Next day the Chinaman returned and expressed his very great joy, because the beginning of the book had been so interesting. As we know, the Chinese have a great regard for honouring their ancestors, and that must indeed be a special man, who had an ancestral tree of such importance and covering so many centuries! This had at once awakened his special interest in the history of such a man. The beginning had therefore inclined him to continue reading with double interest.

So everything in Holy Scripture has its significance and importance. A word of the Bible which at the moment may not mean very much for one person, may for another be of perhaps special importance. The Bible is not God's book only for certain individuals, but for *all*. Therefore it must contain suitable messages for everyone, and everything in it is God-given, profitable, and necessary.

We do not overlook the problems arising from such a faith,

especially those geological and chronological. But unsolved problems are no hindrance to faith relying on Christ and the testimony of His apostles. Problems which seemed insoluble have often been suddenly cleared up, and the Bible has been justified where it had been accused of scientific or historical errors. In a letter to Jerome, Augustine justly said: "If here or there I stumble upon something which seems not to agree with the truth, I make no doubt that either the copy is faulty, or the translator did not express exactly the thought of the original, or that I do not understand the matter." In any case faith can wait.

Thus the question concerning the Millennial kingdom is in large measure a question of inspiration. Eschatology and faith in inspiration are inseparable.

The expectation of a visible kingdom of God on the theatre of this earth is evident in the Old and New Testaments. In a hundred places it is the subject. To "spiritualize" them all is contrary to accurate exegesis. The promises of the first coming of Christ were fulfilled literally. Christ came literally from Bethlehem (Mic. 5 : 2), rode literally on an ass into Jerusalem. (Zech. 9: 9), was literally betrayed for thirty pieces of silver (Zech. 11: 12), and on the cross was literally pierced in hands and feet (Psa. 22: 16). They literally cast lots for His garments (Psa. 22: 18), literally His bones were not broken (Psa. 34: 20), and literally His side was pierced by a spear. (Zech. 12: 10).

Combined with these prophesies of the first coming, there often stand in the *very same sentence* prophecies of the second coming, and by the plain meaning of the words, and by their later fulfilment in the life of Jesus of Nazareth, it is evident that the first part of such sentences is to be taken literally. Who therefore can justify the taking merely "spiritually" of the second part of one and the same sentence (e.g. Luke 1: 31–33)? Who gives us the right to take Jews to mean Christians, Jerusalem to mean now only the church, and Canaan heaven? No, the "spiritual-izing" of these promises of the Messianic kingdom, given out of free grace and evidently understood literally, and a transference of them to some other corporate system, were nothing else than a veiled breach of covenant by God as regards Israel. But this is impossible.

It is quite evident that the Old Testament prophets expected above all else a *spiritual* renewing and conversion of Israel (Zech. 13: 1; Ezek. 36: 26; Isa. 4: 4); to which in the New Testament Paul especially refers (II Cor. 3: 16; Rom. 11: 24–26); and it is likewise true that they announced a *spiritual* renewing of the nations (Zeph. 3: 9; Isa. 2: 4; etc.). But equally plainly, and in statements completely beyond misunderstanding, numerous prophecies announced for the End-times also a return of Israel to the land of their fathers and a *national* and *territorial* reinstatement (Isa. 11: 11, etc.).

In plain words which admit of no other possible explanation they declare that for the Messianic End time they expected a reuniting of the Two-tribed kingdom with the Ten-tribed kingdom and the sovereignty of the Messiah over the whole Twelve-tribed people in a single proper civil institution and in racial national unity (Ezek 37: 15-24).

With indisputable clarity they proclaim it as a Divine message that those who had been scattered to all quarters of the world would be brought back, and this to their *own* land (Ezek. 28: 25), the land of their *fathers* (Jer. 16: 15), *this* land (Jer. 32: 41), the land of Israel (Ezek. 11: 17), in Gilead and on Lebanon. These terms can mean only the well known geographical area in Western Asia in which Israel formerly dwelled and which is unmistakably indicated by these unequivocal expressions (Zech. 10: 10).

They further declare that the central place of worship will be in Jerusalem. And not indeed for Israel alone but also for the renewed nations (Isa. 2: 1-3; 27: 13; Zech. 14: 16), and that from this renewed people of God, Israel, dwelling in the Holy land, there will go forth powerful influences upon all nations (Mic. 4: 1-4; 5: 8; Zech. 12: 6). It were no difficult task to multiply these proofs. Sound exegesis cannot overlook this Old Testament prophetic expectation of an earthly, territorial, national restoration of Israel. But of course all these prophecies do not apply to unconverted Israel, but only to the at last spiritually renewed Israel believing upon Messiah.

Similarly it is undeniable that the *Revelation* of John expects a kingdom of God that lies *between* the appearing of the Lord in glory and the proper renewing of the universe. For, first in chapter 19 it speaks of a return of Christ as the glorious Victor, Who, accompanied by hosts of angels, descends from the opened heaven, breaks His foes to pieces, and as King of kings and Lord of lords displays His conquering power. Only after this, in the beginning and middle of chapter 20, it speaks of the kingdom of the thousand years (20: 3-7), which it thus quite plainly sets forth as a consequence of the victory so pictured; and not till then, at the end of chapter 20, and in chapter 21, after the catastrophic final events, does it speak of the great white throne, of world collapse, world transfiguration, and world renewing (20: 11-15; 21).

Therefore the well-known German theologian Professor Paul Althaus says justly: "The Biblical argument cannot be refuted by asserting that the passages named do not speak of an End time period prior to the consummation. As to I Cor. 15: 23–25 one may perhaps ask how far the thought of an intermediate kingdom stands behind the intimation; but there can be no doubt as to Rev. 20: 4–7." But when, in spite of this, building on "internal" reasons, Althaus and many others reject a visible Millennial kingdom they can do this only (if they think it through logically, which Althaus does) on the presupposition of an enfeebled view of inspiration influenced to a certain degree by Higher Criticism. The prophet, including John the Apostle, "was, indeed, just mistaken" (Althaus.)

In fact, to "spiritualize" these promises—perhaps by referring to Israel having failed to accept the Messiah and being in consequence set aside—and to transfer them in this "spiritual" form to another body corporate, the church, would mean nothing else, than that these promises of the kingdom *in their plain literal Old Testament sense will never be fulfilled!* By a logical explanation of the actual meaning of Old Testament prophecy, it remains wholly unavoidable to declare with Paul Althaus (who is one of the leading representatives of the method of spiritualization) that "history has taken a quite other course than the book of Daniel expected . . . In contradistinction to the older theologians it must be stated plainly that the Old Testament contains sometimes even 'erroneous' beliefs, prophecies by God-called prophets which God according to their plain Old Testament meaning does *not* fulfil, expectations which He disappoints. Also expectations, which the prophet was quite certain he had received from God have 'failed.' Their 'spiritual' fulfilment in Christ signifies at the same time, that in their Old Testament sense they will *not* be fulfilled . . . One must say definitely that the 'fulfilment' of the Old Testament in Christ is at the same time a critique and annulment of those prophecies as to their earthly national realization. The promises of a high earthly standing for Israel are, and will be, not only fulfilled 'spiritually' in Christ . . . but through this spiritual fulfilment their earthly and national form is broken to pieces. . . . When Jesus vehemently rejected the national Messianic ideal of His contemporaries, He thereby stood in measure also against the great prophets. Indeed, it amounts to an actual opposition and conflict. There is another spirit, an antagonism for which there can be found no reconciliation as if there might come later in a Millennial kingdom what had not yet been fulfilled in Christ. . . . Since Christ is come the hour for the fulfilment of the vision of Ezekiel (ch. 40–48) of a new priestly Jerusalem can never come."

In these words—which we certainly can only repudiate—

there is laid bare, consistently and unmistakably, the only logical, fundamental background of the denial of the Millennial kingdom and of all *pure* spiritualizing of the meaning of Old Testament prophecy. This is said under the presupposition that the Old Testament prophetic passages are really taken in the sense in which the prophets meant them and which they expressed. *Correct exegesis of prophecy and the method of spiritualizing can logically unite only upon the basis of a certain acknowledgment of Higher Criticism.*

So here we stand unavoidably before a threefold choice:

Either false exposition of prophecy, and then, indeed, the possibility of a method of spiritualizing, even with personal full belief in the inspiration of the prophetic words;

or a correct exposition of prophecy, and then however, the possibility of pure spiritualizing, only involving acceptance of a certain measure of Biblical criticism, presuming that the problems are logically thought through to their deepest roots (as e.g. Althaus correctly does);

or finally, right exposition of prophecy united with belief in full inspiration, but then indeed necessarily an expectation of a literal fulfilment of these promises, acknowledged as meant literally, and therefore to be fulfilled literally in a visible kingdom of God in the End days.

A fourth possibility can scarcely exist.

Therefore Paul Althaus says quite justly that "where one defends the old conception of inspiration one must naturally refuse all sifting of Old Testament prophecy: the New Testament then *completes* indeed these old prophetic messages through fulfilment and newly added promises, but it does not *sift* them."

Out of the great number of the representatives of the spiritualization method we have quoted especially Professor Althaus because he, as a scholar of high scientific rank, clearly sees and frankly admits the actual, original meaning of the Old Testament prophecies, without, unscientifically, trying to attribute to them a sense which is alien to them; and because he, as a really logical thinker, thinks problems right through to their depths, and has also the courage to express the principal foundation on which this spiritualizing method necessarily stands, if the Old Testament texts are really taken in their indisputable, obvious sense. Not all representatives of the spiritualization method see and express this with the same clarity, transparency, and consistency. But here the position is set forth absolutely clearly. (For further remarks on the method of spiritualization see Part III).

But *we*, in agreement with a very great number of Bible-believing scientific expositors and students of Scripture of the various Christian Churches, Free Churches, and assemblies, declare that *all* words of prophecy must find their fulfilment. They must be fulfilled literally, actually, completely, and in the same sense in which they were meant originally. The fact that, in addition to this, God often fulfils a prophecy in a still higher, spiritual, eternal degree, surpassing the Spirit-given wording of the message and the understanding of even the prophet himself, is no proof that thereby the original, literal meaning is dissolved and that the expectations, as far as God Himself through this inspired prophecy has evoked them, will ever be disappointed. No, God, the Eternal, Unchangeable and Faithful One, always keeps His word, and does this in the same sense as He first gave it. But it is His abounding grace that frequently He surpasses that meaning, and surprises expectant faith by the unfolding of greater blessings first indeed hidden, but already from the beginning immanent, and in their final display infinitely richer. "The gifts of grace and the call of God are beyond recall" (Rom. 11: 29).

Naturally the full explanation of prophecy will not come before the fulfilment. The exact details, stages, and sequence of all the separate intervening events God has not revealed. But in joyful confidence faith can look into the future with assurance that its main lines God has made known. The goal will be duly reached, the kingdom of God will triumph. The redemptive plan of the Eternal, which has advanced through ages and periods of revelation, will be completed until God shall be all in all (I Cor. 15: 28)

To our powers of thought and perception it may not be easy to picture to ourselves the details of such an earthly kingdom of the heavenly Christ. It may also be difficult for us to comprehend intelligently how in this our world, which is still temporal and material, and among men who are yet in the flesh, there shall be a kingdom of God in which the forces of sin and death shall be indeed weakened but not yet entirely destroyed (Isa. 65: 17, 20; comp. *The Triumph of the Crucified*, p. 170). In general this whole Biblical doctrine of a future earthly kingdom of God's Messianic King, arising from the house of David, may be for many a thorn indeed a stone of stumbling. Especially will it be a vexation to the modern mind with its scientific reasoning, its philosophical view of history, its racial and national feelings, all the more since today in many lands Antisemitism in a certain measure is still present, even if concealed.

Nevertheless this "difficulty" of faith in the Bible cannot be simply set aside by reversing the sense of the Messianic prophecies concerned, and still less by stigmatizing the whole doctrine as fantastic and fanatical. The "difficulty" can be removed solely and only by faith bowing to the Divine word. But thereby faith will perceive that ecclesiastical and theological science has not seldom prepared its own difficulty of conception and faith by approaching this part of the Divine revelation with false presuppositions. But this friction between theology and the Bible can be overcome by a believing acknowledgment of the whole of prophetic Scripture.

In this mighty development Christ is the centre. He is the central sun of the whole Bible. All the books of Holy Scripture bear witness to Him (John 5: 39). Often in just those Old Testament places where at first sight it does not at all appear so, the instruction of the Holy Spirit in the New Testament shows that there also Christ was the subject (Heb. 7; Matt. 2: 15). This is seen, for example, in the appearing of Melchizedek (Gen. 14: 18–24), or in the testimony of Hosea concerning Israel that God called His Son out of Egypt (Hos. 11: 1), and in many other places.

Here again it is often the delicacies and details of the text which reveal not only a general but a quite special inspiration which attaches to the single words, sentences, and grammatical connexions. Only such belief in full inspiration could enable Paul to give his proof from Scripture in the Galatian letter in that form which he used (Gal. 3: 16). He wrote: "Now the [Divine] promises were given to Abraham, and to his seed. He saith not 'and to seeds' in the plural, but refers to a single person, 'and to his seed', which is Christ." Thus Paul sees the Messianic prophecies of the Old Covenant as Divinely and exactly ordered even to the smallest details of the text, indeed to the singular and plural endings of the words. In fact *Hebrews* goes so far that not only the speech but also the silence of the Old Testament is Divinely inspired; for the chief Scriptural proof for the high priesthood of Melchizedek being everlasting it draws from what is *not* stated in the sacred text, even from the fact that the historical account of the Melchizedek of Abraham's time mentions neither his father nor his mother, nor the beginning nor end of his life, so that thus the priest-king of Salem, so far as the Biblical record is concerned, appears likewise without father or mother or genealogy, "having neither beginning of days nor end of life"; so that precisely in this respect he is (typologically) like the Son of God (Heb. 7: 3; Gen. 14: 18–24). The Scriptural principle which is the basis of such proofs is entirely that of full inspiration. "The writer's conception apparently goes so far as to believe that the Spirit of God infused and ordered not only the factual form of sacred *history* but also of its written description, and this in such degree that not only the positive statements but also the actual silences have typical Messianic import" (Prof. J. H. Kurtz).

It is further testimony to the wonderful ordering of the sacred text that at times the prophets did not themselves understand the things they prophesied, so that they pondered and "searched diligently what or what manner of time it was to which the Spirit of Christ working in them referred." And because they evidently did not gain rest as to their own message and its meaning, it was revealed to them as a general explanation that "through their service they did not impart to themselves but to *you* what is now proclaimed to you" (I Pet. 1: 11, 12). This fact lifts above all doubt that, according to the testimony of the New Testament, the inspiration of the prophets goes far beyond bare "thoughts" or "personal" inspiration, and rises to the choice of even the words being guided by the Spirit of God. For when at times the prophetic message contained what the prophets themselves did not understand, and when their words, in which their message must perforce be clothed, held more than they themselves comprehended, this was only possible by the *very words* being prompted and ordered by the Spirit of God.

Thus from the practical attitude of the New Testament to the letter of the Old Testament it arises that, for the apostles of Jesus Christ, belief in a full inspiration—without indeed laying down a defined doctrinal formula—was yet a tacit presupposition. In the New Testament faith in a full inspiration is not found as a dogmatic theological formula but certainly as a practical spiritual possession. Only in his second epistle to Timothy does Paul come very close to a formal declaration as to the inspiration of the Old Testament as the Holy Book of God: "*All* Scripture is given by inspiration of God (Gr. *theopneustos*, God-breathed, God-inspired) and is profitable for teaching, for reproof, for correction, for instruction which is in righteousness" (II Tim. 3: 16, 17; see also 1 Cor. 2: 13).

CHAPTER XXI

INSPIRATION ACCEPTED BY THE LORD HIMSELF AND HIS APOSTLES

*W*E *believe in a reliable, full inspiration on the authority of the Lord Jesus and His apostles.*

Hundreds of times the Old Testament declares "Thus saith the Lord!" Christ Himself asserted that "the *Scripture* [that which is *written*, not merely the thought or theme] cannot be broken" (John 10: 34, 35; Gk. *graphē*, from *grapho* to write). Here He refers to a word of the Bible which comes in only this single place in the whole Old Testament. So according to the conception of the Lord whoever breaks the force of this one word, which comes only once in one psalm (82: 6), dissolves the whole organism of the "Scripture." The Bible may be compared to the seamless robe of Jesus, or to a carpet or a house. One has only to step off the carpet at one place to be off it all, or to go out of only one door to be outside of the whole house. Thus firm was the belief of Christ in the organic character of the "Scripture." To the disciples He said: "all things must needs be fulfilled which are *written* in the law of Moses and the prophets and the psalms concerning Me . . . Thus it is *written* that the Christ should suffer, and rise again from the dead the third day" (Luke 24: 44–47). In the Sermon on the Mount He had said: "Verily I say unto you, Till heaven and earth pass away, one letter or one dash shall in no wise pass away from the law till all things be accomplished" (Matt. 5: 18).

For Christ, the personal living word (John 1: 1, 14), one "jot" or one "tittle" of the *written* word had more value than all starry worlds or sun systems of the whole universe. Here we have authoritative proof in especially weighty form; and Paul, His greatest apostle, confesses, "I believe in *all* things which are *written* in the law and the prophets" (Acts 24: 14). Therefore faith in the Holy Scripture as being revelation, and in its indestructible authority, is no unspiritual, narrow-minded deifying of the letter but has on its side the greatest minds in history, including the Son of God Himself. "The revelation stands, nay, it *continues* for us in the Scripture: it is continuing—there is no avoiding it—in the Bible texts, in the words and sentences, in that which the prophets and apostles desired to say, and have said, as their testimony."

It is foolish to object by quoting the words of Paul that "the letter killeth" (II Cor. 3: 6); for there "letter" says nothing as regards the sacred text and the manner of its inspiration, but refers simply to the Old Testament law as it presents externally its demand which results in the death of the still unrenewed man.   This is in constrast to the spiritual revelation of the new covenant as it witnesses in the renewed man organically, inwardly, and makes him to live.

And has not Christ Himself most plainly acknowledged just those parts of the Old Testament which today are most hotly attacked, such as the historicity of Adam and Eve (Matt. 19: 8; John 8: 44), the fact of the Flood (Matt. 24: 37, 38), the miraculous experience of the prophet Jonah (Matt. 12: 39, 40)?   Did He not most strikingly acknowledge the book of Daniel?   For from this very book, today so much attacked by unbelief, He chose the chief symbolic designation of His own person ("Son of man," Dan. 7: 13, 14; Matt. 26: 64), yea, He associated Himself with this book by the single oath which He took during His life on earth (Matt. 26: 63, 64).   And again, it is in this very book of Daniel that there is rooted the chief description of the message of Christ, "kingdom of heaven" (kingly realm, lordship of the heavens, Dan. 4: 26; "the heavens do rule").

Then also the most part of His references to Isaiah are drawn from the *second* part of the book of this prophet (chs. 40–66), which modern unbelief or half-belief ascribes to the so-called "Deutero-Isaiah" (Gr. *deuteros* = second).   But the Lord, as also Paul, select passages from this second part and say "Isaiah says" (Rom. 10: 16 with Isa. 53: 1; Rom. 10: 20 with Isa. 65: 1; Luke 4: 18 with Isa. 61: 1; John 12: 38 with Isa. 53: 1; John 1: 23 with Isa. 40: 3).

It is further striking that all three quotations with which in the temptation Jesus smote the enemy come from the book of Deuteronomy, the very portion of the Pentateuch (five books of Moses) which unbelief declares to be not genuine (Matt. 4: 4 with Deut. 8: 3; Matt. 4: 7 with Deut. 6: 16; Matt. 4: 10 with Deut. 6: 13).

All this testimony acquires a yet more convincing force from the fact that the Lord and His apostles treat the first chapters of the Bible, and so many other attacked portions of the Old Testament, not only as reports of real historical events, but even draw from them doctrinal inferences.   The fact that man was made in the image of God (Jas. 3: 9 with Gen. 1: 27), the God-appointed order of monogamy (Matt. 19: 4–9 with Gen. 2: 23, 24), the serpent nature of Satan (Rev. 20: 2 "that old Serpent" with Gen. 3), the sentence of death that has been passed upon mankind (I Cor. 15: 21, 22), the organic character of the church of

Christ (Christ the "last Adam"; Rom. 5: 12–21; I Cor. 15: 21, 22), the transfiguration of the body of those raised from the dead (I Cor. 15: 45–49)—how great and central are all those Biblical appointments and truths.   And by Christ and His apostles they were all connected with historical accounts from the ancient Bible history, partly as fulfilment, partly as opposed thereto. Therefore said Prof. Ebrard, "Is the New Testament truth? Then Gen. 1–3 is history."

It is impossible to maintain an unbroken faith in Christ and at the same time to put away this evident fact, perhaps with the help of certain speculations concerning the self-humiliation (*kenosis*) of Christ, or by denying the freedom from error of the incarnate Son of God, or even by believing that, against His better knowledge (!), for educative purposes, or in condescension, Christ accommodated Himself to the errors of His contemporaries.   That the Lord accommodated Himself to the *language* of His time is evident; but that He accommodated Himself to the *errors* of His time is utterly irreconcilable with His perfect truthfulness and His divinity.   The reliability of the Bible and the reliability of the Lord Jesus belong together.

Thus we open up the question of the Bible centrally, that is, from the centre of the Bible, Jesus Christ.   We believe in the Bible on His account.   From faith in Christ we reach full faith in His Word also.   In Christ, the centre of God's revelation, we have also the centre of a view of the Bible which is according to God.

Moreover, this alone is consistent with faith.   For Christ Himself is the "Logos," the original form of the word, the personal, living "word," the true and faithful Witness (John 1: 1; Rev. 1: 5), the mouth of the eternal truth, yea, the truth itself (John 14: 6).   And it was His Spirit, the Spirit of Christ, Who inspired the prophets (I Pet. 1: 11), and the "testimony of Jesus" is the "spirit of prophecy" (Rev. 19: 10).

But here we stand on the ground of faith.   Even in purely human life, authority stands as something that cannot be "proved" but must be experienced.

Everything living we perceive through intuition (direct, inward sight).   The deity of Jesus of Nazareth, and therewith His unconditional authority in all questions of faith and life, cannot be proved mathematically; but truth proves itself.   Here enters experience of Christ, heart experience.

CHAPTER XXII

INSPIRATION AS DEMONSTRATED BY THE
SPIRITUAL POWER OF THE BIBLE

*W*E *believe in a living, full inspiration because of the spiritual energy that pervades even the smallest portions of the Bible.*

The question is often put as to how the distinguishing of the books of the Bible as "canonical" from all other writings can be established (*canon* = plumbline, standard). Apart from the proof of their inward harmony and historical unity, the answer lies especially in the "testimony of the Holy Spirit" (Lat. *testimonium Spiritus Sancti*). Let a spiritual mind read but once the very valuable writings of the so-called Apostolic Fathers, who were the leaders of early Christianity who followed directly after the generation of the apostles and writers of the New Testament, that is, the letters of Clement, Ignatius, Barnabas, Polycarp, or The Teaching of the Twelve Apostles (*Didache*), the Shepherd of Hermas, the Letter of Diognetus! Let anyone compare, for example, the letters of Ignatius to the Romans or Ephesians with those letters in the New Testament directed to the same churches by Paul, or the letter of Clement to the Corinthians with that of the great apostle to the Gentiles, or the letter of Polycarp to the Philippians with the well-known letter in the New Testament! In spite of valuing most highly all that is truly spiritual, noble, and fine, what a disparity is observable between these writings of only the second century and the New Testament! Or one may compare the Old Testament *Apocrypha* with the Scriptures of the Hebrew canon! Everywhere here the witness of the Holy Spirit stands on the side of the Biblical writings.

Let no one say that by this we fall into the error of an arbitrary subjectivism. In Scripture the testimony of the Holy Spirit is plainly distinguished from that of the human spirit, even of the man redeemed in Christ. "The Spirit Himself witnesses with our spirit that we are children of God," that is, witnesses in agreement with our spirit, which is thus distinguished from the Holy Spirit (Rom. 8: 16). It is the Divine Spirit who acknowledges what Himself produces. The authority of the Holy Spirit is inward, spirit-wrought, direct, self-evidencing. It is not the bare external authority of a book as a merely literary product but is a wholly spiritual authority. As Paul once expressed it in relation to the Old Testament, the Holy Scripture is "God-breathed" (Gr. *theopneustos*, II Tim. 3: 16). Only thus arises the capacity of the Bible to produce supernatural effects. Only thus comes the inward working power of the words of the Bible and the self-testimony of the Holy Spirit in the hearts of believers which takes place in and by means of the Bible. "The heart declares, That is true, even should I suffer for it a hundred deaths" (Luther). Calvin said justly: "The Scripture carries in itself the evidence of the truth, just as black and white each that of its own colour, and sweet and bitter that of its own taste."

The authority of Holy Scripture has its basis in the person of its Divine Author. Its authority is historically founded upon its inspiration. It is objective and permanent. The Bible has its authority in itself.

The subjective conviction of this authority is the result of the inward testimony of the Holy Spirit who unites Himself with the written word in a living and continually active way.

Inspiration of the Holy Spirit and testimony of the Holy Spirit must be therefore distinguished.

The Biblical *inspiration* of the Holy Spirit is a finished activity of God in the past. The inward *testimony* of the Holy Spirit is a continuous working of God in all subsequent times, including our own and the future.

The inspiration of the Holy Spirit refers to the Bible itself. The testimony of the Holy Spirit appeals to its readers and hearers. Through this working of the Holy Spirit these are intended to be brought to the conviction of the inspiration and the authority of the Holy Scripture, and thus to the obedience of faith.

From all this it follows that the Canon of Holy Scripture— from God's side, and thus ideally and actually in itself—was finished and complete from the very first moment when the last New Testament book had come into existence. What had to follow now was only the actual collection of these writings into a single volume, and their general recognition, in the Christian church, as possessing Divine authority, individually and as a unit.

After having overcome certain questions and uncertainties in detail, this aim was reached in the course of the following two centuries. The decisive factor in this development, however, was not human agreement, or decrees of Church councils, but the spirit-wrought authority of the Bible itself, its own Divine life and power, immanent in the books from the very first moment of their origin, as the result of the Divine Inspiration. At the same time this historical process was under the overruling guidance of the exalted Divine Head of the church. The Church itself had in no way to "complete" or even to "create" the Biblical Canon, but simply to *acknowledge* it.

Thus has the Spirit of God united Himself inexplicably but with marvellous strength with the inspiration of the Bible as with no other book, not even with the noblest and best of other Christian writings. In these records of events in past ages there abides something present and living, there weaves and works in them a secret, imperishable energy, even the Spirit of the living God. Therefore the Bible is a living book. "The word of that former time speaks today." "As the organ of the present Christ the Bible stands forth far above the realm of all other historical records and holds an unique place" (Prof. Karl Heim). Here there is no mere once-upon-a-time but a now, no simple yesterday but a today, no mere concern with the beyond but a God-permeated interest with this life. Here is not only a written word but a spiritually living word, not only external letters but speech of the Spirit, spoken inwardly and still speaking. Thus Holy Scripture in a quite incomparable degree shares in the character of the Eternal as ever present.

The Spirit of God has not only inbreathed the written word and given it, but has continued with it. He accompanies it and makes it operative. He makes the bare record to be a bridge with heaven. God *comes* to us now through His word, and the Word that is centuries old remains fresh and eternally young. It is as if it had been written but yesterday, "as if the ink was not yet dry," never growing old, superior to time, ever present.

And it is often quite insignificant remarks, which the reader may have read in passing hundreds of times, that suddenly shine with light, and become a message from God to influence his life, and indeed can change it fundamentally. What a great difference whether God says that He will bless *according to* His riches or only *out of* them (Eph. 3: 16). How much confidence and hope for wandering souls lies in the two small words "until now": "He who says that he is in the light, and hates his brother, is in the darkness *until now*" (I John 2: 9). How much wisdom in caring for souls lies in the small word "partly": "I hear that divisions exist among you; and I *partly* believe it" (I Cor. 11: 18).

And in general, how greatly is faith strengthened when it can lay hold of the *very words* of God's promises! In the history of the kingdom of God has not this reliance upon the whole Word again and again awakened a courageous faith, given wings to joyful confidence, wrought deeds, indeed made history? Was not this attitude of faith the strength of George Müller, Hudson Taylor, August Hermann Francke, Charles Haddon Spurgeon, and of so many other men of God from whose life and work streams of blessing have gone forth to the world and the church? And above all, was not this the victorious weapon of Jesus Himself when in the temptation in the wilderness He conquered the Foe? "It stands written" (Matt. 4: 4, 7, 10). Was not the *written* word His victorious weapon?

An avowed non-Christian sent to a young believer a whole packet of God-denying literature and counselled him to prefer these discussions to the Bible. The young Christian replied to him; "My dear Sir, If you know anything better than the Sermon on the Mount or the parable of the prodigal son, or if you have anything that is more refreshing and fine than the twenty-third Psalm, or, on the whole, gives more light upon the future, and reveals a more merciful and kind Father than does the New Testament, then I beg you to send it to me."

To this marvellous inward spiritual strength the Bible joins its outward invincibility and conquering energy. This also is an experimental proof and testimony of its Divine inspiration.

The Bible is a high mountain range which overtops all other books of the world as if they were but hills or plains. No other writing of the whole earth approaches it in distribution, longevity, and vitality.

The Bible has shown the greatest longevity. For its oldest portions are more than 3,300 years old, yet all in it has the freshness of dew and early youth. It is an "eternally new Old Testament" and an "eternally new New Testament."

The Bible is the most widely-printed book. One single agency (The British and Foreign Bible Society) issued over 600 millions of Bibles and Scripture portions between 1804 and 1954. The present annual global circulation of Bibles, New Testaments, and Scripture portions is about twenty-two millions of copies.

The Bible has the greatest number of translations. About the year 1500 it had been printed in some fourteen languages, about 1600 in forty languages. Two centuries later it was already in 72 languages, and then in the nineteenth century there set in the incomparable and victorious career of the Bible. At the close of this period (about 1900) Bibles or portions of the Bible were available in 567 languages; by 1937 the number of 1,000 was reached; at the present time it is approximately 1,110. All this was in spite of attempts to destroy and prohibit the Bible, in spite of opposition by spiritual, religious, philosophical, and worldly powers, employing police, military, and civil means. What a pleasant irony of the Divine world government that the nineteenth century, the century of exceptional criticism of the Bible in theology, literature, and common propaganda, was at the same time the century of exceptional conquests of the Bible. "He that sitteth in the heavens shall laugh: the Lord shall have them in derision" (Psa. 2: 4).   "In the word of the King there is power" (Eccles. 8: 4).

Thus has the Scripture showed again and again its Divine power. As with Christ the personal word, so in general, and indeed often, has the written word been nailed to the cross, buried, and declared dead. But as with Him, so has it always risen again and still lives. As with the messengers of Jesus Christ in general, so can the books and words of the Bible say with Paul: "through honour and dishonour, through evil report and good report . . . as dying and behold, *we live*" (II Cor. 6: 8, 9).

It is with the Bible as with the sun: ancient and yet always new, always overcoming the night, spreading light and life, eclipsing all other light, in short, the queen in the kingdom of the spirit, the central source of all true, abiding illumination.

> I trust for ever Thy sure promise;
>   Thereon the soul can safely build:
> I know that not one word Thou speakest
>   Shall fall to earth as unfulfilled.
> The hills and mountains all may vanish,
>   The universe collapse and flee,
> But not the smallest word Thou givest,
>   O Lord, shall unaccomplished be.

(Dr. Adolf Morath)

PART III

THE COMING KINGDOM OF GOD

CHAPTER XXIII

VARIETY IN INTERPRETATION OF PROPHECY

In the hope of salvation as presented in the gospel everything is directed to the consummation, the perfecting. In more than 300 places the New Testament speaks of the return of the Lord Jesus. We are "saved in hope" (Rom. 8: 24).

Of this coming final development the Holy Scripture speaks only in great, general, basic lines. It does not impart to us the more exact details. Our curiosity shall not be satisfied, but our hope and sanctification shall ever receive fresh, living, heavenly impulse. Prophecy is not fortune telling. God is a God who loves surprises. Therefore at first He gives to His own only certain partial information (I Cor. 13: 9–12). Of course in these foretastes there lies at the same time a holy anticipatory joy; but the real full revelation comes first with the fulfilment, in the consummation itself. When we then stand in the full light we shall say, "Not the half has been told me" (II Chron. 9: 6). The fulfilment will infinitely surpass all expectation. Till then we are on pilgrimage to the heavenly goal, and view only from afar the pinnacles of the eternal city of God.

Thus the Holy Scripture gives no detailed description of the course and sequence of the final events. We are permitted to discern only the chief stages and chief stations. But even here there is no complete unanimity among all believing Bible expositors. Therefore it becomes us to be careful not to dogmatize, to remain open for fresh instruction from the Scripture, to esteem one another highly, even when there is difference of understanding, and on our side to bow always to every word of God which grants us any new light, or correction of former convictions, or deepening of assured knowledge already gained.

Our comprehensive view of prophetic events, and our conception of the general historic structure of the whole Divine plan of redemption, depends largely upon the basic attitude of the individual to the expectation of a visible kingdom of God upon the theatre of the old earth prior to its dissolution in world destruction and world transformation.   Three differing convictions stand side by side here:

1. The expectation of a personal return of the Lord in glory and power at the beginning and for the purpose of erecting such a visible kingdom of God and Messiah (Pre-Millennialism: Lat. *prae* = before).

2. The belief that the coming of such a golden age will not be effected by a personal appearing of the Lord with visible revelation of His glory, but through the development and progress of mankind, through Christianizing of civilization, through the gradual victory of the gospel in personal, social, and political life, and that only at the end of this brilliant time will Christ appear so as to carry over the history of mankind into the eternal condition of perfection and glory (Post-Millennialism, Lat. *post* = after).

3. The doctrine that an ideal condition of mankind at the end of history on this earth is in no wise to be expected; that thus there will not be a visible kingdom of God on earth at the close of history (Millennium), but that all prophecies of Scripture which have been connected by certain expositors with such a prospect must be "spiritualized" and referred to heaven and eternity (A-Millennial; *a* = without; *anti* = contrary to).

More precise grounds for our belief that it is right to expect the personal return of the Lord before the setting up of the Millennial kingdom (Pre-Millennialism) we have given in our book *The Triumph of the Crucified* pp. 144ff., "The Visible Kingdom of Christ: Its Historic Reality."   But we think it profitable now to discuss briefly the most important objections which are usually offered by those who represent the other two views.   We restrict ourselves to that which is essential, and instead of dealing with these systematically we think it better to discuss them in the form of statement and reply, objection and answer.   We shall simply state distinctly each of the chief objections and then give our attitude to it.   We mention first the lighter objections, which can therefore be dealt with more briefly, and then pass on to the more difficult and decisive questions.

The statements of these questions and doubts concerning the Millennial kingdom, not seldom expressed by believing and serious Bible teachers, are purposely not actual quotations. Deliberately, the wording of these objections is our own.   We thus avoid the character of a dispute.   We would attack no one, but seek mutual understanding.   The form of statement and reply is chosen only so as to make pregnant and clear the different points of view.

As the result of our consideration we believe that we must hold fast the original Christian expectation of a visible earthly kingdom of God. But at the same time our presentation takes a middle course. While maintaining faith in a Millennium it behoves us to offer such proofs as will stand serious examination. Many a time has a good and right cause been weakened by not being based on quite adequate reasons. Here both sides can learn from one another.

It is our hope by the following discussion to further mutual understanding. We hope that in this way some misunderstanding on either side may disappear, and that the original Christian hope may be freed from certain doubts, the hope known among the early Christians, as witnessed especially by the *Revelation* of John and by the post-apostolic fathers and the church fathers of the second and third centuries, such as Papias, Justin, Irenaeus, and Tertullian.

In any case, let all of us who believe on Christ and in the testimony of the prophets, respect and love one another, even if in questions greater or smaller differences in understanding remain. Here it behoves us to listen to one another, to foster mutual understanding and enrichment, and each to esteem the other as higher than himself (Phil 2: 3).

CHAPTER XXIV

"CHILIASTIC EXAGGERATIONS ARE SECTARIAN ERRORS AND OPPOSED TO THE SOBRIETY OF SOUND CHRISTIAN HOPE"

"The teaching concerning the Millennial kingdom is extravagant and unscientific. It is associated with so many exaggerations, often childish fantasies, that one has a direct duty to warn against it. In particular, lay circles and especially certain sects and fanatical movements have made very great misuse of it."

To be sure! In the course of history it has very often happened that just such excesses have brought the whole doctrine into discredit with many. The history of Chiliasm (the doctrine of a Millennial kingdom) shows that in fact very often onesidedness and excrescences have displayed a "bewildered eschatology." This occurred especially in certain fanatical and sectarian movements as early as the time of the Reformation, and later especially with the "Bible Searchers," "Jehovah's Witnesses," and "Seventh Day Adventists."

Such fanatical excesses and fantastic imaginings are met in even the first Christian period, even by men such as Papias of Hierapolis in the second century. Thus Papias, so as to picture the fruitfulness of nature in the Messianic kingdom, mentions a supposed word of the Lord: "Days will come in which vines will have 10,000 rods, and each rod 10,000 branches, and each branch 10,000 clusters, and each cluster 10 bunches, and each bunch 10,000 berries, and each berry when pressed will yield five measures of wine; and if one of the saints takes hold of a bunch another will cry, I am a better bunch, take me and give thanks to the Lord through me" (that is, in the cup of blessing at the Lord's Supper). Similarly one corn of wheat will bear 10,000 ears, and each ear will contain 10,000 corns, and each corn will yield five two-pound measures of fine, clean flour or meal (See Zahn, *The Revelation of John*).

It can be understood that with men such as Origen and Augustine, with their strong Greek philosophical training, and calm legal thinking, such and similar descriptions produced a correspondingly strong reaction, and that they fell into the opposite extreme and wholly denied any right to expect such an earthly kingdom of God, that is, the doctrine of a Millennial kingdom, so that they forthwith "spiritualized" everything. The prophecy of the Millennial kingdom was applied to church history and it was explained that the triumph of Christianity over heathendom in the fourth century was the royal rule of God and that the kingdom of God announced in the Apocalypse had commenced.

Upon this Dr. R. Pache not unjustly remarks that "If it were so we must call the Messianic rule a truly pitiful affair, for it certainly has not the appearance of Satan being bound and not in a position to deceive the nations; or he must—as someone has said—be bound with a terribly long chain," which allows him very much freedom of movement. (*Le Retour de Jésus Christ*, 424).

In any case this stands fast, that the expectation of not only a spiritual but also of an earthly national restoration of Israel, and of a kingdom intervening between the return of Christ (*parousia, epiphany*) and world destruction and world perfecting, was both the original Christian belief and has again and again been distinctly asserted by leaders in the newer Bible-believing theological science. This can only be overlooked by want of care or insufficient acquaintance with the history of theology.

From the history of early Christianity we mention Papias of Hierapolis (about A.D. 140), Justin from Sichem (about 150), Irenaeus (died about 202), Tertullian (died after 222).

In the early Christian centuries Chiliasm first weakened with the strengthening among Christians of Greek philosophical thought. Especially through Clement and Origen of Alexandria in the East (about 250), and through Ticonius (about 400), and Augustine, Bishop of Carthage (died 430), it came in the West, for the official Church, to the extinction of Chiliasm, and the doctrine of the last things came to be a vacuum for official Church theology. Greek sentiment and thought opposed even the conception of a final historical drama and a real Millennial kingdom on this earth.

This of course threw the door wide open to certain fanatical movements. Especially since the Reformation all sorts of sects have advanced remarkable theories as to the Millennium. The guilt of this, however, lies in large measure in the failure of official theology in this region. There arose thereby a vacuum into which fanatical movements pressed. Fanatical movements often flourish through the indifference of orthodox movements to certain Biblical truths.

In the history of earlier Protestantism Campegius Vitringa (Professor of Theology in Leiden, Holland) and Friedrich Adolph Lampe (Professor of Theology in Bremen) became pioneers in the re-discovery of Biblical prophetic truth; both these lived in the seventeenth century. By these the Biblicist Fathers at

Württemberg were influenced, especially Bishop J. A. Bengel (Stuttgart, died 1752) and Bishop Oetinger (died 1782).

Through these last, Chiliasm, sometimes in milder, sometimes in stronger form, found entrance to scientific theology in the nineteenth century. Notable leaders in this were the Lutherans von Hofmann (Professor of Theology in Erlangen, died 1877), F. H. R. Frank (also Professor of Theology in Erlangen, died 1894), K. A. Auberlen (Professor of Theology in Basel, died 1864), as well as K. J. H. A. Ebrard (Professor of Reformed Theology in Erlangen, died 1888), J. T. Beck (Professor of Theology in Tübingen, died 1878), and Bishop Dr. T. Hermann (1924).

In the light of the history of theology it would therefore be an erroneous verdict, overlooking these indisputable facts, if one should awaken an impression, not to say expressly declare, that the expectation of a literal Millennial kingdom is an error found indeed among fanatics or sectaries, "laymen" or untrained Bible teachers, who do not deserve the title "theologian," but not represented or defended by any distinguished believing scientific theologians. To rebut this idea was the reason, in the above detailed statement, for so repeatedly emphasizing the academic offices of the numerous Bible expositors named.

Among later such leaders we mention Dächsel, Modersohn, Professor Bettex, Dr. S. P. Tregelles, John Lillie, D.D., Edward Greswell, B.D., Fellow of Corpus Christi College, Oxford, Benjamin Wills Newton, Henry Alford, D.D., Dean of Canterbury, Dr. Scofield, Dr. Gaebelein, Dr. A. T. Pierson, George Müller, John Nelson Darby, G. H. Pember, Johann de Heer, (Holland), D. L. Moody, Dr. R. A. Torrey, Hudson Taylor. It cannot be said of these Bible teachers and leading men of God in the church of Christ that they were sectaries or merely lay defenders of a "bewildered eschatology."

But above all this it is here to be said: One can never rightly oppose an extreme by going to the opposite extreme. A cause is in no wise refuted by abuse. An extreme may serve to beget another extreme, but this does not justify either the one or the other. While rejecting firmly excrescences of a Biblical doctrine, it becomes us soberly to hold fast to the Biblical doctrine itself.

CHAPTER XXV

"CHRIST IS NO POLITICAL MESSIAH"

"Jesus did not come as a political Messiah, but to do a *spiritual* work. The purposes of His redeeming work were purely spiritual in nature, and the setting up of a visible, earthly, national kingdom of God would stand in contradiction to the essentially spiritual character of His saving work."

No one disputes that the essential nature of the kingdom of God is thoroughly spiritual. Christ came to save from sins, not from political reproach and oppression (Matt. 1: 21; Heb. 9: 24–28). Repentance and a new birth are therefore the basic condition of entrance into this His kingdom (John 3: 3, 5; Matt. 3: 2; 4: 17). Not fleshly birth—quite irrespective of which flesh, whether Jewish or non-Jewish—but new life from above is the prerequisite. It is not a matter of mere subordination to and regulation by new, and doubtless better, political, social, and financial laws, but of regulation by the spiritual law of the new nature (Rom. 8: 1, 2; 14: 17). The Jew is excluded if he be not born again, and the Gentile is included if he is born again (Matt. 3: 9; 8: 11, 12). Thus neither Jew nor Gentile can gain entrance except on the ground of personal new birth. This at once proves that the kingdom of God as Jesus introduced it, is not, as to its essential nature, national but spiritual.

But this does not challenge the fact that there can be a victorious irruption of this spiritual-moral realm into the sphere of culture, society, and even politics. That the *nature* of the kingdom of God is inward and spiritual in no way excludes that there can be an historical revealed form of it, in which it exhibits its inner nature outwardly and visibly; a form in which Christ, the canceller of sin, then leads on His sin-cleansed people of God to triumph over His foes and brings them to exaltation and honour.

And what shall we finally say thereto, if it now pleases God to declare that He, by special manifestations of love and power, shall bring to pass that the One who appeared first of all, of course, as the spiritual Deliverer from the guilt and distress of sin, shall at last stand forth as the Arbiter among the nations (Isa. 2: 4); that His saving and ruling work shall proceed from inward to outward, from personal to collective, from individual life to social life, and therefore shall have decisive influence upon national life, legislation, culture, international relations, questions of war and peace, armaments, social order, and matters judicial?

(Isa. 2: 2-4; 11: 4). How can this be a contradiction? On what ground shall the first fundamentally exclude the second? Is not the earthly and visible equally a portion of the creation of God? Shall the bodily be fundamentally eliminated from the spiritual, living activities of the Eternal? How can we here assert "this *or* that" when the Holy Scripture declares "this *as well as* that?" No, on the contrary: Is not the exact reverse properly *demanded* by a truly strong spiritual life, that it lays hold also of the bodily? In our own individual personality are not the spirit and soul at the same time the life-principle of our body, affecting its outward appearance, indeed in a most decisive measure ruling its physical life and influencing all its activities?

From all this it arises that the above-mentioned objection to the expectation of a final, historical, visible kingdom of God is in no sense a refutation of the testimony of the Old Testament prophets and the Revelation of John to that kingdom. At its basis there lies in this objection a schism in Creation, with a low estimation of the bodily, even as Grecian Platonic philosophy, more especially after the rise of Hellenism, declared that the body is the prison of the soul, and therefore the goal is not deliverance *of* the body but deliverance *from* the body, and so pure spirituality. Thus the objection rests more on Greek thought, but not on Biblical. It is Hellenism, not Christianity; philosophy, not revelation. But the Bible consummates, as its revelation from God, a harmonious joint display of both: of spirit and Nature in their created oneness, of eternity and time, of heaven and earth, of the kingdom of God and history.

God does not halt halfway. He frees from sin—its guilt and punishment, its power and pollution: but then He will also create new world-conditions. He saves spirit and body. The earthly and bodily also shall at last display His glory.

CHAPTER XXVI

"EXPECTATION OF AN EARTHLY KINGDOM
IS UNWORTHY OF THE
HIGH SPIRITUAL CALLING OF THE CHURCH"

"The expectation of an earthly visible kingdom of God is unworthy of a citizen of heaven. The Church is heavenly and therefore is permitted to expect only spiritual blessings. Therefore an earthly, national literal 'material' kingdom has no place in the possessions for which they hope."

THE expectation of a Millennial kingdom is connected less with the perfecting of the church than with the perfecting of Israel, of the nations, of Nature, and the earth. Here we must not intermingle the different historical lines of salvation. In God's kingdom of creation and His plan of salvation there exist different groups of created beings. Israel is not the church. The church is not the nations. Again, the angels are another group. Further, the different kingdoms of Nature are to be distinguished, the starry world, the vegetable world, the animal world

For all of these God has His plans of love and revelations of love. But these differ for each group, and each according to its place in the whole counsel of God. Concerning the place of the church in the Millennial kingdom Holy Scripture says to us nothing direct. It lets us presume only this, that the risen believers will then reign from heaven with the glorified Christ. "The church of Jesus through rapture and resurrection has left the visible earth and entered its heavenly abodes, to which the nature of its glorified bodies corresponds. The Scripture says nothing to the effect that the Lord will bring back His church from their new heavenly home to the earth to live here. The earth is indeed not yet transfigured. Therefore it cannot offer to the Lord of glory or to His transfigured church a suitable dwelling in the full sense of the word. Perhaps Christ and His chosen will occupy a similar relation to the earth as between His resurrection and ascension, that is, that they will appear as often as the earth requires their presence, while their dwelling remains in heaven. But the chief matter is that they will be with the Lord always (I Thess. 4: 17)." (Dr. T. Harbeck.)

But this spiritual perfecting of the church does not exclude that Israel, the nations, and the earth—within the frame of their various orders of life, which differ from that of the church—will jointly experience a visible triumph of the Lord upon the scene of their former history. It is no way unworthy of a citizen of heaven to expect that God will bless and perfect the other groups of His creation, each according to its station and calling.

CHAPTER XXVII

THE SILENCE OF THE NEW TESTAMENT WITH REGARD TO A COMING VISIBLE KINGDOM OF GOD

"The message of the Millennial kingdom is found only *once* in the New Testament. Otherwise the whole New Testament is silent as to this doctrine, both as to the Gospels and the Pauline and other epistles. At all events, apart from Revelation 20 there is nowhere else a single detailed mention."

THE truth and reliability of a Divine word does not depend upon the number of statements which God permits to be made concerning a matter. If God makes a statement only once we have simply to believe it. This shows how faith in inspiration and expectation of the kingdom go together. We remember again the words of Prof. Paul Althaus; "The Biblicist's argument for a Millennial kingdom cannot be refuted by asserting that the passages named do not speak of a period prior to the perfecting. As to I Cor. 15: 23–25, one may perhaps ask how far the thought of an intermediate kingdom stands behind the intimations, but there can be no doubt as to Rev. 20: 4–7."

(*b*) It is also not to be expected in advance that the New Testament shall give a repeated and detailed setting forth of this doctrine. For the chief theme of the New Testament is the church, not Israel and the nations. Therefore it is quite intelligible that in it the message as to the Millennial kingdom is in the background, and that Christ and the Apostles refer to it only occasionally without setting it forth in detail.

(*c*) Nevertheless these few references in the New Testament are quite enough to confirm the expectation of the kingdom of the Old Testament prophets. Thus the Lord Himself said: "ye who have followed Me, in the regeneration when the Son of man shall sit on the throne of His glory, ye also shall sit upon twelve thrones, judging the twelve tribes of Israel" (Matt. 19: 28). And when, after His resurrection, the disciples asked, "Lord, dost Thou at this time restore the kingdom to *Israel*?" (Gr. *basileia*, kingly rule), He did not rebuke them for "fleshly conceptions," or give a general denial of such a visible kingdom of God as they had in mind, but said only, "It is not for you to know times or seasons which the Father has reserved in His own authority" (Acts 1: 6, 7). But precisely this prophetic expression "times or seasons" proves that the kingdom of God will be duly and actually set up. (See more fully *The Triumph of the Crucified*, p. 144 ff.).

(*d*) Moreover, it was entirely unnecessary that the New Testament should give detail instruction upon this subject. For the existing Old Testament pictures were so many and detailed that it was quite needless that the New Testament should repeat them often.

(*e*) Nor is it to be overlooked that, although this passage in the *Revelation* is the only detail passage in the New Testament dealing expressly with the subject, yet such heavy emphasis is placed upon this message as to the Millennial kingdom that the number "one thousand" is given no less than six times (Rev. 20: 2–7). Thus it is most powerfully intimated that here is something of great importance, worthy indeed of the highest consideration.

(*f*) Finally we remark—mentioning this of course only by the way—that the *Revelation* of John was by no means the first or only book of that period in which an intermediate kingdom of the end time, to last for a thousand years, is mentioned. Although it is no Biblical book, and therefore no inspired text, which we now have in mind, it is yet of interest that the doctrine of an intermediate Messianic kingdom was announced in contemporary Judaism and that its duration was to be exactly one thousand years. The Jewish synagogue as early as the first century distinguished between the days of Messiah and the final perfecting in "*Olam ha-ba*," that is, in the world to come. The former were regarded as being limited in duration, the latter as being eternal. Over the duration of that Messianic pre-perfecting the opinions of the Jewish theologians were from the first divided. Rabbi Eliezer of Hyrcanus (about A.D. 90) is the oldest rabbinical authority to maintain that the rule of Messiah will last for one thousand years. Eliezer was one of the most tenacious defenders of ancient tradition, so that he said of himself, "I have never made a statement that I have not taken out of the mouth of my teacher." Thus it is evident that the duration of the interim Messianic period had been taught *before* Eliezer in the Jewish synagogues and so among the Jewish contemporaries of a Paul or a Peter. Therefore it cannot be justly asserted, as it often has been, that the doctrine of a Millennial kingdom is nowhere found apart from the celebrated passage in Revelation 20.

But for ourselves this one reference of Holy Scripture suffices. We have no right to require from God that He must repeat a statement five or ten times before we can believe Him.

CHAPTER XXVIII

"NO ROOM FOR AN INTERMEDIATE KINGDOM OF GOD IN THE NEW TESTAMENT ESCHATOLOGY"

"The New Testament knows only *two* 'ages', the present and the future (Eph. 1: 21; Matt. 12: 32). It describes without a break, that is, without mention of such an intervening period, the appearing of Christ in glory and the entrance into eternity (Matt. 25: 31 and 46), the resurrection of the righteous and the resurrection of the lost (John 5: 28, 29; Acts 24: 15), the punishing of the godless and the reward of the chosen (Matt. 13: 30, 41–43; II Thess. 1: 6.10)."

THIS statement is insufficient in a threefold respect.

(*a*) *First.* It overlooks the passage in the *Revelation* of John (20: 1–6) which speaks quite plainly of such an intervening kingdom, which it places *after* the appearing of the Lord in glory (19: 11–21) and *before* the events of world perfecting (world destruction, world judgment, world transfiguration, 20: 7–21, 8), and thus between the *epiphany* and the full entrance of eternity.

(*b*) *Second.* It is also incorrect that the New Testament speaks of only *two* ages, the present and the future. This is indeed the case in some few particular places (Eph. 1: 21; Luke 20: 34, 35; Matt. 12: 32), but certainly not in the great preponderance of passages.

Much rather, in Eph. 2: 7 Paul speaks of "coming ages," in the plural, not only of "a" coming age. The Epistle to the Hebrews (1: 8) uses the term "the age of the age": "Thy throne, O God, is unto the age of the age," and thus, so to speak, age multiplied by age. In the second prayer in the Ephesian letter (3: 21) Paul uses indeed a still stronger expression: "To Him be the glory in the church and in Christ Jesus unto all the generations of the age of the ages," that is, the singular number joined not only with the singular but with the plural of ages.

And in quite a number of further passages Peter, Paul, John, and the Writer of *Hebrews* set the crown on this form of expression in that they use not only a doubled singular, nor only a union of singular and plural, but employ a doubled plural, "in the ages of the ages." It is the plural of fulness carried to the highest possible degree; plural of plural, multitudes of multitudes of coming ages. Or expressed mathematically, age of ages multiplied by ages (Peter—I Pet. 4: 11; 5: 11. Paul—Gal. 1: 5; Phil. 4: 20; I Tim.

1: 17; II Tim. 4: 18.   John—Rev. 1: 18; 11: 15; 22: 5; etc.
Hebrews—13: 21).

It is to be noted here that one will do justice to such terms of
Scripture only if each be considered carefully in its own sense
and context.

In any case all this shows that the above objection—that the
New Testament knows of only two ages, and therefore has no
room for an intervening period, is utterly feeble.

(c) *Third*.   There is just as little force in referring to the fact
that New Testament prophecy, in numerous places, views
together the appearing of Christ in glory and the entrance upon
eternity, the resurrection of the righteous and the resurrection
of the lost, without mentioning a long interval between.   For
this simply belongs to the nature of the prophetic outlook.   Thus
also Old Testament prophecy mostly described the first coming
of Christ and the second in one single connexion without mentioning the present interval of already nearly two thousands of
years.   Thus Isaiah speaks in the same sentence of the coming
of the Lord as Saviour and His coming as Judge, although in
the fulfilment there lay between the whole New Testament
period (Isa. 61: 1, 2).   Similarly Isa. 53 speaks in one single
connexion of the sufferings and triumph of God's Servant
without indicating any interval, and thus David also in Psalms
2 and 22.

Thus the abovementioned New Testament passages also in no
wise prove that, because they do not mention an interval between
the appearing of the Lord in glory and the entrance upon eternity,
that no such interval can exist.

As in Old Testament prophecy, so here, it is necessary to
observe the law of prophetic perspective.   The prophet, like
the wanderer among high mountains, saw in one view the sum-
mits of mountains lying behind one another without at the time
seeing in detail the valleys that lay between.

It is also necessary to observe that in the history of prophecy
there is progress in revelation and understanding (Matt. 13: 16,
17).   What in the Old Testament, and at times even in the prophecies in the Gospels, was compressed into one picture, as the
prophecy was further unfolded divides more and more into its
details and is more and more clearly declared.   As the Lord
Himself said: "I have yet many things to say unto you, but ye
cannot bear them now.   Howbeit when He, the Spirit of truth,
is come, He shall guide you into all the truth" (John 16: 12, 13).

Thus the Old Testament prophets, and in measure certain
prophecies of the New Testament, view in one both the Millennial
kingdom and the eternal glory.   For them preliminary presenta-

tion and final fulfilment, introduction and main portion, End-time and the other side, the earthly and the heavenly Jerusalem flowed together into one single magnificent picture. They see the final conditions of this side and the eternal beyond as one single, continuous line conditioned by the nature of "this side," and they paint the new creation of the Perfection with the colours of the kingdom of glory of the old creation (comp. Isa. 54: 11, 12 with Rev. 21: 18–21).   It is only the New Testament, especially Rev. 20, which draws a clear diagonal line between the two which separates eternity and time.   This dividing line between the this side and the beyond of the earth is found in the events of world perfecting, that is world destruction, world judgment, and world transformation (Rev. 20: 7–21: 1).

With the same right with which, on account of this joint out-look, one would oppose the reality of an intervening kingdom between the Parousia and the final perfecting, one could oppose the existence of the present interim period of the church between the first and second comings of the Lord which are viewed together in numerous Old Testament prophecies. Yet this church interval is there, and has already lasted nearly two thousands of years.

This all proves that belief in a Millennial kingdom and the correctness of the prophecy of Rev. 20 can in no wise be refuted by such an objection.

CHAPTER XXIX

"THE GOSPEL DISPENSATION EQUALS THE 'LAST DAYS' IN THE NEW TESTAMENT HISTORY OF REDEMPTION"

"The present period, the age of the church, is described in the New Testament as the 'last time' (Acts 2: 16, 17; I John 2: 18). Therefore, since we are already in the 'End time,' there can be no room for a coming intervening kingdom, because after this 'last' there can follow only eternity."

IN the language of Scripture the whole New Testament unfolding of salvation is termed the "last time." The "last days" commenced with the first coming of Christ (Heb. 9: 26; I Pet. 1: 20). The outpouring of the Holy Spirit in Jerusalem at Pentecost was already a fulfilment of Joel's prophecy of the "last days" (Acts 2: 16, 17). In the passage mentioned above (I John 2: 18) and therefore as early as the first century, John explains that "it is a last hour," that is, this is the character of the period.

But this does not exclude that, since the "last days" have already lasted nearly two thousand years, they may, if God so will, likewise endure a further thousand years, even the thousand years of the Millennium after the close of the church period.

In any case, according to Joel 2, the outpouring of the Holy Spirit "upon all flesh," that is, the inclusion of the whole of mankind in the power of the Spirit, "in those days," belongs to the Messianic perfecting. The term "those days," as it is most often used by the Old Testament prophets, is connected unmistakably with the kingdom of Messiah they expected, and with the associated restoration of Israel (so directly after by Joel 3: 1; also Jer. 3: 16; Zech. 8: 23). In the address of Peter at Pentecost the term "last days)" is used as the equivalent of the term "those days" (Acts 2: 17 = Joel 2: 28, 29). Therefore it follows that the kingdom of Messiah, as expected by the prophets and the apostles, belongs to these "last days."

The beginning of the New Testament "end" time was completed only in several different stages. The church age did not, *in its fullest sense* begin with the birth of Christ, nor at Golgotha, yea, nor even Pentecost, but only with the reception into the church of the first wholly heathen believers in the house of the Roman Cornelius at Caesarea (Acts 10), and the revelations given to Paul. Similarly the conclusion of this "end" time can be completed in such a sequence of stages.

That this will be fact is shown most plainly in Rev. 20. We point out again that here there is mention of a kingdom of a thousand years that *follows* the appearing of the Lord in glory and *precedes* world destruction and transformation (19: 11–21; 20: 7–21: 1), which is thus openly described in the Biblical account as coming between these events and for the duration of which the number "a thousand" is given no less than six times.

Thus according to the testimony of the New Testament the "last days" contain two great halves; the period of the church and that of the visible kingdom of God on earth. Only then comes the "day of God," that is, eternity (II Pet. 3: 12, 18).

CHAPTER XXX

"THE PERSONAL RETURN OF CHRIST WILL BE AT THE END, NOT AT THE BEGINNING OF THE MILLENNIUM"

"A twice repeated appearing of the Lord in glory, first at the beginning and a second time at the close of the coming visible kingdom of God on earth, is not to be expected. The kingdom of God comes through development and progress, through Christian-izing of civilization, through improvement of mankind, and the infiltration of all personal, social, and political life with the ideals of the gospel. Only *after* this golden age of righteousness, peace, and general brotherliness is attained will Christ appear and the final glorifying of mankind be effected and men pass into eternity. Therefore a return of Christ to commence and set up the Mil-lennium will not occur."

THIS belief in progress stands in contradiction to experience and to the Scriptures. Until 1914 this doctrine (the Post-Millennial) won very many adherents. But since the fight-ings and catastrophes of two world wars, and especially today in the age of the atom bomb, there is observable an essential change in the whole philosophical attitude and disposition of mankind, and this is ever increasing quite apart from the negative or posi-tive attitude of individual men to the Christian faith. In place of the age of optimistic cultural happiness and enthusiasm over the glorious acquisitions of civilization and culture, and of self-confidence in evolution and progress, there has come widely an age of anxiety and fear. Will mankind not fall finally into the madness of self-destruction and collective suicide? Is it not already only a question of time? For how long can it perhaps be deferred? And will not the end be the collapse of the West as certainly as of the East, the collapse of Europe and America, and at last of all civilization?

Only Utopian fanatics and feeble-witted theorists, strangers to reality, can today defend with conviction the belief in progress. The end of the humanistic illusion is come. World history, precisely with its modern advance in invention and discovery, commerce and technique, in the face of its wickedness, indeed of the increasing godlessness of whole groups of peoples, is an irrefutable disproof of this theory.

(*b*) To this proof from experience is added that from Scripture.

"It is the unmistakable teaching of the Bible that the goal of history is not the product of history, that the kingdom of God does not reach sovereignty through growth and ascent but only after world-wide collapse and catastrophe. Lawlessness will take the upper hand, the love of many will wax cold (Matt. 24: 12), and when the Son of Man comes He will find but *little* faith on earth (Luke 18: 8). Not Christianizing of the world with consequent Christianizing of civilization, but increasing enmity of the world unto the expulsion of Christianity by civilization—this is the path foretold by Biblical prophecy (Rev. 13: 2; II Tim. 3: 1–4; II Pet. 3: 3). 'Let no one mislead you, for the day of the Lord will not come except the *apostasy* come in advance and the *Man of sin* be manifested, *the Son of perdition, the Opposer, the Wicked One,* whom the Lord Jesus, when He comes, will destroy by the breath of His mouth (II Thess. 2: 3, 4, 8).

"'Thus not by reconciliation but *by intensifying of the conflict to the end,* not by the glorifying of human development but by its collapse, not by a compact between God and civilization, but by the shattering of the kingdom of the world by the kingdom of God —this is the manner by which the affairs of the Lord will triumph.' *The Triumph of the Crucified,* p. 117)."

(*c*) The parable of the leaven offers no contradiction to this (Matt. 13: 33). Of course it must be explained in agreement with the whole prophetic teaching of the New Testament.

Leaven is a symbol of the principle of permeation. In all other places in Holy Scripture it is employed as a symbol of evil (e.g. I Cor. 5: 6–8; Matt. 16: 12; Mark 8: 15). If now it is meant to be understood in this sense in the present parable (of the inroad of evil doctrine and evil conduct in the development of the kingdom of God), then in advance this parable cannot be regarded as proof that the "leaven of the gospel," by way of progress and Christianizing society, will gradually permeate the whole world.

But even if, as others explain, the leaven is, as an exception, a symbol here of good (the kingdom of God itself being here compared to leaven), yet is this no proof of the supposed Christian cultural development. For even then the parable must be explained in harmony with the whole prophetic announcement and cannot be set in opposition to the otherwise plain testimonies of Scripture of increasing enmity against God, of an advancing *de*-Christianizing of civilization on to the arrival of *anti*-Christianity, with its universal (!) acceptance by civilized mankind apostatized from God (Rev. 13).

But then this increasing progress of the good, which in such case this parable would assert, can apply only to individual life, not to collective world-development. It would then declare that the royal rule of God, like unto leaven, would permeate and fill the whole life of individuals, till Christ, through the extension of sanctification, would permeate and govern the whole individual personality in spirit, soul, and body (I Thess. 5: 23).

Therefore whether one takes the symbol of leaven in the good or the evil sense, in no case is the parable a proof that the whole remaining prophecies of the New Testament of the increasing apostasy of mankind from God were at all incorrect. At the end of cultural development and progress there stands, not a Christianized civilization, but the world rule of Antichristianity. That in spite of this the kingdom of God will then conquer, will come to pass, according to the express testimony of the Lord Himself, and of Paul and John, only through the mighty manifestation of Christ the Victor returning in glory (Matt. 24: 29–31; II Thess. 2: 8; Rev. 19: 11–21).

It is in the light of such clear testimonies of the New Testament that a symbolic passage such as the parable of the leaven must be explained. Symbolic passages of Holy Scripture must be interpreted by the light of plain passages. One must explain Scripture by Scripture, dark passages by clear, such as admit of more than one meaning by such as allow of only one meaning, symbolic utterances by direct statements, and therefore parables by non-parabolic passages. This is an indispensable principle of all sound exposition of Scripture.

To the question itself whether in this parable leaven represents good or evil we take here no attitude. In our present connexion it is enough to prove that, whichever sense one here gives to the symbol, the doctrine of the cultural progress of Christianity as above defined cannot appeal to this passage as a Biblical basis.

CHAPTER XXXI

LITERAL AND SPIRITUAL ISRAEL

"How can it be expected that Israel will experience a literal, national restoration seeing that it is to the *spiritual* Israel that God grants His blessings? God has never given His promises simply to the literal Israel merely because they were Israelites after the flesh. Upon this the Scripture speaks expressly, especially in the Gospels and the Pauline epistles: 'Think not to say within yourselves, We have Abraham to our father: for I say unto you that God is able of these stones to raise up children to Abraham' (Matt. 3: 9; comp. John 8: 39). 'For He is not a Jew who is one outwardly; neither is that circumcision which is outward in the flesh: but he is a Jew, who is one inwardly; and circumcision is that of the heart, in the spirit, not in the flesh' (Rom. 2: 28, 29; comp. Rev. 3: 9). 'Not all who are from Israel are Israel: neither because they are Abraham's seed, are they all children . . . not the children of the flesh are children of God; but the children of the promise are reckoned for a seed' (Rom. 9: 6-8).

"Therefore there is not to be expected for Israel as a people any outward, national, territorial restoration, but it is to the believing remnant, that is, the spiritual Israel, that the hope of Israel belongs, and this in a purely spiritual manner. This is fulfilled to the believing from Israel who belong to the New Testament church, and to the Gentiles whom God adds through the gospel and faith, and thus creates the New Testament people of God, the 'Israel after the spirit.' 'For *we* are the circumcision, who worship God through the Spirit . . . and have no confidence in the flesh' (Phil. 3: 3). 'They who are of faith, these are sons of Abraham' (Gal. 3: 7; comp. 6: 16).

"Thus not the whole literal Israel is in the true sense Israel. Physical birth has no eternal value with God, but the spiritual birth; not the literal circumcision as an external observance, but the spiritual circumcision of the heart (Col. 2: 11); therefore in no case the merely literal and outward but the spiritual and inward."

D OUBTLESS! No one denies it. God's promises were never unconditional. This is a principle of His government in all times. The realization of the promises is always bound up with the faith of the receiver. In this the faith of the creature is indeed in no sense a desert, an equivalent, a "work," which annuls the character of the free grace of God. But it is the empty hand which the creature stretches out to God and in which He, out of free mercy, places the unmerited gift of His love. But if this empty hand be not stretched out, then God does not give His gifts of grace. Faith is indeed, not the basis but the condition of being blessed.

It is thus with Israel.   No one will say that it is the literal Israel as such that will have a standing of blessing in the coming kingdom of God, merely on the ground that they are literal children of Abraham.   No, the promises of God given to him will only then and there be fulfilled when and where faith is present in Israel.

Therefore the counsel of God takes effect first in only the kernel of the nation believing in the Messiah.   Through unbelief the great mass shut themselves out from the promised possession. Upon this follows judgment.   Only a "shoot out of the root" remains, the "holy seed," the believing "remnant," out of which new life springs forth (Isa. 6: 13).

(b) But it was not with the spiritual Israel only, but with the literal in general that God established the covenant of the law at Sinai.   "Behold, days come, saith the Lord, that I will make a new covenant with the house of Israel, and with the house of Judah: not according to the covenant that I made with their fathers in the day that I took them by the hand to bring them out of the land of Egypt; which My covenant they have broken" (Jer. 31: 31, 32).   Thus it was the very ones who later broke the covenant with whom God had made it, that is, with the literal Israel as a nation, not merely with the "true" Israel, the later "remnant," the "spiritual seed" of the patriarchs.   In the same way God's "firstborn son," whom Pharaoh was to release, was certainly not only the pious in Israel, but Jacob's whole bodily descendants who had lived some centuries in Egypt, the land of oppression (Exod. 4: 22).

God's "son" whom, according to the prophet Hosea, He had called out of Egypt, was likewise not only the "spiritual" Israel, but at the same time the company of men who presently offered unto the Baalim and burned incense to the carved images (Hos. 11: 1, 2).   But above all, the whole structure of the history in the second book of Moses concerning the giving of the law at Sinai itself proves that God concluded His covenant not with merely a portion, namely with the believing among the bodily descendants of Abraham, but unmistakably with Israel as a people, with the entire company of the bodily descendants of the patriarch whom with uplifted hand He had brought out of Egypt.   There is no difficulty in multiplying the proofs.   One has only to read a single passage such as 1 Cor. 10: 3-5.

Of course the great mass of Israel as a nation has gone the way of unbelief and must finally be broken out of the noble olive tree of the kingdom of God (Rom. 11: 20).   Like the Pharisees of the time of Christ, these, by so doing, make the counsel of God of none effect for themselves (Luke 7: 30).   But this does not alter the fact that God on His part originally included them in the scope of His covenant.

(*c*) Seeing that the grace of God confers its free gift only upon faith, the practical outworking is that Israel's national calling can only operate where true faith is present in Israel. Therefore now only the small company of believers, the remnant,[1] become the representatives of the ideal "Israel." Therefore this insignificant minority becomes the theocratic kernel of the nation, its heart, its true essence, its centre, its representative before God, the true "Israel." Thus thenceforth in the eyes of God only that is really "Israel" which is so inwardly (Rom. 2: 28, 29; 9: 6–8; Rev. 3: 9), and only the circumcision of the heart is counted as circumcision (Phil. 3: 3; Col. 2: 11).

(*d*) Nevertheless these two points of view, the national and the spiritual, in no way exclude each other. Exactly here is one of the chief faults in the opposition to a future national restoration of Israel, that a contradiction is created which in fact does not exist; so that one does not reach the synthesis of these two opposite poles, their harmonious outlook, the release from tension.

What the Scripture testifies is, that the spiritual will at last occupy the whole frame of the national and literal (Isa. 11: 9; Zech. 8: 3; 14: 20, 21; Joel 3: 17), and the national and literal will reach its fulfilment and transfiguration only through and after this glorious victory of the spiritual (Ezek. 37: 15–24; Isa. 11: 11–13). This will come to pass through the future conversion of Israel as a nation by the appearing of Messiah (Rev. 1: 7; Zech. 12: 10–14; Hos. 3: 5); and thus the "Jewish miracle" will be wrought, and in this the saying of Adolf Saphir will reach its climax that "the history of Israel is the history of miracle, as it is the miracle of history" (Isa. 52: 8). Thus first will the practical synthesis be found. The tension in the Biblical-prophetic outlook for Israel between "spiritual" and "national-literal" will be resolved only eschatologically, that is, by the history of the End.

Naturally there is no salvation for Israel merely because they are bodily descendants of Abraham. Much rather does the whole prophecy of blessing of the Old Testament refer to the transformed and renewed Israel. The Old Testament gives not a single promise of rule and blessing to the *un*converted Israel, neither while dwelling in the land nor while scattered among the nations because of their sins.

But what shall we finally say if it pleases God to declare that one day, through special manifestations of His glory, the whole

[1] Isa. 1: 9; 6: 13; 10: 21; 11: 11; I Kings 19: 18; Ezek. 5: 1–4; Rom. 11: 1–10.

of Jacob's bodily descendants then living on earth, shall attain
to faith through sight of the returning Messiah: that the people
who pierced Messiah shall at last confess Him (Rev. 1: 7), and
the "natural" branches which were broken off shall be regrafted
into "their own olive tree," and so "all Israel shall be saved"?
(Rom. 11: 21, 23, 24).

It is quite impossible to apply to the church spiritually the
term "all Israel" used by Paul in this passage. The fourfold
use in the context of the same term "Israel" makes clear in advance that Paul everywhere here uses the word in the same
sense of the national, literal Israel. At the beginning (ver. 1) he
declares, "I also am an Israelite, of the seed of Abraham, of the
tribe of Benjamin," where the word "Israelite" can only be
meant in its literal sense of the apostle's national association.
Only a few verses later (7) he says, "What Israel sought that it
did not attain," which again can refer only to the literal, earthly,
national Israel. And in the immediate context of the section
where he uses the term "all Israel" he has spoken directly of
Israel in contrast to the Gentiles, so that this also beyond doubt
can refer only to the earthly, literal people ("hardening in part
[only] hath befallen Israel [and only] until the fulness of the
Gentiles" has come in: ver. 25). And when he then, in the
conclusion which he draws from the fact, immediately, in the
very same sentence, declares that thus "all Israel" shall be saved,
this closest possible connexion makes it completely incontestable that here, also, as in the three other places of this chapter,
he speaks of Israel literal, not in some "spiritualized" sense,
(that is, perhaps, the church).

From the wider connexion also of Romans 11 it further arises
beyond doubt that the apostle speaks of the literal Israel (in part
believing, in part unbelieving), even of the "natural branches"
which have remained in "their own" olive tree, as well as of the
"natural branches" which have been broken off from "their
own" olive tree; so that at present only a *portion* of this Israel
will be saved through faith; but by like faith, at the time of the
End, when the broken off branches have been again ingrafted,
then *all* Israel shall be saved. The expression "all" stands in
unmistakable contrast to the former two-fold division, that is,
the natural branches which have remained in the olive tree and
those which have been broken off.

So shall this two-fold division be at last removed. Through
the conversion of the Jews at the appearing of Messiah the faith
of the little remnant extends to the whole body. *The literal
Israel has thus become spiritual Israel.* Abraham's descendants
according to the flesh have by conversion and regeneration

become true sons of the patriarch and thus at the same time Israel according to the spirit (Gal. 3: 9). Thenceforth the national is identical with the spiritual. *The "remnant" has become the whole people*, and the saved national people are at the same time both literal descendants of Abraham and also his spiritual seed.

Thus is relieved the seeming conflict in the prophetic statements. Only in this manner will justice be done to the whole of these two lines of God-given prophetic words:

on the one side the strong emphasis, expecially by John the Baptist, by the Lord Himself, and by Paul, that the bodily and the national is not the decisive factor, but the genuinely spiritual and inward; and

on the other side the equally strong emphasis by many prophets that with the setting up of the coming kingdom of God there is connected a national restoration of Israel. The national will be spirit-filled and the spiritual will extend itself victoriously through the whole range of the literal and national. But by this our opening objection to the restoration of the national Israel in the visible kingdom of Messiah loses all force.

L

"SPIRITUALIZATION IS THE METHOD OF NEW TESTAMENT INTERPRETATION OF OLD TESTAMENT KINGDOM PROPHECY"

"It is quite plain that the Old Testament writers have often employed pictorial language. The New Testament writers (though by no means always) have applied their quotations from Old Testament prophecies not only literally to the last times and the future but spiritually and morally to the present. To a wide extent 'spiritualizing' is the New Testament method of exposition. Does it not follow from this that the Old Testament prophecies of the kingdom are not usually to be understood literally but symbolically and typically; so that a literal fulfilment in a possibly still coming kingdom of God at the end was never meant and therefore is not to be expected?"

IT is quite evident that the Old Testament prophets often employ figurative language, and with the highest effect apply it in manifold forms—types, metaphors, allegories. Quite often their message rises indeed to the highest forms of human speech. Prophecy and poetry unite and form magnificant works of art, such as belong to the highest pinnacles of all human literature (especially Isaiah.)

At the background of all figurative speech stands the revelation of God in Nature. As an outflow of the Divine will Nature is the material expression of the thoughts of the Creator. The spiritual laws of the Eternal are reflected in the world of Nature. There is so fundamental a parallelism between the infinite and the finite, the ideal and the actual, that the visible becomes direct embodiment of the invisible, a mentally comprehensible figure of what is beyond our comprehension. Therefore human language in general constantly sets the material and the spiritual side by side and interweaves them. Thus speech humanizes the material and speaks of a "laughing" sun and "cheerful" brook; and conversely it sometimes applies material epithets to human attributes, and speaks of a "cold" unkindness, a "sunny" disposition, or a "radiant" joy. Similarly Isaiah carries the bodily into the spiritual and speaks of a "festering" wound of sin (1: 6), as conversely he brings the natural into the human and speaks of Israel as "budding" and "blooming" (27: 6). The psalmists and other prophets so speak. At times their language ascends to the use of living personification and then they shape these personifications according to certain chief human features and activities. Thus they speak of jubilant mountains (Isa. 49: 13), exulting fields and singing trees (Psa. 96: 12), of deserts rejoicing and singing (Isa. 35: 1), indeed of the trees of the field clapping their hands (Isa. 55: 12). Hosea declares that corn, new wine, and oil will "hear" the prayers of men asking them for food (Hos. 2: 22). It is poetical language when Joel declares that the mountains will run with new wine and flow with milk (Joel 3: 18).

(b) To the essence of the prophetic style of presentation belongs further a frequent application of types. This is the ground on which in not a few places the New Testament spiritualizes the Old Testament kingdom prophecies and applies them to the present period of the church. Only so can certain arrangements and appointments by the Lord Himself be rightly understood.

Thus the twelve disciples of Jesus correspond to the twelve patriarchs, being so to speak, ancestors of a new people of God; and the sending forth of the 70 disciples (Luke 10) somehow reminds us of the 70 elders of Israel.

Thus the literal Israel is at the same time a type of a spiritual people of God; on which account Paul names the members of the New Testament church (spiritual) "sons of Abraham," even in a letter addressed to Gentile Christians (Gal. 3: 26, 29); and Peter applies to the New Testament church the great titles of honour of the Old Testament people of God: "chosen race," "royal priesthood," "holy nation" (I Pet. 2: 9, comp. Exod. 19: 6; Isa. 43: 21). Similarly John states that the Lord has made us to be "kings and priests" (Rev. 1: 6; 5: 10) and Paul calls Christ the "passover lamb" (I Cor. 5: 7). The Lord's Supper is a parallel to the Passover, and baptism to the passage through the Red Sea (I Cor. 10: 1, 2). This whole typical connexion is the ground upon which Jesus introduced His Supper just at the feast of Passover, so that the New Testament holy festival came on the day of the Old Testament holy festival, indeed, as its continuation, fulfilment, and transfiguration.

Thus all the three great apostolic leaders, Peter, Paul, and John, see in the New Testament church a royal and holy "priesthood" taking this expression from the Old Testament calling of Israel (I Pet. 2: 4, 5; Rom 15: 16; Rev. 1: 6; 5: 10). Both Peter and Paul view their acts of worship and practical devotion as spiritual "sacrifices" (I Pet. 2: 5), as "sacrificial victims" (Rom. 12: 1), as "drink offerings" (Phil. 2: 17; Gr. *spendomai*), as does the Writer of *Hebrews* (13: 15, 16). Indeed Paul applies the prophecy of the royal rule of "the root of Jesse, who arises to rule over the nations" (Isa. 11: 10), as direct ground for the acceptance of believing Gentiles in this age of the church, and draws from it the conclusion that the believing Jews should receive these believing Gentiles, and so there be mutual acceptance by both groups (Rom. 15: 12, 7).

Likewise circumcision is regarded by Paul as a type of a spiritual experience of the members of the New Testament church.   This experience deals with something invisible, spiritual, inward, to which New Testament baptism has relationship.   According to to Paul circumcision is not a direct type of baptism, but as he expresses it in the Colossian letter, of something which is "not made with hands."   No one however can baptize, whether it be infants or believers, without using his hands.   But it is indeed a type of that "cutting off of the impulse to sin, even to the very root of our existence," or as Paul says, "of the putting off of the body of the flesh" (Col. 2: 11), that is, the surrender of our old life unto death, our basic and practical fellowship with Christ as the Crucified One, Who both died and rose again for us.

The same truth is the essential spiritual germ of the original Christian baptism, in the one aspect of its meaning represented by the act of immersion, which is symbolic burial (Rom. 6: 3, 4). The other aspect of its meaning is fellowship of life with the Risen One, represented by coming up out of the water, which act is symbolic resurrection.

The relationship of circumcision and baptism is therefore as follows: Both refer to the "putting away of the old man"; circumcision indeed in the *fore*view of the Old Testament preparation for salvation, but the original Christian baptism looking *back*wards from the New Testament experience of salvation, namely on the principle of fellowship with the Cross of Christ realized by faith.

Thus they both have in common the same central spiritual truth.   But they do not stand in direct relation to each other as type and fulfilment (antitype), but are as two fingerposts standing at a certain distance from one another with a common centre lying between, the one (circumcision) pointing forwards, the other (baptism) backwards.   But neither points directly to the other.

In all this indeed "spiritualizing" of a type is found in its noblest and deepest sense (Col. 2: 11; Phil. 3: 3).

(*c*) Sometimes, though but seldom, prophetic speech goes so far that it employs even the name of the original type itself to describe the antitype, retaining the same description.   Christ, the Davidic Messiah king, is by Ezekiel and Hosea called simply "David": "afterward shall the children of Israel return and seek Jehovah their God and David their king" (Hos. 3: 5; Ezek. 37: 24, 22).   So the name of an Old Testament person was used to point to a New Testament person who was not literally the same person and did not literally bear the same name. Christ is the announced David but not the literal David.

The reason for this joint use of these names is to emphasize heavily the correspondence between type and antitype, prophetic symbol and fulfilment. But such an individual instance is in no way proof that consequently the whole of Old Testament prophecy of the kingdom in general is not to be taken literally. Moreover even in this particular case there is no merely "spiritual" fulfilment. For the New Testament David (= Christ) is a literal person, even Jesus of Nazareth.

(d) Thus the Old Testament is full of symbols and types. They are persons, acts, arrangements, and events. In the New Testament the Lord Himself refers to this, as also Paul, and especially the *Hebrews* epistle.

In this respect there are types with single, double, and even treble New Testament fulfilments. Not seldom they have a near, then a later, and at last a final fulfilment; first a fulfilment following immediately, then one at a remoter distance, and at last a complete fulfilment. So have they also different *forms* of fulfilment—spiritual, literal, and super-historical-eternal. And there are different *times* and *stages* of fulfilment—prior fulfilment, enlarged fulfilment, and complete fulfilment.

All this arises from the unity of the whole plan in Biblical history and the educative wisdom of God, who in all prior developments has always the final goal in view, and it arises from the planned, progressive, actual carrying forward of the revelation to the established eternal goals of perfection.

(1) Types with one New Testament fulfilment are the serpent lifted up in the wilderness, which pointed to the Cross (John 3: 14); the Passover lamb as pointing to Christ and His sacrificial death (I Cor. 5: 7, 8); Adam as the first head of mankind, as the counterpart of Christ as the "last" Adam (Rom. 5: 12-21; I Cor. 15: 45).

(2) Of typical prophecy with *double* fulfilment the prophecy concerning Immanuel is an example. For the Immanuel announced by Isaiah is first a little Jewish boy of Isaiah's time, that is, the eighth century B.C., who would still be quite young at the collapse of the kingdoms of Damascus and north Israel (Damascus conquered 732 B.C., Samaria destroyed 722 B.C. See Isa. 7: 14, 16, comp. 4-8). But at the same time this boy became a type of the great Immanuel, the Messiah, whose birth was likewise in poverty and simplicity, whose contemporaries were likewise in political oppression and distress, but whose life and service likewise stands under the promises and faithfulness of Jehovah,

so that His task and victory will merge finally into ocean-wide salvation and glorious triumph (Isa. 8: 8; 10: 9, 6; Matt 1: 21-23).

A further typical prophecy with double meaning is the word in Hosea, "Out of Egypt have I called my son" (11: 1). In the meaning of the prophet there is here a backward view at the exodus of Israel from Egypt under Moses. But at the same time there was here a God-intended foreview, not unknown indeed to Hosea himself, of the early days of Messiah (Matt 2: 15; comp. I Pet. 1: 11, 12).

(3) Numerous prophecies of the Old Testament have even a *threefold* accomplishment. To these belong very many prophecies of the kingdom.

In the meaning of the prophet such belong mostly to the earthly kingdom of God in Israel at the End time. But this kingdom of God of the preliminary Perfecting he often sees in one picture with eternity (Isa. 65: 17, 20; 66: 22; comp. *The Triumph of the Crucified* p. 143 and p. 169 of this present book).

According to the New Testament however the period of the church is already a spiritual advance fulfilment; for the New Testament writers connect many Old Testament prophecies of the kingdom with the present age of the gospel (see p. 171 ff).

Moreover, because, in addition to all this, many prophetic words have a pronounced reference to the contemporary affairs of the prophet himself (comp. the "first" Immanuel of Isa. 7), it must be said that Old Testament kingdom prophecy has a fourfold reference and must therefore have a fourfold explanation:

i. Historical and contemporary, to the circumstances of the prophet himself:

ii. Spiritual and typical, to the period of the church:

iii. Literal, to the closing history of Israel and the nations in the coming kingdom of God on the old earth:

iv. Eternal, to the new heavens and the new earth.

But it would be precipitate if from the fact that the New Testament speaks of a spiritual fulfilment of the Old Testament kingdom prophecies the conclusion were drawn that this is the complete fulfilment and no further fulfilment is to be expected. With the same right one could as well deny their application to an eternal and ultimate fulfilment, which however no one does and which, on the contrary, every sound Bible expositor regards as their essential and chief meaning.

Much rather by this manifold fulfilment of Old Testament prophecy it is proved that "on the way to the consummation each stage in turn is first of all a porch. The Old Testament is the vestibule to the church age; the church age is the vestibule to the visible earthly kingdom of God, But even that visible earthly kingdom of God is not the final goal, but likewise only a vestibule. Only in eternity, in the new heaven and on the new earth, is the royal palace of perfection opened" (*The Dawn of World Redemption*, p. 147).

(*e*) From all this it arises that:

According to the Scripture both the literal and symbolic spiritual explanations are justified in principle. In any case all prophecy, whether literal or spiritual, will have actual, matter-of-fact fulfilment.

In reality no one on either side explains everything as *only* literal or *only* spiritual. Much rather do all on both sides defend both explanations. The difference is that what on the one side is the rule, on the other side is the exception.

And here must both sides beware of extremes. Extravagancies have been known on both sides. But this never justifies the other side in going to the opposite extreme.

There is no iron rule applicable to all details to settle when the literal or the symbolic explanation is alone justified. Decision can be reached in each case only by careful exegesis made with regard to the local context and to the whole of Scripture. As a pilot between two rocks there serves here the principle: "Each word is to be taken in its simplest, literal significance unless the wording, context, or other related passages of Scripture make clear that it is to be understood otherwise." Or we think of that sound rule of reliable exposition: "If the literal sense of a passage gives simple common sense, seek no other sense. Take each word in its original, common, simple sense, unless plain facts from the context demand another sense." Neglect of this law leads to uncertainty, confusion, and arbitrariness. But if this law be observed and rightly applied God's Word unfolds itself as a harmonious and connected whole.

In most cases the context and the general thought will make clear in advance to the impartial reader whether the statement is literal or figurative. For example, to take a drastic instance, when Isaiah, in his prophecy concerning the Forerunner of Messiah (40: 4), says that "every valley shall be exalted, and every mountain and hill shall be made low," it is obvious that this is meant figuratively, and that he is not speaking of ground levelling operations (comp. Luke 3: 2–6). Or when Zechariah declares that in the coming kingdom of Messiah ten Gentiles will take hold of the skirt of one Jew, it is clear that, while the expression is drastic and impressive, it is not intended literally, but means that the nations will perceive how much God has blessed saved Israel and that through Israel help and salvation can become their portion also (Zech. 8: 23).

On the other hand it is equally clear that prophecy must be meant literally when, with the most distinct mention of quite well-known lands and districts, and with direct use of their political and geographical names, such as Gilead and Lebanon, it declares that in the time of Messiah Israel will live in the regions thus unmistakably indicated. And it does this yet further by distinct emphasis on the expressions "this" land (Jer. 32: 41), "their *own* land" (Ezek. 28: 25), "the land of their *fathers*" (Jer. 16: 15).

It is said that "they shall dwell in their *own* land, which I have given to my servant Jacob" (Ezek. 28: 25); "I will bring them back to *their* land, which I have given to their *fathers*" (Jer. 16: 15); "I will plant them in *this* land" (Jer. 32: 41). The context in these three places makes clear that it is not the return from Babylon that is meant, but the future and final salvation of Israel. For the first passage defines the time as "when I shall gather the house of Israel from among the *peoples* among whom they have been scattered"; and the second says that they shall dwell in "their" fatherland "when the Lord has brought out the children of Israel from the land of the north and from all the lands" where they were driven. This goes far beyond the region of Babylon, as does also the third passage, carrying on the thought to the final salvation of the people by the immediately previous statement "I will make with them an eternal covenant."

Again we read: "I will bring them back into the land of Gilead and to Lebanon" (Zech. 10: 10). The prophet Zechariah through whom God gave this last prophecy, began his ministry not earlier than fifteen years *after* the return from the captivity in Babylon (in the second year of Darius, 512 B.C., Zech. 1. 1; Ezra 4: 24; 5: 1). This makes clear that the return of which he, from his point of time, speaks as being still future must lie *later* than the return from Babylon, and therefore must still be future.

(*f*) From all this it follows that the presence in the prophets of numerous symbolic and typical forms of speech creates no objection to the expectation of a final and visible kingdom of God. On the contrary, the many magnificent symbolic and typical expressions in prophecy only show how important and glorious this coming kingdom will be, how they all rejoiced in it in advance and set forth its splendour in such gorgeously coloured prophetic symbols.

(*g*) It is right that the literal conception must acknowledge that symbolic explanation of some details is justified.

It is further right that the literal conception must guard against a too vigorous introduction of fanciful elaborate details into the Millennium.

It is also right that the literal conception must not give to the Millennium an excessive importance in relation to eternity. For even the Millennium is still but a portico to eternity. It is the first, lesser, and likewise the introductory period of the coming kingdom of God. For of all the literality and historicity, of all the brilliance and might of the Millennial kingdom it must be said, that the true essential *core* of the Perfecting is not the earthly kingdom of God on the old earth (this first stage of the coming kingdom of God), but the eternal, of which that will be only the court and porch of the second and chief portion of the coming kingdom of God, even the nations on the new earth with the new Jerusalem there.

In this sense the kingdom prophecies of the Old Testament, when they speak of a coming visible kingdom of glory on the old earth, are at the same time quite often a typical prophecy of the complete Perfecting on the new earth. For were it not so we should face a fact simply beyond explanation, even that the whole of the Old Testament kingdom prophecies would refer to only a very short period of one thousand years and say virtually nothing of the real and final goal of history. But no; it is at the same time typical prophecy of eternity. In this deepest and noblest sense "spiritualizing" is decidedly in place.

Thus these two kinds of prophetic explanation are by no means irreconcilable. In prophecy literal and symbolical speech unite in harmony.

But as regards the earthly kingdom of God, it is not at all contradicted by the following facts:

that the prophets often expressed their message in the form of symbols and types. This rather shows

that the prophetic message often moves on the highest heights of the spirit, emotions, and perceptions;

that from one common outlook they combine the earthly and the heavenly into one magnificent picture;

that the earthly and the present are a type and introduction of the heavenly and the future;

that of these heavenly and future things God, in condescending and educative wisdom, has given in advance types and parables;

that up to eternity everything is preparation and introduction, preliminary stage and prior exhibition, porch, portico, vestibule;

that therefore before that actual complete fulfilment, in these prior stages numerous prior fulfilments have place;

that all things, growing and advancing, go onward to the

final goals, and that therefore the last time, indeed eternity itself, is presented in all these introductory stages and pre-developments;

that therefore in all its preparatory ways and prior exhibitions, even before the arrival of the perfect day, eternity more or less clearly shines forth like the light of dawn.

> Eternity in time
> Ever clear doth shine;
> That to us the small be smaller,
> And the great appear as greater!
> Blest eternity!

CHAPTER XXXIII

"THE PRESENT GOSPEL DISPENSATION IS NO 'MYSTERY' BUT WAS FORETOLD BY OLD TESTAMENT PROPHECY"

"The New Testament applies many prophecies of the Old Testament to the present dispensation of the gospel. Does it not follow that for their fulfilment a still future kingdom age is not only not required but is excluded, so that after the period of the church no kingdom age can possibly be expected?"

HERE also it is needful for both sides to guard against an extreme. It would be one-sided to say that the Old Testament kingdom prophecies never speak of the blessings which we enjoy in the present age of the gospel. This would in no way do justice to the manner in which the New Testament cites the Old Testament prophecies.

On the other hand it would be likewise one-sided to declare that, because they speak of these now present blessings, henceforth no further, and perhaps still larger, fulfilment than the present can come.

In other words, it were one-sided to apply the Old Testament kingdom prophecies to the future, the Millennium, alone, and to separate them from the present gospel age; and equally one-sided to apply them solely to the gospel age, to spiritualize them entirely, thus to separate them from the Millennium and to oppose a literal fulfilment.

The one would stand in opposition to the New Testament way of applying Old Testament prophecy; the other to the Old Testament text itself, even to the unmistakable connexion of the text and to the meaning that the prophets themselves intended and to the fulfilment that they quite plainly expected.

(b) The New Testament often states plainly that the Old Testament prophets spoke of "these days," and therefore not only of the final kingdom of Messiah. In this it applies the term "these days" to the present period of the church.

Thus the early praying church in Jerusalem said that the hatred of Jews and Gentiles against the Messiah, of which David had prophesied in the second Psalm, had found fulfilment "in *this* city" in the rejection of Jesus and the persecution of His followers, and thus in the earthly days of the Lord and the immediately following time of the first church, that is, in the present age of salvation (Acts 4: 26–28).

Paul declares the same of this second psalm, even that the fulfilment had started early in this present age, for he says that the word "Thou art my son, this day have I begotten thee" was fulfilled in the resurrection of Jesus (Acts 13: 33).

Similarly, on the day of Pentecost Peter declared concerning the prophecy of Joel of the outpouring of the Holy Spirit "in the last days," that "*this* is that which was spoken through the prophet Joel" (Acts 2: 16, 17; Joel 2: 28, 29). Thus the beginning of the present age brought a fulfilment of this Old Testament prophecy. A short time later, this same Peter declared that "all the prophets, from Samuel and those who followed, as many as have spoken, have announced '*these* days'." (Acts 3: 34) Thus the foretelling of "these days" he connected not with David only, but also with Samuel and *all* the following prophets.

Moreover, the "gospel of God" as announced by Paul, the pioneer apostle of the present age, was, according to his own testimony in the Roman epistle, "promised before by God through His prophets in holy writings" (Rom. 1: 1, 2). In Antioch he based the transfer of his message from Jews to Gentiles upon a reference to an Old Testament prophetic word: "We turn to the Gentiles; *for* so has the Lord commanded: 'I have set thee for a light to the nations'" (Isa. 49: 6; Acts 13: 47). Thus he saw a fulfilling of Isaiah's prophecy in his own preaching to the Gentiles in this present age. Indeed, he, the chief evangelist of the church age, testified before king Agrippa concerning his own message that he said "nothing but what Moses and the prophets had spoken" (Acts 26: 22, 23).

The duty of Jewish and Gentile Christians of this church period to receive one another (Rom. 15: 7–13) Paul established by a series of separate Old Testament prophecies which he applied to the conversion of Gentiles in this present age, among which was even the kingdom prophecy of Isaiah concerning the coming "Shoot out of the root of Jesse which standeth to rule over the nations" (Isa. 11: 10).

And Peter, writing in his first epistle to readers who, like ourselves, lived after Pentecost, and therefore in the present age of the gospel, testifies (Eph. 1: 12) that the Old Testament prophets had indeed received no light as to what time, or what manner of time, the Spirit of Christ which was in them signified, but that they had prophesied of the "salvation" and the "grace that should come unto you," and "for you" had ministered the things which "*now*" have been announced unto "you" through those who preached the gospel unto "you" through the Holy Spirit sent forth from heaven. All this being after Pentecost means in the present age of grace, and the "you" includes us of the present time.

(*d*) Similarly it is clear that David knew of an age to intervene between the ascension of Messiah and of His final triumph in glory, for he wrote: "Sit thou at My right hand *until* I make thine enemies thy footstool" (Psa. 110: 1). We in particular who believe in a visible kingdom of God on the theatre of the old earth ought clearly to recognize this. It is this time of waiting which *Hebrews* also refers to the present age of the gospel (Heb. 10: 13).

In emphasizing this we by no means transfer New Testament knowledge backward from the time of fulfilment into the consciousness of Old Testament prophets. For David, who, as Peter declared on the day of Pentecost, was also a prophet (Acts 2: 30), had "known" of the kingdom of Messiah and "foreseen" His resurrection (ver. 31). In this, as Psalm 110 shows, David had recognized that *before* the triumphant kingdom of Messiah there would be a period in which He would sit on the throne of God in heaven and act as the Priest-King after the order of Melchizedek, even "until" God should put His enemies under His feet. Furthermore, the psalm shows that David knew that this priestly rule of Messiah would be introduced by His ascension: "Set thyself at My right hand."

In addition David had known that Messiah would die. For "foreseeing" (Acts 2: 31) he spake of the resurrection of Messiah, which could not have been save in connexion with knowledge of His death (Psa. 16: 8–11). Finally, after the mission to him of the prophet Nathan (II Sam. 7: 16) David had the knowledge that Messiah would be his "son," a member of his house, and thus would be born as man.

Thus David had seen all three chief Messianic periods:

the first, the birth of Christ as man and as son of David, His death, His resurrection, His ascension:

the second, the waiting period, following the ascension, when Messiah sits as Priest-King at the right hand of God in heaven:

the third, the victory of His kingdom, the subduing of His enemies and the triumph of His glory.

Thus it is not possible to assert that the whole present age of the gospel was completely hidden from the Old Testament prophets and had been an absolute "mystery" (secret). Much rather had they, at least David, known of the existence of such a period before the setting up of the kingdom, even though, of course, the details of this intervening period were not clearly known by them.

(*e*) In any case they had known of a coming conversion of the

Gentiles. As a rule they viewed this conversion in one picture with the salvation of Israel. Yet they nowhere expressly say that this conversion of the Gentiles can only be *after* the salvation and renewal of Israel as a nation. As regards the sequence of events, the separate stages in the carrying out of these promises, and as to certain further important details to be added later, no light was granted to them. The "times" in the history of the fulfilment were hidden from them (I Pet. 1: 11, 12).

Above all it was not yet revealed to them that in this present time of which they spoke the principle would rule of the equality of Jews and Gentiles in the people of God. Nowhere in the Old Testament was it said expressly that the Gentiles could be received into the people of God without law-keeping and circumcision, that is, directly as Gentiles and solely on the ground of faith. Complete silence reigned as to whether Gentiles must first become Jews so as to gain admission into the kingdom of Messiah. Not a single prophecy in the whole Old Testament deals with and gives light on this question. In the past the principle of the non-circumcision of believing Gentiles in the church of God was an absolute secret.

In harmony with this fact Paul, writing to the Ephesians, expresses himself with extraordinary exactness. He does not state that the Old Testament prophets had known nothing at all of what would take place in this present age of grace, but he says that this had not been *so* made known to the sons of men "*as* it hath now been revealed to His holy apostles and prophets through the Spirit," and in especial measure to Paul himself (Eph. 3: 4-6). The general fact of the call of the Gentiles was already known in the Old Testament, but not the details connected with this call. Upon these the New Testament first gives full revelation.

Therefore the "mystery" of which Paul speaks in Ephesians 3 was that the Gentile believers should receive a completely equal standing in the Christan church with Jewish believers. They are "*fellow*-heirs, *fellow*-members of the body, and *fellow*-partakers of the promise in Christ Jesus through the gospel" (Eph. 3: 6). By this prefix "fellow" (Gr. *syn*) Paul expresses the closest possible union and indistinguishable equality between Jews and Gentiles in the church.

But now, because precisely this principle of equality is one of the most essential characteristics of the New Testament church, it must be acknowledged that none of the Old Testament prophets had foreseen that, in the coming period, *such* a building of God would arise; and in *this* sense although not the fact that such a New Testament people of God (church of God, *ecclesia*) would exist, but its composition, nature, and principle of organic fellowship, was in the Old Testament a "mystery" not yet revealed.

This makes intelligible why the New Testament, with its God-inspired and extraordinarily careful manner of expression, never describes the present age *as such* as a "mystery," nor calls the *ecclesia as such* a "mystery"; but only terms "mysteries" certain individual principles and detail truths *connected* with the present age and *concerning* the church, although these are in the highest degree essential and truly important.

Thus the "great mystery" of Eph. 5: 32 is not the *ecclesia as such* but the *relation* of love between Christ and the *ecclesia*: "This mystery is great, but I speak in regard of [*concerning*] Christ *and* the *ecclesia*." Exactly so in the earthly life, not the existence of the husband and wife as such is a "mystery" but the relation of love which binds them together.

(*f*) In like manner the New Testament knows nothing of an "offer" to the Jewish people by the Lord, at the beginning of His public ministry, to set up the earthly kingdom of Messiah, which offer being refused by the Jews the kingdom was consequently "postponed" to a later time; so that then the present gospel age would have been inserted like a parenthesis, as something quite unforeseen and never announced. There are three chief reasons to the contrary.

(1) The silence of the Bible: In the whole Bible there is no single place which speaks distinctly of such an "offer" and "postponement" of the earthly kingdom. Rather do all the explanations related to this idea rest upon inexact attention to the wording of certain passages of Scripture or upon inferences drawn from them.

(2) An offer of and setting up of Messiah's kingdom before Golgotha was simply not possible. For no kingdom of glory could come without the forgiveness of sins. But forgiveness of sins was possible only on the ground of the substitutionary atoning death of Christ, and from the beginning He had come for this very purpose that He should give His life a ransom for many (Matt. 20: 28). Therefore such an offer would have been a proposal by God Himself which would have stood in strongest opposition to the most decisive principles of His own plan of redemption. Consequently from His very entrance into the world, the Cross stood before the eyes of the Lord as the very first of all matters (Heb. 10: 5–10). First rejection, than exaltation: first the crown of thorns, then the royal crown. Therefore also John the Baptist, the preparer of His way, had from the

beginning thus announced Him, saying, "Behold, the *lamb* of God who beareth away the sin of the world" (John 1: 29). From the very first the sequence was the same: Through Cross to crown; through repentance to salvation. Only through forgiveness of sin to the glory. Never the reverse.

(3) Furthermore, the exact wording of the preaching of the kingdom is to be observed: Both John the Baptist and Jesus had declared: "Repent, *for* the kingdom of the heavens *has* drawn near"[1] (Matt. 3: 1, 2; 4: 17). They did not say, "*If* you repent *then* the kingdom of the heavens will draw near." The repentance of man was not the condition for the coming of the kingdom, but the coming of the kingdom was the ground of the demand for repentance. The kingdom itself had come in either case. "The kingdom of the heavens *has* drawn near." Unbelief could not alter this. "But into whatsoever city ye shall enter, and they receive you not, go out into the streets thereof and say, Even the dust of your city that cleaveth to our feet we do wipe off against you: howbeit know this, that the kingdom of God *has* come nigh" (Luke 10: 10, 11). For each individual entrance into this kingdom was conditional upon his repentance. Each individual had the possibility to submit himself to the kingly rule of God and so to be blessed, or, as the Pharisees did, "to make the counsel of God of none effect" *for himself* (Luke 7: 30).

In any case we must here guard ourselves from a precipitate equalizing of "kingdom" with "Millennial kingdom." The kingdom of God will indeed have in the end time its appearance in visible glory. But in its essence it is the royal estate of God in general, His sovereign kingship as the ruling and saving God, which sovereignty He displays in different times and dispensations in ever new forms. Therefore the term "kingdom of God" includes of course the Millennial kingdom, but at the same time comprises much more than this. Only the immediate context can make clear from case to case what particular historical form of the kingdom is meant; whether the Old Testament kingdom (Matt. 21: 43), or the present spiritual kingdom (in "mysteries": Matt. 13: 11), or the visible kingdom of the future (Luke 19: 11), or the eternal kingdom.

In reference to the *national* history of Israel the present period of the church is indeed a parenthesis. For until its restoration Israel as a people is set aside, "till the fulness of the Gentiles has come in" (Rom. 11: 25, 26). "Jerusalem shall be trodden down of the Gentiles until the times of the Gentiles be fulfilled" (= have run out: Luke 21: 24). But this is not on the ground of

---

[1] *ēngiken*, perfect; has drawn near.

a rejection by the Jews of a supposed offer by Jesus of the visible kingdom of Messiah, but on account of the spiritual and moral rejection of His person and His message by the unbelief of His Jewish contemporaries.

But all this God had foreseen from eternity. Therefore everything was included in His plan and was correspondingly announced through the Old Testament prophets, even if in very hidden form.

(g) But the opposite extreme must be equally avoided. The fact remains that in the period of the New Testament church Old Testament prophecies of the conversion of the Gentiles are being fulfilled. But, as both experience and Scripture testify, this applies first of all to the salvation of *individuals*: "God will *take out* of the nations a people for His name" (Acts 15: 14). But this does not contradict the other fact that, in the course of the carrying through of this His one inclusive plan for the Gentiles, God will hereafter cause a still greater ingathering of Gentiles, in which the nations *as nations* will be converted, and, with Israel as a *people*, will stand under one common covenant of blessing and peace under the one sovereignty of Messiah as King of Israel and King of mankind (Isa. 19: 23–25).

Therefore the fact that the New Testament applies to the present age numerous Old Testament prophecies of the conversion of Gentiles, in no wise contradicts a visible kingdom of God composed of all mankind in the Millennium. The Old Testament prophets foretold only quite in general a conversion of Gentiles. But on the question how this would be carried out in detail, in what stages and in what sections of time, by what measures and in what increasing degree, they said nothing precise. Therefore such general prophecies, and their application in the New Testament, can form no warrant to deprive of their original significance by "spiritualizing" other Old Testament promises, the evident sense of which is a national conversion of both Israel and the other nations in one visible Messianic kingdom of God, or to oppose them as "mistaken prophecies."

(h) At the same time these prophecies look on into eternity. Even the Millennial kingdom is only a portico to the Perfecting. Only then will the promise of the conversion of the nations have reached its full realization.

Thus the carrying through of the Old Testament promises for the nations of the world will be completed in three great and mighty stages:[1]

[1] For fuller details see *The Dawn of World Redemption*, p. 146–55.

M

In the present gospel age, through salvation of many individuals and their incorporation into the organism of the church.

In the coming visible kingdom of God of the pre-perfecting, the Millennium, through the renewing of whole nations and their subordinate yet associated position with Israel under the kingly rule of Messiah, Who will have appeared in glory.

In eternity, in the conditions of the new world, as nations on the new earth who will live in the light of the new Jerusalem, the city of God come down from heaven.

CHAPTER XXXIV

"RE-ESTABLISHMENT OF TEMPLE SERVICE IS CONTRARY TO THE TEACHING OF *HEBREWS*"

"The Old Testament prophecies of a future Temple service and sacrifices, especially by Ezekiel, cannot be taken literally because this would be in contradiction of the teaching in the *Hebrews*. This declares that by the one sacrifice of Christ the many Old Testament sacrifices were for ever fulfilled and thereby abolished (Heb. 10: 1–8, 14, 18).

"This also arises from the relationship of 'shadow' and 'substance,' as the New Testament characterizes the connexion between the Old Testament sacrificial system and the redeeming work of Christ (Col. 2: 16, 17; Heb. 10:1). For must not the shadow fade when the substance, the essential, has appeared? How can both shadow and substance be in force at the same time? What virtue shall a prophetic symbol, a type, have when it has been fulfilled? Why shall they who have the essential turn back to the shadow? What significance shall the blood of rams and bullocks (which in any case cannot take away sin: Heb. 10: 4) have after the sacrifice of Christ has been offered, which can take away sin? Would it not therefore be simply without sense or significance to reinstate the Old Testament sacrifices after Golgotha?

"Must one not always accept a figurative meaning in places where a literal meaning would lead to consequences which are in opposition to truths elsewhere revealed in Scripture?"

THE last sentence above would be in order if we could be sure in advance that we understand fully the final end of all God's revelations. But this is by no means the case. Things Divine often meet us in the form of paradoxes. With our mental capacity limited as to time and space we are not in a position fully to comprehend things super-spatial and super-temporal. Therefore in the Scripture there are at times parallel lines which do not meet in time but only in infinity. In such cases we have the duty to allow these passages simply to stand in accord with the evident meaning of their words, and to wait patiently till fuller light will be granted at the dawn of eternity (I Cor. 13: 9, 10). In any case caution is necessary.

(*b*) As regards the prophecies of a future temple service in time of Messiah, in numerous places they go into such detail that for every impartial reader a purely spiritual meaning is completely excluded. Isaiah speaks of an "altar" of God in the coming Messianic kingdom and of a "place of His sanctuary" which He will adorn (60: 7, 13). He speaks of the "oblation," of "priests and Levites," of "new moons" and "sabbaths" on which all flesh will come to worship the Lord (66: 20, 21, 23). Jeremiah also speaks of "priests and Levites," of burnt-offerings, meal-offerings, and "sacrifices" in the kingdom of the "shoot of David" then to reign in righteousness (33: 15, 18, 21, 22). Above all, Ezekiel pictures a future temple with so very many particulars and measurements that it will be simply impossible to declare that all this is only figurative and must therefore be "spiritualized."

At the Passover there shall be offered daily exactly seven bullocks and seven rams as a sin-offering, and likewise exactly seven bullocks and seven rams as a burnt-offering. In that coming temple service, as Ezekiel sees it, the meal offering will consist of one ephah of fine meal and one hin of oil. At the feast of Tabernacles, the date of which, exactly as formerly, is fixed for the fifteenth day of the seventh month, the same sacrifices will be offered (Ezek. 45: 21–25).

But other numbers apply to the usual weekdays. Each morning only one lamb shall be offered, and its accompanying meal-offering shall not be of a whole ephah, but of only a sixth thereof, and of oil not a whole hin but of only one third (46: 13, 14).

On the sabbath the prince shall bring exactly six lambs and one ram, and for each ram again one ephah of fine flour and one hin of oil. On the new moon the numbers are again different. Then it shall be one bullock, six lambs, and one ram (46: 4–7).

He who enters through the north gate shall go out through the south gate, while he who enters through the south gate shall go out through the north gate (46: 9).

In the forecourt there shall be four tables on the one side and four tables on the other side, together eight tables; and in addition four stone tables, each one and a half ells long and broad and one ell high. Even the fork-shaped double pegs are mentioned, each a handbreadth wide, on which are hanged the slaughtered beasts, evidently to draw off the skin (40: 39–43).

Blood shall be used; unleavened bread shall be eaten (45: 19, 21). Salt shall be sprinkled, and fire employed (43: 24, 21).

The priesthood shall be in the hands of the sons of Zadok of the tribe of Levi (43: 19; 44: 15; comp. II am. 15: 24).

And what shall we say of the individual measurements of the temple itself, as Ezekiel gives them? The whole area shall be a square of 500 rods (42: 15–20). The first threshold of the east door shall be exactly one rod wide. At the entrance of the door there shall be six guardrooms for the guards, three over against three, each one rod long and one broad, and between the indivi-

dual guardrooms a space of five ells. The narrow windows of
these guardrooms shall have gratings, and the pillars shall be
ornamented with carved palms (40: 6, 7, 10, 16).

The great gate shall have a breadth of ten ells, and the length
of the gate shall be thirteen ells. On the outer edge of the stone
pavement of the forecourt there shall be thirty chambers (40:
11, 17).

The altar of incense shall be three ells high and two long and
wide (41: 22). The altar of burnt offering is described with
special exactness. It shall rise in three tiers, above a pedestal
one ell high. The first tier shall be one ell above the pedestal;
the second and smaller, shall be two ells above the first; and the
third, and smallest, shall be four ells above the second; and so
the whole altar shall be seven ells high. The third and upper
tier, the hearth for the fire, shall be a square of twelve ells, pro-
vided with four horns on the four corners. The pedestal and
the upper tier have railings half an ell high (43: 13–17).

Shall we continue? It would be very easy to extend this list
of details and measurements, but the foregoing will suffice to
show that a true reading of these prophetic statements puts
beyond all doubt that a *purely* figurative spiritualizing is here
wholly impossible, but that the prophet expected an actual
future temple with precisely the given details, and a future
system of sacrifices with the numerous particular appointments.
That many are so easily satisfied with the explanation that these
prophecies of Ezekiel of a coming temple service are to be
understood purely figuratively, and refer exclusively to the
spiritual priesthood of the New Testament church, has in many
cases its ground in the fact that many readers of the Bible have
simply never read these passages of Ezekiel with continuity and
care. It is on this account that we have quoted above so many
details and small items, in order to convey to the reader the
impression that these prophetic passages unevadably impart.

We stand here really before an inescapable alternative: *Either*
the prophet himself was mistaken in his expectation of a coming
temple service, and his prophecy in the sense in which he himself
meant it will never be fulfilled; *or* God, in the time of Messiah,
will fulfil literally these prophecies of the temple according to
their intended literal meaning. There is no other choice possible.

(*c*) It is also impossible to attempt to maintain the literality of
the temple as seen by Ezekiel while denying its application to
the future in the End times, by applying it to the temple of
Zerubbabel which was to be built shortly after the time of
Ezekiel (536–516 B.C.) by those who returned from captivity in
Babylon (so Prof. Hengstenberg). For the measurements of the

temple of Zerubbabel in no way agree with those of Ezekiel. According to Ezra 6: 3 the temple of Zerubbabel was sixty ells high and sixty ells broad, whereas Ezekiel 41: 12, 13 gives quite different figures (seventy, ninety, one hundred ells). Also the descriptions of Zerubbabel's temple as given in the books of Maccabees draw a completely different picture (I *Macc.* 4: 47, 60; comp. *Sirach* 50: 1f). Moreover the descriptions of Zerubbabel's temple as given in the book of *Ezra* mention only its backward connexion with the ground plan of the Tabernacle and Solomon's temple, but never mention the temple of Ezekiel's vision as its ground plan and pattern.

(*d*) It is clear that with all this, and particularly in view of *Hebrews*, there still remain unsolved questions. But unsolved questions should never be a hindrance to faith. They can never justify us in disrobing a passage of its evidently intended and real meaning by an inadmissible spiritualizing. Even when in certain cases it is not possible to reach a complete and satisfying explanation we ought still to hold fast the manifest sense of a prophetic statement. The attitude that becomes us is to wait patiently till the fulfilment brings full light.

Yet in spite of this literality the symbolic will be the chief matter in that coming temple. Its literalness does not oppose its spiritual significance. Precisely in its symbolic numbers it will be a wonderful setting forth of spiritual realities. Here both belong together, literality and symbolism. Neither the first excludes the second nor the second the first. Together they represent an organism as of body and spirit.

In the Tabernacle of Moses symbolism and typology had likewise been its real, chief significance; nevertheless it had been a literal tent consisting of visible materials with literal measurements. So also here must they both be viewed together:
the literality of the outward and material and yet its essential purpose being for spiritual ends:
The clothing of eternal spiritual truths in material forms and yet the full reality of this literal material.

(*e*) But perhaps we can at least already perceive the general direction in which one day the resolution of these questions may be shown. Certainly the *Hebrews'* epistle says, "Where forgiveness of sins is there is no more offering for sin" (Heb. 10: 18). But this in no way proves that there can be no more symbolic actions in Divine service after the redeeming work of Christ, such as Ezek. 40–44 very plainly indicate.

Symbolic actions in Divine service are still possible even *since* Golgotha. It is true that they are no more, as in the Old Testament typological sense, prophetic symbols looking *forward* to the expected Redeemer, but rather, in the New Testament sense, symbolic acts looking *backward* to the accomplished work of this Redeemer. For if after Golgotha no further symbolic acts of Divine service were possible, with which spiritual blessings are associated for believers, where then were the possibility for the church of New Testament baptism and the Lord's Supper? Are not these last likewise outward, visible symbolic acts with which, even today, as a matter of fact, through the Holy Spirit God-given blessings are associated for the believer?

Certainly it is true that, according to Ezekiel, the future sacrifices foretold by him are not merely symbolic acts which will simply serve to bring to mind and remembrance the work of Christ, but they are actually united with God's grant of atonement and forgiveness of sin (Ezek. 43: 21–27; 45: 17). But just so, according to the teaching of the New Testament, do the acts of baptism and the Lord's Supper go beyond the *merely* symbolic and the fact of remembrance and are associated with the reception of Divine blessings (see esp. I Cor. 10: 16–21). So the reference to *Hebrews* offers no cogent, fundamental, irrefutable objection to a future literal temple service. It is only proved that these acts will then have an entirely new meaning and an entirely new outlook. In their Mosaic, pre-Christian, Old Testament sense sacrifices and priesthood will never return. The "old covenant" is for ever gone and will never again arise and be re-established. Much rather will everything take place in the spirit of the "new covenant." The old forms will be filled with a completely new spirit.

Within the circles of Bible-believing, scientific theology, Auberlen (formerly Professor of Lutheran theology in the University of Basel) was one of the chief pioneers of the expectation of a visible kingdom of God on the still untransformed earth. He described as follows the relationship of this new temple service in the Millennium to the preceding economies of law and grace: "That which in the times of the old covenant came to pass only in an *external* manner, in the 'letter'; that which, in the reverse, in the time of the church was withdrawn into the *internal* hidden essence of the spirit; this in the time of the Millennial kingdom will exhibit and display itself both *outwardly* and at the same time in a *spiritual* manner. Under the old covenant the whole life of the people of Israel in its different appearances, in the house and the civil sphere, in a more *external* way and measure, in labour, art, literature and and culture, was governed and characterized by religious laws. The church had above all to press for the renewing of the *heart*. But in the Millennial kingdom all these *outward* regions of life will be truly Christianized from *within*." (See Lange's *Bibelwerk* on Ezekiel 46). Thus in high degree they will then be harmoniously united, the external and the internal, the visible appearance and the invisible spiritual life of the heart.

(*f*) Finally we must assert that, however the prophecies of Ezekiel are to be understood, they are by no means the decisive basis for the expectation of a visible earthly kingdom of God. Ezekiel's prophecies do indeed belong to the most significant pictures of certain central details of this Millennium; but the Millennium itself has its chief roots in other prophecies. Some of the most important examples of these we shall briefly enumerate on pp. 192 ff. For a fuller account we refer the reader to *The Triumph of the Crucified*, 144–69, (especially 144–53).

CHAPTER XXXV

CHRIST'S PRESENT SPIRITUAL KINGDOM AND OLD TESTAMENT PROPHECIES OF A DAVIDIC KINGDOM

"The kingship of Christ on the 'throne of David' will not begin first at His appearing in glory but began already at His ascension, and thus not first at the end of the present age of the gospel but at its commencement. This applies also to the building again of 'the tabernacle of David which is fallen' (Acts 15: 16) and Christ's royal rule over the nations as the 'shoot out of the root of Jesse'" (Rom. 15: 12; Isa. 11: 10).

WE do not underestimate the importance of this objection "Thou shalt call his name Jesus. He shall be great and shall be called the Son of the Most High: and the Lord God shall give unto Him the throne of His father David: and he shall reign over the house of Jacob for ever; and of his kingdom there shall be no end" (Luke 1: 32, 33).

"After these things I will return,

"And I will build again the tabernacle of David, which is fallen; . . . that the residue of man may seek after the Lord,

"And all the Gentiles upon whom my name is called, saith the Lord" (Amos. 11: 12; Acts 15: 16–18).

"There shall be the root of Jesse,

"And he that ariseth to rule over the Gentiles" (Rom. 15: 12; Isa. 11: 10).

Two opposing explanations of these New Testament passages are current.

According to the one the rule (kingship) of Messiah will begin only at the setting up of His kingdom in glory at His return in the End time.

According to the other the Davidic kingship of Messiah began at the ascension and exaltation of the Divine Son of David to the right hand of the throne of the Majesty in the heavens.

The two explanations agree that the expressions "throne of David" and "tabernacle of David" are not to be taken literally but figuratively. They agree further that the Davidic kingship will experience an extension in area and glory through the Davidic, Messianic God-King.

The principal difference is threefold;

First, as to the degree of this extension, that is, as to its circumference, as regards what persons and lands are included, to what extent Israel, to what extent the other nations.

Then as to the *form* of this rule, whether it will be only inward and spiritual, or, in addition, visible and external, indeed, even historical and political.

And third, as to the dating of this Davidic kingship of the Son of David, whether its commencement is to be placed at the ascension and Pentecost or only at the future parousia and epiphany.

Within the scope of our present task, that is, in answering the question as to the Biblical warrant for expecting a visible kingdom of God on this earth, the most decisive factor is that it is easy to show that *both* explanations can well agree in expecting such a Millennium, in the sense that the one teaches it directly and the other by no means necessarily contradicts it but can fit harmoniously into it. Here again however both sides must guard against extremes and from drawing inferences which the Bible itself does not draw.

Our only task here is to show this as regards both explanations. To take an exact and positive attitude to the numerous separate questions involved is here not required, indeed would go beyond the scope of our work. Our present object is not detail exegesis but answering the question as to the Biblical warrant for the original Christian hope of a visible earthly kingdom of God, and replying to certain objections raised by believing expositors of Scripture.

It is perfectly clear that the expression "throne of David" as it regards the rule of the Messiah is not meant literally. No one asserts—not even the most extreme defender of belief in a Millinnial kingdom—that it will be the same actual throne upon which David sat a thousand years before Christ. So that in any case the term "throne of David" is to be taken figuratively of the royal rule of Messiah as a descendant of David and as heir to his kingdom.

At the gathering in Jerusalem, James cited the prophecy of Amos: "In that day will I raise up the tabernacle of David that is fallen, and close up the breaches thereof, and I will raise up its ruins, and I will build it as in the days of old" (Acts 15: 13–16; Amos 9: 11). What is meant by this "tabernacle of David?"

Doubtless not a literal structure which David in his day may have owned or occupied, but this term also is to be understood figuratively. It is certainly not to be taken as meaning simply the earthly national political "State" over which David ruled, but it points to his "house," his "royal house," his "royal dynasty," as we speak of the "house" of Windsor, or of Hapsburg, or of Hohenzollern. Thus God had made known to David through the prophet Nathan that "Jehovah will build thee a house," which in the immediate context is explained as "royal house," meaning "royal dynasty": "And it shall come to pass . . . I will set up thy seed after thee . . . and I will establish his kingdom . . . and I will establish his throne for ever" (I Chron. 17: 10b–14).

After the collapse of the Jewish State (586 B.C.) this royal house of David, formerly so mighty, had become a ruined hut.[1] David's family itself had sunk into poor and socially humble circumstances, so that when Christ appeared He was reared as a member of an artisan family descended from David.

But now the prophecy announces that God will build again this royal house. He will revive the former brilliance of David's royal dynasty. This will come to pass through the coming Son of David, Christ the Messiah king; and the kingdom which this Son of David will receive will be far wider and more glorious than ever was that of His ancestor David. As to this last point also there is full agreement among Bible teachers.

To this everyone will agree who refers the spiritual kingship of Christ to this age of the *church*. For it is a fact that, in addition to the believing from Israel, there are now the thousands of thousands, indeed ten thousands of ten thousands of all people and tongues who, through the Holy Spirit, call Christ their royal Lord (I Cor. 12: 3), so that the scope of this spiritual kingdom of the Messiah is far wider and includes far more of our race than the limited kingdom of the original David.

Moreover, all who connect the kingdom promises given to David solely with the future, the *Millennium*, will affirm this mighty extension of the kingdom of David's Son beyond that of His ancestor. For it is precisely in the literal Millennium that the rule of Messiah on the throne of David will likewise embrace a wider area than the former kingdom of David, because when He then sits on the throne of David He will be the Arbiter between the nations and Divine King of all mankind (Isa. 2: 4; Zeph. 3: 9; Zech. 14: 9). Moreover, because the church will have been raised bodily from the dead before the beginning of the thousand years (I Thess. 4: 14–17), the first resurrection having taken place immediately before the Millennial kingdom (Rev. 20: 4–6), therefore the rule of Messiah will include not only the general unglorified inhabitants of the earth but also men risen from the dead. As Himself raised bodily from the dead and glorified in heaven He will rule at the same time over the raised and glorified.

---

[1] The word here used for "tabernacle" has nothing to do with the tabernacle of Moses. The same word is found in Isa. 1: 8 in the sense of a simple hut in a vineyard.

Thus in any case the royal rule of Messiah on "David's throne" will extend beyond that of the original David and his original kingdom. "Christ on David's throne" embraces much more than "David on David's throne" embraced. With the exaltation of the Heir to David's throne there is connected a glorifying of David's throne.

In all other instances the antitype is greater than its type. Every fulfilment surpasses its promise. The "body" always exceeds its "shadow" (Col. 2: 17); the New Testament reality excels its prior Old Testament representation. In infinite degree this is the case with Christ. As the "Lord" of his ancestor He surpasses him in incomparable degree as to both His person and sovereignty (Matt. 22: 42-45).

In what period and in what manner will the Messiah build again the "fallen tabernacle" of David, that is, restore the former glory of David's house and his kingly rule?

As proof that the conversion of the nations was in harmony with the word of God, James, at that meeting in Jerusalem, referred to the word quoted from the prophet Amos. Through his account of the events in the house of Cornelius Peter had given the proof from experience, and James then added the proof from Scripture: "To this [that is, the conversion of the Gentiles] agree the words of the prophets; as it is written, After these things I will return, and I will build again the tabernacle of David, which is fallen . . . that the residue of men may seek after the Lord, and all the Gentiles, upon whom My name is called, saith the Lord" (Acts 15: 15-18).

By this argument James shows that the conversion of the Gentiles *fits in* to the general scheme of historical events as announced by the prophets. The prophesying of Scripture, including its Davidic kingdom prophecies, *left room* for the period of the preaching of the good news among the nations. In the meaning of the prophet himself the expression "rebuild [the royal rule of] the house of David" was doubtless connected with the restoration of Israel as a people and its kingdom after the time of judgment. This will take place "after this," that is, after the destruction of the sinful kingdom of Israel from off the face of the earth, with the sifting of the house of Israel among the nations, and the death by the sword of all the sinners among them who say, "The evil shall not overtake nor prevent [come upon] us," of which events the prophet had *immediately before* spoken (Amos 9: 8-10). In this context the announcement of the prophet that "in that day," "after this," the fallen tabernacle of David will be rebuilt is without question to be understood of Israel in the End time. It is further beyond dispute that the application by James of this word of the prophecy would in no degree change or deny this original and plain meaning. From this point of view, and in conjunction with the period of New Testament evangelizing, there are five successive stages of events:

1. The judgment upon and destruction of the sinful kingdom of Israel.

2. The visiting by God of the Gentiles to take out of them a people for His name. This is the gathering out of the church in the present period of the gospel.

3. The return of the Lord: after this "I will return."

4. The rebuilding and raising up of the tabernacle (house, royal dynasty, kingly rule) of David, that is, the reinstatement of the Davidic throne over the house of Israel.

5. The conversion to God of the residue of men, in connexion with this restoration of Israel and re-establishment of the Davidic kingdom.

In this sense this whole passage becomes a testimony *for* the setting up in the End time of a visible kingdom of God embracing Israel and all mankind.

But according to the explanation of many other Bible teachers, James goes beyond this to a direct application of this passage in Amos concerning the rebuilding of the tabernacle of David to the present age of the gospel, and in the events in the house of Cornelius he sees a certain measure of fulfilment of this Old Testament passage. After Peter had given his account of the first conversion of persons entirely Gentile James says: "Simeon hath rehearsed how first God did visit the Gentiles, to take out of them a people for His name. And to *this* agree the words of the prophets": that is, the words of the prophets agree with this visitation of the nations of which Peter has now spoken, and so with the taking out a people for His name from among the peoples in this present dispensation. The words of the prophets in view were especially those from Amos 9: 8–10: "After these things I will return, and I will build again the tabernacle of David . . . that the residue of men may seek the Lord." Jesus the Son of Mary, the humble maiden out of the impoverished race (tabernacle) of David, is at the same time the Saviour of the world. "Salvation comes from the Jews" (John 4: 22). Christ, the Messiah of Israel, Who comes from the royal house of David, is the Redeemer upon Whom the believing Gentiles trust.

In this connexion James says not that the Old Testament prophets only silently "leave room" for a period for the conversion of the Gentiles, to precede the rebuilding of the tabernacle of David, of which period they themselves, however, say nothing, but that they "agree" therewith, and therefore of it they *speak*. Were it otherwise the words of the prophets, of which James cites Amos as a chief example, would indeed have had no reference at all to the present events directly in question, for which however James wished just then to give proof from Scripture. Thus he combines the restoration of the kingdom, coming out of the house of David, with the saving activity of the Lord Jesus Christ as the Redeemer of the world in the present age of the gospel.

Paul similarly applies a prophecy as to the Root of Jesse to the present age of the church and the conversion of the heathen (Rom. 15: 12). His exhortation that in the present age of the church Jewish and Gentile Christians should mutually receive one another he bases upon the fact, among other things, that Jesus, the Root of Jesse, has set the Gentile Christians also under His kingly rule: "Receive ye one another, even as Christ also received you . . . a minister of the circumcision . . . that the Gentiles might glorify God for His mercy; as it is written . . . There shall be the Root of Jesse, and He that ariseth to rule over the Gentiles; on Him shall the Gentiles hope" (Rom. 15: 7-9, 12; Isa. 11: 10). This form of argument by the apostle was only possible if he applied this kingly rule of Jesus, as the Root of Jesse, the ancestor of David, already to the present age of the church.

In Antioch the same apostle declared "that God raised Him [Christ] up from the dead . . . He hath *thus* [in this manner] spoken, 'I will give you the holy and sure blessings of David'", that is, the inviolable mercies promised to David (Acts 13: 34; Isa. 55: 3). Here also he unites the fundamental fulfilment of this prophecy concerning the "sure mercies of David" not at all first with the return of the Lord in glory at the beginning of His second appearing but with His resurrection at the close of His first coming. He had done the same immediately before in the same address at Antioch with a word from David's psalm (Acts 4: 25): "We bring you good tidings of the promise made unto the fathers, how that God hath fulfilled the same unto our children, in that He raised up Jesus; as also it is written in the second psalm, Thou art My Son, this day have I begotten Thee" (Acts 13: 32, 33; Psa. 2: 7).

But in reality, as regards the question of the Millennium, these two explanations of the words of James are not at all irreconcilable. No one disputes that an application of Old Testament, including the Davidic, prophecies to the present age is justifiable, that indeed the dispensation of the gospel brings in a certain sense a fulfilment of not a few prophecies of the old covenant. For the present period of salvation is at once an introduction to and a preliminary spiritual exhibition of the coming Perfecting, and the conversion of individual Gentiles in this present period is at the same time a prophecy of the yet greater conversion of Gentiles in the Millennium, so that in a certain sense they belong together.

And is it not clearly to be recognized in other places also in the Prophets that they have not merely a single but a double, and at times indeed a threefold fulfilment? Are there not other prophetic sayings also, which in the meaning of the prophet doubtless refer to the Messianic kingdom of glory, similarly applied in the New Testament to the period of the church, *without* thereby opposing their literal application to the End time? Therefore if James perhaps regards the conversion of Gentiles in the age of the church as a pre-fulfilment of the prophecy of Amos, there is strictly no more a denial of their future complete fulfilment in the End time, as meant by the prophet himself, than in these other similar applications in the New Testament of other words of Old Testament prophecy. We refer the reader to our former discussion of the spiritualizing method of the New Testament; pp. 165 f.

If Christ, as the One come out of the seed of David and, as Paul further testifies, as the Root of Jesse (Rom. 1: 3; II Tim. 2: 8), already *through the Holy Spirit* rules over the individual believers from Israel and the nations (Rom. 15: 12), because these are even *today* translated out of the kingdom of darkness into the kingdom [*basileia*, comp. *basileus* king] of the Son of God's love (Col. 1: 13), how is it thereby denied that a time will come when He will establish His sovereignty on the "throne of David" over *all* Israel and over *all* nations, not only spiritually but visibly, and thereby the promise to rebuild the tabernacle of David also be fulfilled visibly?

How shall here the one exclude the other? Has the throne of David *not* been on earth, but in heaven? How shall a prior spiritual fulfilment serve to prove that a final complete fulfilment is no more to be expected? Is it not wholly incontestable that, even if these promises can have a prior spiritual fulfilment in the period of the New Testament church, the Old Testament prophets themselves, on the ground of the inspired wording of their prophecies, expected a *literal* fulfilment in a renewed Israel and in saved nations in a visible kingdom of God, and that therefore they cannot be disappointed by God?

No, here the second belongs to the first, and is indeed the conclusion and perfection of the first. The kingly rule of the highly exalted Son of David shall embrace not only the realm of the spiritual and moral, but shall also permeate the outward and visible. This universality belongs to a true complete exercise of His Davidic kingly rule. The earthly and visible is also God's creative work. And in general it belongs to the completeness and full vigour of everything inward which is really strong and true, that it never remains restricted to the spiritual and invisible, but advances from this, so to speak, as from "above," till it fills and transfigures the outward and lower also.

Quite irrespective, therefore, of whether James applied the fulfilment of the promise as to the conversion of the residue of mankind, connected with the rebuilding of the tabernacle (house, royal dynasty, kingly rule) of David, simply to the End time or to the present age of the gospel also, proof is given above that in no case is there a denial of a coming visible kingdom of God. But with this breaks down the objection to the Millennium which is raised from this aspect. And for our present discussion this is again the essential matter.

But in addition to all this it must be expressly declared that *these figurative forms of speech, such as "tabernacle of David," are in no wise the decisive ground for expecting a Millennial kingdom.* Fundamental to this are:

1. The definite statements of the prophets concerning a future national reuniting of the two-tribed and ten-tribed kingdoms in the time of Messiah. (Ezek. 37: 15–24; Hos. 1: 11; Jer. 3: 18; Zech. 10: 6).

2. The definite testimony of the prophets that in the time of Messiah Israel will again dwell in the land of their *fathers* (Jer. 16: 15), in *their own* land (Ezek. 28: 25), in *this* land (Jer. 32: 41), in the land of *Gilead* and on the *Lebanon* (Zech. 10: 10).

3. The equally clear announcement that this will be effected only by its being associated with the glorious appearing of Messiah (Zech. 14: 4; Dan. 7: 13, 14; Matt. 26: 24; 24: 30; Rev. 1: 7) and with the inward renewing of Israel (Hos. 3: 5; Isa. 4: 4; 11: 9; Ezek. 36: 26; Zech. 13: 1).

4. The announcement, equally beyond misunderstanding, that in connexion with this inward and outward renewing of Israel there will be a conversion and renewal of the other nations. (Isa. 2: 3, 4; 19: 23–25; Zeph. 3: 9; Zech. 14: 9; Mal. 1: 11).

5. The God-given inspired interpretation of the dream visions in the book of Daniel. Speaking of the "kingdom of the Son of man," which follows the four Wild Beast empires of man's

previous history, it says (Dan. 7: 27): "Then will the kingdom
and the authority and the dominion over the kingdoms *under the
whole heaven* be given to the people of the saints of the Most
High."   Also the dream vision of Nebuchadnezzar declares that
the stone which shatters the feet of the imperial image finally
becomes a great mountain which "fills the whole *earth*," so that
the kingdom of God occupies the whole area which the kingdoms
of the world together had formerly occupied (Dan. 2: 35,
38, 39).

To this is to be added from the New Testament:

6. The unmistakable answer of the Lord Jesus to His disciples
when they asked, "Lord, dost thou at this time restore the
kingdom to *Israel*?" (Acts 1: 6).   He did not reprove them for
earthly or even fleshly conceptions, nor deny the coming of a
visible kingdom of God such as they had in mind, but said only,
"It is not for you to know the times and seasons, which the
Father has set in his own authority."   Thus He did not reject
their expectation of a visible earthly kingdom but only their
curiosity and impatience in this expectation.   By this His prophetic term "times or seasons" the Lord Himself testified that
in due time the kingdom of Israel will in fact be established.

Because we are here giving a summary we give one final
further reference:

7. The testimony of the *Revelation* of John.   It is wholly incontestable that here there is mention of a Millennial kingdom
which is placed *after* the return of Christ in glory and *before* the
destruction of the universe (Rev. 19: 11–21; 20: 4–6, 9–11),
which therefore—this is the unmistakable meaning of the sacred
writer himself—will be set up in the End time as an *intermediate*
kingdom, *between* the parousia and world transfiguration, and
on the theatre of this old earth.

The conclusion and perfecting of this royal and wondrous
work will then be the descent of the heavenly Jerusalem to the
new earth.   This is the eternal home of the Perfected, out of
Israel as well as the church.   It is the transfiguring of the
Israelitic Old Testament Holy of Holies (comp. the cube), the
prototype and the perfecting of ancient Israel.   Therefore the
names of the twelve tribes of Israel stand on its gates (Rev. 21: 12).
For "salvation is from the Jews" (John 4: 22), and therefore
He who testifies concerning all these things, including the consummation, is called "the root and the offspring of David, the
bright, the morning star" (Rev. 22: 16).

But this all comes to pass not for the honour of Israel but for
God and His glory.   "Thus saith the Lord Jehovah: 'I do not

this for your sake, O house of Israel, but for mine holy name'" (Ezek. 36: 22).

The spring of salvation is heavenly, yet the ocean into which its stream merges is worldwide, embracing all mankind. In this Israel is both the receiver and the channel of blessing. Therefore all praise belongs to God alone.

APPENDIX

THE large, bright, many-coloured circle which forms the chief part of the Chart is the actual setting forth of the plan of redemption. The blue starry background signifies only that this plan reaches beyond the earth and man out into the super-earthly cosmos, the universe.

A. THE GENERAL CHIEF DIVISIONS OF THE CHART

World creation, world redemption, world consummation—this is the threefold yet harmonious content of the Divine revelation. Everything comes from God (world creation); everything is wrought by God (world preservation, world redemption); everything tends back toward God (ideal appointment for world-consummation). Thus God is beginning and end, original and goal of the whole universal process. Therefore the Alpha and Omega, the A and O, at the summit of the whole circle of the Chart. Alpha is the first and Omega the last letter of the Greek alphabet.

The triangle which is shown as the background of the A and O, in delicate, subdued colour, points to the inexplicable mystery of the tri-unity in the Divine Being.

But inasmuch as everything comes from God, and, according to His ideal appointment, is for Him, and tends back toward Him, the whole revelation and course of history is like a mighty circular movement. This is the reason why we have not chosen to represent matters on our Chart as a horizontal level, but in the form of a circle, so that the whole is to be read as the dial of a universal clock, just as we, by the use of watches and clocks, are accustomed to read the sequence of time (hours and minutes) not in a horizontal line but in a circle.

That the lake of fire, on the right, is outside of this great circular movement indicates that we find no warrant in the Scripture for the doctrine of the final salvation of all. Thus the form of a circular movement typifies the *ideal* intention of the whole development, but it finds its actual practical realization only where the creature accepts in living faith God's saving work in Christ, the crucified and risen One.

It is in Christ that God carries out all His counsels. Therefore the Son is the central sun in the whole course of events. He is Mediator of world creation, world preservation, world redemption, and world consummation: and because in prospect of the Fall God had from eternity foreseen Him as the Lamb of God, therefore the Cross attaches to this sun, and the covenant faithfulness of God, the symbol of which according to Scripture is the rainbow, guarantees the completion of this Divine plan of salvation. Therefore in our drawing Christ, the central sun, the Cross, and the rainbow are found together.

This plan of God extends beyond the earthly creation. Although it has the earth and man as its crystallization point, yet is it not limited to them. It is not bound to the earth and restricted to man. Sun, moon, and stars, indeed the invisible world of angels and "heavenly things," are in some way united with the history of salvation, though the manner and measure of this is for the present undiscoverable by us (Heb. 1: 14; 9: 23; Isa. 30: 26). This universal connexion of the plan of redemption is indicated in our Chart by the actual circle of revealed history being set in a background of stars, with the four Cherubim who symbolize the highest creaturely living powers (ox, lion, eagle, man[1]), forms which are allotted to the four quarters of the heavens, as are the chief constellations of stars.

Of the history of the earth Holy Scripture gives that only which is taking place in the period between the creation of man and world perfecting. This only can be discerned, that the origin of evil must have come at some point in the earliest world development, and that it had certain catastrophic effects prior to the history of man.[2] Therefore our Chart shows in detail, and in plainly drawn form, only the revealed middle section of the history of the earth (from the origin of evil to its overthrow), while the prehistoric and the post-mundane eternity is only lightly indicated by luminous but ever-retreating rings of light, that is, as unfoldings which, in the course of primeval aeons, gradually appeared out of the eternity of God, and in the course of future aeons will again merge into the eternity of God. They shine forth from the ocean of light of the Divine infinity, and in the ocean of light of the Divine infinity they again mingle. Everything else is hidden in the mysteries of pre-mundane and post-mundane eternity.

This is the meaning of the two extended fields of light on both sides of the upper half of the whole circle of the Chart, which unite the pinnacle of the whole (A and O) and the middle section. This last is given in details which illustrate the revealed course of history. The field of light with its rings on the left refers to the original condition of the earth before the inrush of sin, the field of light with its rings on the right refers to the perfected condition of the (new) earth after sin has been overcome. In this coming glory the heavenly Jerusalem will be on the new earth as the capital of a transfigured universe. In the picture-language of the book of *Revelation* this is represented by the space symbol of a cube, the most perfect form of space (equal on all sides, and thus the symbol of harmony and perfection, transparent as crystal, Rev. 21: 11).

In this mighty movement from God to God the Cross of Christ is the centre of all history. Not indeed as to time, but spiritually and really, and therefore as to the history of salvation, it is the centre of all world events. The Cross is the one, incomparable, central event in universal history, surpassing all else in significance. Therefore in the Chart it stands not only as the middle point of the long extended section which represents the course of history, but in size and height

---

[1] The last marked in the early Christian attitude of prayer with both hands uplifted: see I Tim. 2: 8.

[2] Consider the fact of death shown in the geological strata.

it surpasses in the drawing all other representations of events in the whole plan of redemption. Its being black in colour points to the darkness of death that Christ suffered for us, and by which, descending into the black "death line," He brought to nought him who has the power of death, the Devil (Heb. 2: 14).

"INRI" *Jesus Nazarenus Rex Judaeorum*—Jesus of Nazareth the King of the Jews. This inscription over the cross in Latin, Greek, and Hebrew, is—though wholly unintended by man—a testimony by God of the universal value of Golgotha. He Who came out of Israel is at the same time the Saviour of the world (John 4: 42). Therefore should He be proclaimed in all languages of the earth. As such we preach Christ the crucified (I Cor. 1: 23). Therefore all salvation is in the message of the Cross alone (Acts 4: 12).

B. THE DIFFERENT COLOURED SECTIONS AND SEPARATE LINES OF THE CHART

The Green Areas

The green areas represent the chief sections in the history of the nations. As long as the human race as a whole was still in the circle of light of the direct revelation of God the corresponding fields are undivided and of one colour. It was thus in the original revelation from the creation of man to the call of Abraham. It will be thus after the rapture of the church in the time of the End, and especially after the readmission of the nations at the beginning of the Millennial kingdom. In the interval between Abraham and the completion of the church God takes His separate way with Israel and the people of His New Testament covenant, whilst the nations, as regards revelation, are passed by and excluded. The Chart indicates this in that for these periods the areas are divided: the lower green half points to the nations, as being set aside, the upper blue half shows God's separate way with the Old Testament people of His choice and with the New Testament church.

In the second green section the two names, Cainites and Sethites, are shown in the form of two diverging lines which indicate the two chief lines of ancient mankind after Adam, of which the one lived in unbelief (Cain, Gen. 4: 17–24), and the other for a time in faith (Gen. 5), until later these also were conquered by unbelief, and both (with the exception of the family of Noah) perished in the Flood. The summit of Cainite rebellion was Lamech (Gen. 4: 19–24), the pinnacle of Sethite piety was Enoch (Gen. 5: 22–24).

After the Flood there was a fresh distribution of the human race according to three chief families, those of Shem, Ham and Japheth (Gen. 10). But when mankind in combined strength would erect in the tower of Babel a token of godless self-glorifying, God destroyed their oneness and prepared for the setting aside of the nations and the call of Abraham.

In the green areas beneath, which represent the history of the nations for the last centuries before the first coming of Christ, stand the symbols of the world-kingdoms of the prophecies of Daniel, in such form that at the same time the monarchical image of Nebuchadnezzar is jointly displayed. This is shown by each of the wild beasts standing on a metal base, the kinds of metal corresponding to the metals of Nebuchadnezzar's image. That is:

the Babylonian lion stands on gold,
    the golden head (606–536 B.C.);
the Medo-Persian bear stands on silver,
    the silver breast and arms (536–333);
The Greek-Macedonian panther stands on copper,
    the copper belly and loins,
        (333: from the battle of the Issus to the second century B.C.);
the last and fearful monster is on iron,
    the iron legs and feet, the
        supreme power of Rome, especially from second century B.C.;
        202, battle of Zama, with victory over Carthage;
        133, Pergamum inherited: determination of dominance in the
            East;
        31, Augustus becomes sole ruler, with the beginning of the
            empire.

The Latin number LXX (70) above the wild-beast symbol of the third kingdom intimates that during the existence of the Hellenistic kingdom of the Ptolemies, which arose out of the empire of Alexander the Great, there was made, between 250 and 150 B.C., the Greek translation of the Old Testament which became later the Bible of early Christianity, being used by Paul and the first Christians. On grounds not yet clearly known it bears the name "Septuagint" (Lat. 70).

The iron line passes from the symbol of the fourth world empire right through the green section of the present age (found beneath the seven golden lampstands) and merges into the time of the Antichristian world system. This indicates that the fourth world empire, in the meaning of the prophecies, lasts to the end of the present dispensation. The Antichristian system itself is shown at the end of the iron line by the two symbolic beasts of Revelation 13 and the "tower" of the "Babel" of the last days (Rev. 19). After its destruction, the two beasts of Rev. 13 will be cast into the lake of fire, that is, the Antichrist and the false prophet. This is expressed in the Chart by the two black lines which pass from these two beast symbols into the lake of fire (Rev. 19: 20).

With the re-acceptance of the nations and their reception into the visible kingdom of God the restriction of the Divine revelation, which set in with Abraham, has an end and the universalism of salvation begins again. Therefore in the Chart there is no longer a twofold partition of the green sections into two parallel divisions, differently coloured (green and blue), but, as for the period of universalism of the original revelation, so now again for the period of the universalism of the End revelation, simply a single-coloured, undivided whole. The royal crown in the centre of this section signifies that this re-acceptance of the nations is the time of the kingly rule of Messiah's kingdom, that is, the time of the visible rule of the God-King reigning in glory.

Terrible is then the revolt of the nations in the "little season" after the Millennial kingdom (Rev. 20: 7–10). *Gog and Magog*, according to the Scripture, will take the lead in this last revolt of mankind. The

outcome will be flaming destruction and world judgment.   But out
of this final catastrophe, and after the final judgment before the great
white throne, God will cause a new earth to arise, and on this new
earth there will be renewed nations walking in the light of the heavenly
Jerusalem (Rev. 21: 1, 24; 22: 2).

The red line

The history of Israel is shown by the red band passing through the
whole revelation from the time of Abraham.   None of the peoples
was available for God so that it could be called by Him.   And so by
a free decision (Rom. 9) He began His new and special way with one
man (Abraham).   Therefore the red line begins as it were with a
point, which only in the following period broadens into a continuous
band.

The division of the kingdom after the death of Solomon (tenth
century B.C.) is indicated by the red band being from that time divided
by a central black line.

Where the red band sinks from its normal level the periods are
indicated in which the descendants of Abraham are not in their land
but in Gentile lands.   This occurs three times in Israel's history.
In consequence the red line sinks three times below the green area of
the nations:

First, shortly after the time of the Patriarchs, the sojourn in Egypt
(about 1700–1500 B.C.).

Then in a double collapse, captivity (exile) in Mesopotamia:

Carrying away of the ten northern tribes of Israel to Assyria, 722 B.C.
Carrying away of the two southern tribes of Judah to Babylon,
586 B.C.

Finally, since the destruction of Jerusalem in A.D. 70, dispersion among
the nations everywhere.

By this (since 722) the ten tribes of the northern kingdom simply
disappear among the nations ("the lost ten tribes").   Their red line is,
so to say, gradually lost in the green background, first to emerge again
in the End time immediately before the setting up of Messiah's kingdom, then to unite with the red line of the two tribes, rising again at
the same time, both to merge ultimately together in the visible kingdom of God.

After the destruction of Jerusalem by Nebuchadnezzar (586) the line
of the two tribes sinks likewise into the green area of the nations,
but it is not lost there in the general green surface but soon rises again.
This indicates their return under Zerubbabel and Joshua at the close
of the seventy years, as well as under Ezra (457) and Nehemiah
(445).

Then this red line of the restored people remains at its normal
level, that is, Israel remains in the land until the day of Messiah and
the beginning of His church.   But then, on account of its rejection of
the Messiah, the people was placed under judgment.   In A.D. 70 Jerusalem was destroyed, and after the defeat of the false Messiah, Bar
Kochba, the Jewish State was dissolved and the people dispersed
(135).   Now the line of the southern, two-tribed people also sinks
completely into the green area of the nations, and, like the red line

of the ten tribes, appears again only at the close of the present age.
But the goal is that they both shall flow together into the kingdom
of Messiah, in which Jesus of Nazareth, the God-King and Messiah,
shall be crowned with the gold and silver crown of kingship and
priesthood.

The four dates at the end of the green sections, where the red
gradually reappears amidst the green, point to four chief events in
which we see milestones and chief stages in the history of Israel at the
opening of the End time.

1791. Removal by the French National Assembly of all special laws
against the Jews.

1897. Founding of Zionism.

1917. The Balfour Declaration.   Palestine declared to be the national
home of the Jewish people.

1948. Founding of the State of Israel.

Thus the triple descent of the red line indicates Israel's path of
judgment and grief in Egypt, Mesopotamia, and the nations in general,
But even as in the course of history all the chief races of the world
have worked together in Israel's judgment and distress—the Hamites
in Egypt, the Shemites in Assyria and Babylon, the Japhetites in the
Roman and general exile—so at last will God's mercy triumph over
sin and judgment and all will at last, together with Israel, be blessed
in the coming kingdom of glory (Isa. 2: 2–4; 19: 24, 25).

The White Line

In the Divine worship of the Old Testament white is the chief
colour of the priesthood.   For it is the colour of the light, of purity
and holiness, and therefore the symbolic colour of the invisible,
spiritual, Divine world.   And the priesthood was designed simply
to represent and restore intercourse with God as the Holy One and
with His world of light.

For the carrying out of this duty, and answering to the requirements and possibilities of any given historical situation, God from time
to time appointed ever new forms of temple and priesthood.   These
various temples in their historical sequence are introduced into the
white line on the Chart.   Our chief concern is with seven exhibitions
of the Temple idea, omitting the temple of Rev. 11: 1, 2.

1. The Tabernacle of Moses (1500 to 1000);

2. The Temple of Solomon (1000 to 586);

3. The Temple of Zerubbabel (516 B.C. to A.D. 70), rebuilt by
Herod (John 2: 20);

4. The temple of the body of Jesus (John 2: 21);

5. The spiritual temple of the church:
(a) the church entire (Eph. 2: 21),
(b) the local church (I Cor. 3: 16, 17),
(c) the individual Christian (I Cor. 6: 19).

6. The Temple of Ezekiel, in the Millennial kingdom (Ezek.
40–44);

7. The new Jerusalem as temple (the heavenly Most Holy Place,
   and therefore symbolically a cube: Rev. 21: 16, 22).
   "Behold, the tabernacle of God is with men."

The Golden Line

The golden line exhibits the history of the glorified Christ.   The
Son of God came down from the heavenly glory (see on the Chart the
birth star of Messiah), went to the Cross, there gave up His life, descended in the black line of death.   But as the Holy One He could not
remain in death.   It is as if out of the black death line a golden line of
glory suddenly arises (see Chart).   It goes first to the earth, continues
there only a quite short time (between resurrection and ascension),
and then in exaltation mounts to the very heavenly places (Eph. 1: 20).
There it remains throughout the whole period of the church dispensation.   But then Christ will descend to take His church to Himself.
The golden line likewise descends, and unites with the blue line of
the people of God who, in the rapture, have ascended to the air (I Thess.
4: 17).   Now they are both for ever together, the golden line of Christ
and the blue line of the church.   Together with His church Christ
now reveals Himself fully by the setting up of His kingdom (Col. 3: 4).
Together with His church He will live in the eternal glory.   So the
golden line, united with the blue, immediately before the setting up
of the visible kingdom, comes down from the air to the earth.   Then
this double line turns again upward and remains above the green
section that represents the Millennium, and merges finally into the
new universe.   There Christ will reign with His church for ever.

The Blue Line

The blue line which arises in the blue section of the seven golden
lampstands indicates the future history of the church.   In the present
period the people of God, seen according to His purpose, are like
seven golden lampstands, precious in His eyes, shining with clear
testimony before the world, filled with the oil, the Spirit of God, as
the living, Divine energy of their light (Rev. 1: 20).   The goal for the
church is its being glorified.   We shall be caught away in the clouds
to the Lord in the air, and so shall we be ever with Him (I Thess. 4: 17).
The blue line which ascends out of the blue area of the golden lampstands will, speaking figuratively, unite in the air with the golden
line of the history of the glorified Christ descending from heaven, and
thenceforth both lines will remain permanently together.   Then the
blue line, together with the golden line, will descend to the earth at
the descent of the glorified Christ to establish His visible kingdom
of glory on the earth.   Thus both lines remain united in heaven
during the period of the Messianic kingdom.   And after the events
at the end of the world both lines will go in common into the glory
of the new earth.   The throne of God and of the Lamb will be on
the new transfigured earth (II Tim. 2: 12; Rev. 22: 5).

The Black Serpentine Line

The Holy Scripture speaks with much reserve regarding the origin
of evil and the transcendental background of the developments on

earth. But it intimates that Satan came originally from the hand of God, a pure, unblemished creation (Ezek. 28: 14, 15), but that, at some point in the prehistoric ages, he fell away from God and thus passed under the Divine wrath. The lightning flash on the drawing speaks of this original downfall of Satan and the consequent judgment of God. Since the fall of man at the tree of knowledge demonic powers pressed into human history in three chief connexions: as demonizing world history, as the power of death, as the rule of wicked spirits in the region of the air (Eph. 2: 2; 6: 12). Therefore in the Chart the black serpent-line starts at the tree of knowledge, as the scene of the overthrow of man, and issues in three directions:

(1) downward in the black line of death; for death is the wages of sin (Rom. 6: 23), and from that time Satan has the power of death (Heb. 2: 14). Hence Satan's power in the kingdom of death:

(2) within the history of the universe, for thenceforth the development of mankind has been under the curse of the demonic (see Dan. 10: 13, 20). Hence Satan's power in the sins of men:

(3) in the heavenly places; for Satan is the prince of the power of the air (Eph. 2: 2; 6: 12). Hence Satan's power in the lower heavenly regions.

Thenceforth through all pre-Christian times the serpent line continues as the demonic influence acting upon man from the air. The decisive battle took place at the Cross (Gen. 3: 15). Thenceforth in principle Satan is a conquered foe (Col. 2: 15; John 12: 31–33). This is shown on the Chart in that the numbers (2, 3, 4, 5), which show the chief historic periods *before* the victory of the Cross, stand *beneath* the serpent-line, whereas the numbers (6 and 7) which give the New Testament sections of revelation are *above* the serpent-line.

In the End time Satan, being defeated by the archangel Michael, will be cast out of the heavenly places to the earth (Rev. 12: 7–9). In the time immediately succeeding he will work in especial manner upon the earth and will incite the God-defying world-system of Antichristianity (Rev. 13). But then, after the defeat of this by the appearing of the Lord in glory, Satan will be bound, and during the Millennial kingdom will be held in fetters in the Abyss (Rev. 20: 1–3). For only a "little season" after the Millennium he will be again set free; but he will be completely vanquished and his end will be to be cast into the lake of fire for ever (Rev. 20: 7–10).

Thus shortly before the time of Antichrist the serpent-line turns abruptly out of the heavenly places and is forced downward. Then for a while, that is, during the time of Antichrist, it winds about on earth, and then, after the collapse of Antichristendom, it is forced quite beneath. Then the line, as expressed on the Drawing, runs under the green section of the Millennium, thereafter turns again upward on to the earth, causes the revolt under Gog and Magog, and at last in the final battle is cast into the lake of fire for ever. "The Devil, who deceived them [Gog and Magog] was cast into the lake of fire and brimstone . . . and Death and Hades were cast into the lake of fire. This is the second death, the lake of fire" (Rev. 20: 10, 14).

C. THE CHIEF DETAILS OF THE CHART, ARRANGED ACCORDING TO
                           THE CHAPTERS

We conclude with a concise summary of the most important details
of the Chart arranged in the order in which they are found in the
chapters of the book, so that text and Chart may be mutually explana-
tory.

1. *Heaven and earth in God's plan*
The eternal God—the A and the O.
      The trinitarian triangle.
      Christ the centre of salvation.
      The rainbow.
      The starry world as the background of revelation.
      The four cherubic symbols, ox, lion, eagle, man.
      The earth before the entrance of sin and after its conquest.

2. *Seven Chief Methods in God's Revelation to Mankind*
      Three dark regions of the demonic.
      Seven periods in the whole great circle.
      The first and the last sections of the circle undivided and
        of one colour (green).   Double-colour and parallel course
        of two divisions of the middle section (green and blue);
        the last from Abraham to the rapture.

3. *The Mystery of the People of Israel*
      The red line.

4. *The History of the Temple of God*
      The white line.
      The gold and silver crown of the Priest King.
      The cube of the Most Holy Place (Jerusalem).

5. *The Testimony to Christ of the Old Testament.*

6. *The nations before God*
      The green area.
      The symbols of the wild beasts.
      The early Babylonian and final Babylonian tower.

7. *The History of Christ*
      The birth star of the Messiah.
      The Cross (INRI) and its rays of light.
      The golden line.

8. *The present complete salvation in Christ.*

9. *The Church of the Living God*
      The seven golden lampstands.
      The blue line.

10. *The days of God.*

11. *The Judgment Seat of Christ and the Great White Throne*
      The two thrones.

12. *The Triumph of the Kingdom of God.*

13. *Satan, the Adversary of God*
    The flaming lightning flash.
    The black serpent-line.
    The death line.
    The lake of fire.

14. *God's universal plan of the Kingdom and the Church.*

INDEX